END OF EMPIRE

END OF EMPIRE

END OF EMPIRE

The Demise of the Soviet Union

G. R. Urban

in conversation with leading thinkers of our time

THE AMERICAN UNIVERSITY PRESS

Copyright © 1993 by
The American University Press
4400 Massachusetts Avenue, N.W.
McDowell Room 117
Washington, D.C. 20016

Distributed by arrangement with
National Book Network
4720 Boston Way
Lanham, MD 20706

3 Henrietta Street
London WC2E 8LU England

Library of Congress Cataloging-in-Publication Data

End of empire : the demise of the Soviet Union / G.R. Urban in
  conversation with leading thinkers of our time.
        p.   cm.
  Includes bibliographical references and index.
    1. Soviet Union—History—1985–1991.
    I. Urban, G. R. (George R.), 1921–   .
DK286.E53   1993   947.085'4—dc20   92–33436 CIP

ISBN 1–879383–11–X (cloth : alk. paper)

 The paper used in this publication meets the minimum requirements of
American National Standard for Information Sciences—Permanence
of Paper for Printed Library Materials, ANSI Z39.48–1984.

Contents

Preface

The conversations collected in this volume were conducted between 1988 and 1991—a momentous period in modern history. A detail here and a forecast there will inevitably strike the reader as dated. I have, nevertheless, not attempted to bring these colloquies up to date because their value seems to reside precisely in the glimpses they offer us of the seismic events that shook the Soviet empire and the world while these events were still unfolding.

How, then, should we characterize these conversations? They are, in the narrow perspective, and with the partial exception of Sidney Hook's autobiographical statement, dispatches from the zone of turbulence; but from a larger perspective they appear to us as elements of the turbulence itself. In a different metaphor, we see two cameras in operation—one to read the "facts" as they appear to experienced observers, and another to read the observers.

My interlocutors and I were too close to the scene of action not to err in some of our tentative forecasts; but I am persuaded that imperfect and even false predictions can be as revealing as (and sometimes more revealing than) sound ones, because they draw our attention to the rich variety of human choices and underline the openness of history.

I record with great regret that Sidney Hook and Elie Kedourie passed away while this symposium was being prepared for publication. Their profound and fearless scholarship will long be remembered.

G. R. Urban

Acknowledgments

All chapters in this volume, with the exception of the introduction, were broadcast in full or in part by Radio Free Europe/Radio Liberty Inc. whose cooperation has been invaluable. "Aftermaths of Empire" appeared in *Encounter*, December 1989; "A Tale of Two Empires" in *The World Today*, May 1990; What is 'Soviet'—What is 'Russian'?" in *Encounter*, May 1990; "End of the Bolshevik Utopia" in *The World Today*, October 1991; a section of " 'The Best World We Have Yet Had' " in *Report on the USSR*, May 31, 1991 (RFE/RL Inc. Research Institute); "Nationalism and the Balance of Power" in *State and Nation in Multiethnic Societies* (see note, p. 101).

I am especially indebted to the Heritage Foundation for encouragement and assistance.

Introduction: The Cold War in Perspective

G. R. Urban

One could wish that the pursuit of contemporary history were less strewn with obstacles and the prospect of ruined reputations. The contemporary historian is, after all, tangling with the texture of his own environment and should be able to take advantage of that absence of self-consciousness and ease of communication that make for familiarity and shrewd judgement. Not so. If, as Benedetto Croce observed, all history is contemporary history, then it is equally true that all contemporary history is in the process of becoming history. This makes the contemporary historian himself part of the story and lands him with added handicaps. Observer and observed alike, he will be suspect in the eyes of his successors as much as he is suspect in the eyes of those who make history around him.

If the historian "proper" can take comfort from the fact that he has gained distance and his eyes are firmly looking backwards, his "contemporary" colleague is subject to a whole spectrum of assumptions, open and hidden influences which can, unless he has luck and possesses unusual integrity, play havoc with his evidence. Try as he might to catch his subject now from this, now from that angle, the turbulent flow of events will leave his curiosity unsatisfied, his analysis incomplete, and his judgements contingent. He will ruefully discover that "for the historian it is easier to trace the disintegration of old attitudes and patterns than the formation of new ones."[1] There are, nevertheless, times when the sheer magnitude and decisiveness of events call for a stock-taking—when familiar landmarks vanish, established patterns of being and thinking are abandoned, long-forgotten loyalties, ambitions, and forms of speech come back to life, and new ones clamour for our attention. The fall of the Soviet system and empire is clearly one such time, and lucky the historian who, having been involved in shaping some of the action, has lived to narrate the tale. I like to think of myself as one of those chroniclers-in-combat-fatigues whose work in the "field" has not entirely warped his sense of "what actually happened," and whom students of the many faces of Utopia in our century may read with curiosity and perhaps a modicum of profit. History can be understood as what people have done and what historians have written. In a small way, I have had my feet planted in both. In contemplating the pitfalls of my craft, I am consoled by R. W. Seton-Watson's observation many years ago that, from the time of Thucydides onward, some of the best history has been contemporary history.[2]

The dialogues assembled in this symposium attempt to catch the mood and plot the future of the unravelling Soviet Empire from two main points of perception—from the "belly of the beast," and from the observation posts of students of imperial decline and social disintegration. Milovan Djilas and Sidney Hook come into the first category; Adam Ulam, Hugh Trevor-Roper, Elie Kedourie, and Karl Popper are in the second; while Otto von Habsburg fits in some measure into both.

The uses of the dialogue format have been explained elsewhere.[3] Its shortcomings are obvious. It cannot compete in thoroughness with the well-researched, uninterrupted narrative, and it is (unless pursued by a man of Plato's genius) too short of breath to articulate the might-have-beens, to compare or to reflect. My own trust in its place in the historiography of our time is nevertheless unshaken. The testimony of the runner has an authenticity about it which neither the timekeeper nor the umpire can match. A systematic account of the race, though important at a different level of understanding, is but a pallid reflection of the experience of those who took part. I am not saying it is inferior or superior—it is different and complementary. The challenge-and-response method promotes clarity, brevity, and discipline. It is hard on evasion and penalises double-talk; it is a truth detector in the whole field of doctored memories and mendacity. What it loses in breadth, it gains in incisiveness.

In this, as in earlier books, I have been led by my (not always disinterested) curiosity to identify "on the hoof" those feelings and ideas behind the words and deeds of my contemporaries which either would not or could not reach the bracing air of consciousness and open discussion. In doing so I have tried neither to pry, "unveil," nor debunk—much less to reduce my story to a "distillation of rumour."[4] Whether these traps have been truly avoided, with the excavation of the truth unimpeded, is for the reader to judge.

Our age is not short of documentation. Archivists complain of a surfeit, historians of indigestion. What we know much less about are the true sources of private thought and public action: On what assumptions, in the possession of what information, under the influence of what beliefs and pressures, did people take this or that course of action or abstain from doing so? It is these sources that are more likely to become accessible under the immediate challenge of the spoken word and in the immediate vicinity of action, than they are to the efforts of the historian working from a more distant perspective. All this goes *a fortiori* for things connected with what used to be the Soviet and Soviet-dominated world, where fear, mendacity and self-censorship cast an almost impenetrable haze over the roots as well as the results of the deeds and misdeeds of men.

* * *

Milovan Djilas and Sidney Hook, different though they are in background and character, talk to us from within the framework of socialism and communism. They are heretics of a creed they once keenly embraced, and tell a particularly instructive story. Seeing the father of communist dissent and the principal scourge of the "progressivite" Western Left address us jointly from this particular juxtaposition imparts to their message a credibility all its own. It is a credibility which flows from the Design of History examined—but found wanting; Soviet Man embraced—but repudiated; and the notion of the ends justifying all and any means rejected as a monster of the Utopian imagination. Djilas's long insistence (in the teeth of convergence theorists) that communism of the Soviet type cannot be reformed, only destroyed, has been fully vindicated by history. Sidney Hook died just before the final disintegration of the Soviet system, but he would, in my judgement, question whether the idea of totalitarianism has died with it. He would argue that the need for Utopia is a debilitating but constant factor in human affairs, and he would foresee a time when supporters of a new seamless dispensation would contend that communism had not really failed because it had never been tried. They would point to the corruption of the true faith by tsarism in Russia, and the emperor cult in China, as the real causes of the ideology's disappointing performance. Hence the creed would survive and attract disciples because there would always be idealists and malcontents united in the cry, "There must be a better world than consumerism and the stock exchange." While recognizing these constant longings and delusions in the minds of men, Hook would have no truck with them. He would say, as indeed he did, that the central problem of our time is no longer the choice between capitalism and socialism, but the defence and enrichment of a free and open society against totalitarianism. Hook's speculative question whether a German victory in 1918 would not have served mankind better than did Germany's defeat—because a German victory might have forestalled both Hitler and Stalin—is another telling aspect of his conviction that totalitarianism is the overarching evil of our time, compared to which balance-of-power politics and even the national interest should weigh lightly in a moral person's universe.

Two of the three historians in this volume take a more sceptical view of the good that may issue from the disintegration of the Soviet Empire. Hugh Trevor-Roper and Elie Kedourie see the maintenance of world stability through the balance of power to be more important after the Soviet collapse than the advance of nationhood to statehood—especially the promotion of fledgling nations to the condition of mini-states. Trevor-Roper and Kedourie do not regret the demise of Soviet supremacy—on the contrary, they feel that its disappearance was long overdue, but they doubt whether true sovereignty is possible among states of unequal size, wealth, and power. Hence their reading of the post-Soviet landscape is more detached from moral commitment than are the interpretations of Hook and Djilas. People are what they are, they appear to be saying, hence they have to be kept in order. Morality is a bonus; it is fine to have it but we cannot count on it.

Kedourie and Trevor-Roper are true conservatives. They do not believe that the nature of man is open to improvement or that individuals or societies learn from the crimes and mistakes of their kith and kin—much less from those of others. To Winston Churchill's rhetorical question, "Is it the only lesson of history that mankind is unteachable?,"[5] Kedourie seems to answer that the notion of teachability is irrelevant to the course of human affairs. Nations and states have their natural interests on which the good or bad intent of politicians and the affinities and antipathies of social systems have but limited influence. "Human nature being what it is," Kedourie writes, "balance-of-power politics is the best mechanism men have so far invented for keeping a semblance of order in the world."

Hugh Trevor-Roper's answer to Churchill's question is less apocalyptic: Nations and elites on the path of imperialistic aggrandizement do not go on trying to spread their power indefinitely. After the first defeat of imperialistic expansion, the sons distance themselves from the crusading spirit of their fathers and opt for a quiet life. But when the grandsons come along, the taste of defeat is forgotten and the spirit of militancy is suffused with fresh enthusiasm. A second attempt is made, but when that too is checked, imperialism expires.

We do not gather from this cyclical view of expansionism whether aggression expires because nations are teachable, or merely because they are too exhausted to persist. Trevor-Roper tells us that his theory holds true for Spain, France, and Germany, but the vital question remains: Can we use it to forecast future Russian behaviour? This, we are told, must stay unanswered, partly because the multiplicity and trickiness of historical occasions allow us to make only the most general forecasts, and partly because the analogy with recent Western imperialisms is necessarily incomplete and thus misleading. ''What we can safely say is that under Brezhnev the Soviet Union acquired . . . a maritime empire . . . But this has proved to be an imperial overstretch which the Soviet economy could not sustain. Hence the Gorbachev retrenchment. Whether the next Russian generation will summon the energy for another try is a matter of conjecture.''

It is Adam Ulam whose fear of the destabilizing effects of the collapse of the Soviet imperial order is least pronounced—he seems to have, indeed, no such fear at all. He does not believe, as some Western leaders did until quite recently, that the rapid disintegration of the USSR poses so great a threat to world stability that our dislike of the Soviet system should now be tempered by our even greater dislike of world disorder. It is well to remember that on the ''Soviet watch'' we have been poorly served by our leaders since at least 1989. With the exception of the Germans, they have shown themselves initially incapable of grasping the new Soviet and the post-Soviet scene and reluctant to act on them in time and constructively.

It was, historically speaking, only yesterday that France and Britain tried to thwart German unification; that Willy Brandt called the prospect of reunification ''the specific lie-in-the-soul *(Lebenslüge)* of the second German Republic''[6]; that the opposition German Social Democrats and the governing East German Communists took up common positions on security and ideology[7]; that several leaders of NATO states insisted that the Warsaw Pact remain intact; and that both the American president and a British prime minister pooh-poohed any idea of an independent Ukraine and were markedly reluctant to recognize the breakup of Yugoslavia. Even today (1992), the chief proponents of keeping the former Soviet armed forces strong and under a single command are Western politicians. Their words are enthusiastically quoted by ex-Soviet generals and marshals (of all people) in support of their resolve to preserve what is, in effect, the Red Army.[8] Who would have thought it possible even five years ago that the unproven threat of nuclear proliferation would so unnerve our leaders that they would go to great lengths to uphold the power of essentially the same Red Army we spent untold amounts of energy and money to render ineffective over nearly half a century?

Speaking in 1989, Ulam rejects the "better-the-Union-than-anarchy" type of reasoning on the grounds that the breakdown of a militant ideological empire is manifestly less destabilizing than its continuing existence would be. Nor does he go along with those who believe that Russo-fascism is the most likely successor to the Soviet system. Could Russians want to resuscitate the evil they have just buried? Ulam takes the view that Russia under Stalin has already undergone one terrible experience of fascism in the guise of internationalism. "Nations," he says, "do not make the same mistake twice." But that, of course, is begging the question.

The one residual "practitioner" of imperial rule in this symposium, Otto von Habsburg, also sees the idea of Bolshevism as utterly exhausted and its protagonists discredited; but he fears that the collectivist heritage is strong and might survive, draped in the colours of Mother Russia, as a form of nazism. All the signs, he claims, are there: Unreconstructed Communists, Slavophiles, and generals bereft of their command and their self-confidence might join forces and push the post-colonial democracies into civil war and worse. Would so cataclysmic a denouement follow the pattern of the disintegration of the Austro-Hungarian Monarchy? Was the Soviet state, despite its totalitarian characteristics, nevertheless a guarantor of international stability similar to the Ottoman and Habsburg empires? Otto von Habsburg denies any resemblance. Certainly in its last half-century, Austria-Hungary was a multicultural and multinational state, whereas the Soviet Union has been an old-fashioned colonial empire under Russian tutelage and with national frustrations and dissensions built into its very foundations. With the fall of the colossus, international order might, von Habsburg implies, be momentarily disturbed, but he believes with Ulam that mankind stands to gain immeasurably more from the fall of a crusading despotism than to lose from the uncertain anchorage it provided for the international balance of power.

Nevertheless, Otto von Habsburg's perception of the post-imperial world is guarded and sombre. He believes that the catchment area of a new Russian imperialism (if such were to arise) would be markedly smaller than the erstwhile international appeal of the communist system; hence, the substitution of Russian for Soviet imperialism would still enlarge the estate of human freedom. In the meantime, however, the disintegration of the *ancien régime* might involve the whole of Europe and much of the world in unpredictable upheavals: "I foresee cataclysmic developments which may not remain isolated. That is why I feel European unification must be pursued with speed and determination so that, by the time all these things come to pass, we in Europe have a modicum of security. Politically and psychologically, the collapse of a great empire produces a chain reaction just as terrible in its effects as a nuclear meltdown. A political Chernobyl is what we have to brace ourselves for."

My conversation with Sir Karl Popper concerns itself with the post-Soviet state only in its final section, but in it Sir Karl appears to reconfirm, under perhaps unduly provocative questioning, his belief in piecemeal change and piecemeal social engineering even when the system to be reformed is an economically bankrupt, tyrannical communist one.

In a way, Popper's consistency is admirable. He made his famous distinction between piecemeal social engineering and holistic planning many years ago in the context of warning Western democratic societies against the illiberal consequences of remodelling the whole of society from a Utopian blueprint; that warning in turn followed from his critique of the deterministic view of history and, more particularly, his refusal to accept the existence of laws, especially evolutionary laws, in the historical activities of men.[9] He now sticks to the idea of gradualism even when faced with the need to dismantle the consequences of the most repellent example of Utopian planning—the Stalinist model of society and the command economy.

Popper's thinking is, therefore, all of a piece, but is it reasonable? How can he square his profound humanism with wishing to prolong, no matter how briefly, the misery and injustices of the Soviet system on the grounds that it is better to change despotism by "piecemeal tinkering" than by wholesale reform? And it is not that gradualism in Central and Eastern Europe has not been tried. The evidence from Yugoslavia, Hungary, and Poland is unanimous in showing that it was precisely the ineffectiveness of half measures, of "muddling through," of combining the command system with free-market capitalism, that

turned the gradualist communist societies into disaster areas and led
to the clamour for rapid, indeed revolutionary, capitalist change. The
failure of "feasible" market socialism was as spectacular and full of
lessons for the future as the collapse of the undiluted Soviet model
itself. And yet, Popper may be proved right by history, at least over
the short term. Judging by the collectivist and egalitarian hangover
which still determines attitudes in the whole area, it may well be that
the "mending and making do" prescription that Popper embraces will
be the one which the former communist societies will settle for as the
first phase of their emancipation. He has certainly supplied grist to the
mill of social democratic solutions of the kind Gorbachev favoured and
began, without success, to put in train in the last year of his rule. If
Popper is right, the self-liberation of the post-Soviet world will be
exceedingly slow and partial. We have several examples of dictatorships thriving under free-market conditions, but none of free, pluralistic democracies thriving or surviving in the absence of a free market.

                                 *   *   *

But let me put the questions raised here on broader ground and ask,
How do the judgements of Western observers and politicians over the
last quarter-century stand up to the record of the Soviet system as it is
now known to us?

Let it be said at once that in every Western country there were small
groups of scholars whose courage to tell the truth about the Soviet
Union never deserted them—not in the face of the opprobrium of their
peers; not in the face of threats to their chances of academic accepta-
bility or promotion; not in the face of the threat of financial penalties
by foundations and other sponsors; and not in the face of innuendoes
and ridicule by the Soviet system itself, frequently echoed by Western
clients in the media and elsewhere. Suffice it to name, among other
resilient spirits, Raymond Aron, George Bailey, Alain Besançon, Robert F. Byrnes, Robert Conquest, William Griffith, Ronald Hingley,
Leopold Labedz, Walter Laqueur, Richard Pipes, Leonard Schapiro,
Hugh Seton-Watson, Robert Tucker, and Adam Ulam.

Such salutary fortitude, however, was untypical. Halfway houses
were sought and found where none existed. The urge not to see what
was too unpleasant to see and not to damage what was, wrongly,
thought to be a lasting global "peace order" was great. Many of our
policy- and opinion-makers had so convinced themselves of the military superiority of the Soviet Union, and even of the long-term un-
stoppability of the march of "socialism," that their fine rhetoric about
the solidity of our defences, about human rights and international law,

was seldom accompanied by deeds more dignified or effective than preemptive compromise or reassuring fudge before elections. We were told, for example, that a more robust Western response to the occupation of Czechoslovakia or the invasion of Afghanistan would result in global confrontation, and our television audiences were treated to spine-chilling scenarios of the incineration of our towns and the genetic disaster that would follow if we stood up to Soviet expansionism. We frightened ourselves beyond the limits of enjoyment, but we did not frighten Brezhnev or the Politburo. While Soviet power was acquiring a maritime dimension, we did nothing, until Ronald Reagan's election, to discourage it.

The chances of global nuclear confrontation were, in my view, never entirely serious with the exception of the Cuban Missile Crisis of 1962, but the moral demobilization of our side was. We were superior in all things except the number of conventional divisions, yet we worked ourselves up into a fine state of inferiority, fear, and guilt. Fame and big money were made by using our freedoms to savage the reputation of American presidents, but the crimes and infamy attaching to the names of Soviet leaders were treated with detachment. "Unveiling" Nixon was a paying and career-building proposition; taking the lid off Brezhnev would have caused no great indignation in American living rooms and brought in no accolades. Our media pundits treated with derision anyone pointing to "reds under the beds" as dinosaurs of the Cold War—but the reds were there all right, well-supplied with funds from Moscow, as we now know from the revelations of the former Soviet Party Central Committee, and continued to be there well into the rule of Gorbachev.

Foreign broadcasting policy was another field in which a mood of atonement for sins never committed luxuriated. "Propaganda" was out—"public diplomacy" was in. To avoid misunderstandings, the name of Radio Liberation was changed at an early stage to Radio Liberty, and Radio Free Europe's station identification was attenuated from "This is Radio Free Europe, the voice of free Poland," etc., to "This is Radio Free Europe." Liberty after 1956 was not to be confused with liberation.

We surrounded our broadcasters with so many guidelines, warnings, and inducements to self-censorship that it became fair game to quote pejorative views about our presidents and prime ministers (running ourselves down was supposed to increase our credibility), but poor form to tell the truth about Brezhnev's unsteady hand on the tiller, the antics of the Brezhnev clan, the tyrannical rule of Ceausescu, or the corrupt practices of Zhivkov. There was a time under détente when the policy controllers of Radio Free Europe would not put Alexander Solzhenitsyn directly on the air because his views were judged to be nationalistic, illiberal, and confrontational; and the Board for International Broadcasting had a chairman in the person of John A. Gronouski, who proposed in 1977–78 to make airtime available to Soviet and East European Communist officials whenever they believed that the programmes of Radio Free Europe or Radio Liberty had been unfair.[10] The idea eventually was repudiated by Congress, but it was a sign of utter political disorientation at the top of the U.S. policy-making establishment that it should have been raised in the first place.

As late as 1984, under Mr. Reagan's presidency, a senior White House official let it be known that Radio Free Europe had been right under détente to maintain self-imposed silence about the presence of Soviet troops in Hungary, and wrong to have resumed broadcasting about it. Such unnecessary talk, it was said, might embarrass Kádár. The Radios were not under White House supervision; the advice was ignored. The Liberal Left's finest hour came with its campaign in the mid-1980s against Radio Liberty. Its purpose was to discourage Radio Liberty from giving Russian and Ukrainian national consciousness their due. "Nationalism," it was said, would promote the disintegration of the Soviet Empire to which liberal opinion was opposed. But such fears were no more surprising than the attitude of the State Department itself, which had never been quite happy about the legitimacy and mission of the two Radios. On even days of the calendar, voices of robust support came from sections of the Reagan Administration; on uneven ones, doubts surfaced from the unquiet waters of the State Department. Ambassadors and former ambassadors were pressed into service to warn and to discourage. Bogus elections in Eastern Europe were to be given credit as "progressive," useful, or almost free, on the basis of the argument that it was in the American interest not to alienate governments with which the U.S. had friendly relations and which were, in any case, firmly entrenched in power. The very mission of the two broadcasting stations was qualified by an astonishing caveat which, if strictly followed, would have rendered their work nonsensical from the beginning. Part III of the Policy Guidelines for the 1970s, laid down with Congressional approval by the Board for International Broadcasting, stated: "RFE/RL have no mandate to advocate the establishment or disestablishment of any particular system, form of state organization, or ideology in the areas to which they broadcast."[11]

One important strand in the academically induced soft approach to the Soviet Union was the notion, slowly insinuated in the 1970s, that it was unprofessional, not to say wicked, to look upon the Soviet system as totalitarian. "Pluralistic," we were told, was the correct way of thinking about it—pluralistic in its own way, with personal factions, elites, and interest groups providing democratic choice. Only "anti-communists," with the hidden agenda of destroying socialism, would impute totalitarian tendencies to it, it was said. "To state that the Soviet Union is now characterized by a type of pluralism . . . reminds us that the changes that some see as evidence of petrification of an ideological system could also be cited as evidence of evolution toward a more Western system," Jerry F. Hough observed in 1979 of the first phase of the Brezhnev era.[12] The right way of analyzing the Soviet Union was to see it as a many-layered, modernizing, albeit sometimes elite-dominated society which, like so many other agrarian underde-veloped countries, saw itself compelled to exact sacrifices on a scale Western nations would perhaps not tolerate but which were within the threshold of tolerance of Russians, Ukrainians, etc. "In broad compar-ative terms the Soviet Union has, in fact, been a 'modern participatory state,' " Hough wrote, quoting Gabriel A. Almond and Sidney Verba.[13] "Whatever our final conclusions about the distribution of power among different strata of the Soviet population, it is absolutely clear that we should not be speaking as if there were some sharp line between some elite which shares in political power and a mass which has none."[14]

There is, in 1992, no need to waste too many words on exculpations of this kind. If there is one unanimous verdict reaching us through countless channels from the successor states to the Soviet Union, it is that the Soviet system was indeed totalitarian, that ordinary people were powerless, and that even after the fall of the system, the heritage of totalitarian thinking is a profound obstacle to reform.

Another beguiling hypothesis came from the dissident ex-Soviet philosopher Alexander Zinoviev. It may be summarized in the state-ment that the Soviet system was quite adequate to the conditions of Russia and the republics associated with it and was here to stay. Zinoviev denied that, with the exception of the Baltic states, the spirit of national independence could be a source of trouble for the system. He rejected any notion that the non-Russian republics had been Russi-fied. He was passionately convinced that it was the minority nations that lorded it over Russia, which they regarded and treated as a colony. He predicted that the Soviet Empire would disintegrate, but insisted that the system would survive. He stated in 1984, "I am sure that the

Communist system has a future. . . . More than that, I feel confident
that the Communist system will eventually embrace the whole of
mankind." As one who was born into Soviet society, Zinoviev observed, he knew that the system "cannot be destroyed in a thousand
years."[15] Zinoviev was, to be sure, no appeaser of the Soviet Union.
His was a bad case of *déformation professionnelle*. Having devoted so
much of his life to the study of the Soviet system, and having built so
much of his reputation on his (so he thought) unique understanding of
it, he found it hard to imagine that a time might come when his skills
would be no longer in demand.

Another nonappeaser, but a Eurocommunist of sorts unless I misread his meaning, was Stephen F. Cohen, whose significant work on
Bukharin carried the clear implication that there was a desirable
Bukharinist alternative to Stalinism both in the Soviet Union and for
Western Europe. He did not like the system, but neither did he seek to
overturn it. He found in Bukharin "an ancestral symbol in the search
for a non-Stalinist alternative," and believed the system could be
reformed and applied to modern conditions. "The real potential of a
Bukharinist alternative today is in the Soviet Union itself," he wrote
in 1979. "The idea of a Bukharinist alternative is loose, from Moscow
to West Europe. It is as though Bukharin had hurled Danton's curse:
'You have laid hands on my whole life. May it rise and challenge
you.' "[16]

Under Gorbachev, Bukharin was eventually rehabilitated, but Bukharinist ideas had singularly little impact on restructuring in the Soviet
Union, and no impact at all on West European Communists. Danton's
ghost did not rise and challenge anyone, but the hope that it might do
so was a significant indication of the ideological sympathies of certain
influential sections of American scholarship.

There were, furthermore, those in Western Europe, and especially
the U.S., who were too uneducated to have theoretical or methodological axes to grind, but had so profound a hatred for American institutions and American presidents—especially Richard Nixon and Ronald
Reagan—that they sought to clothe all things Soviet in a favourable
light on the basis that "this will outrage Nixon" or "undermine the
self-confidence of the military-industrial complex". The publicity sur-
rounding the final phase of the Vietnam War and the student upheavals
of 1968 were the finest fruits of this self-hatred, but government
misanalyses of the Soviet system and of Soviet intentions were frequently no less striking.

At a more gullible level, we could hear arguments to the effect that it was only under Soviet conditions that one could be truly religious, because only a state that persecuted religion took it seriously. In the liberal West, it was said, permissiveness and consumerism had side-lined the church and subverted the need for religious commitment. The Soviet system re-created the church of the catacombs, and Christians should be grateful for their tribulations. Some well-known writers and intellectuals uttered similar opinions. Graham Greene, for example, held the view that writers in the USSR were thought to be so important that they were shut up in prison and often died there. In America, on the other hand, writers could live to a ripe old age, whatever their challenge to the mighty, because they did not matter.[17]

And what was one to make of those timorous souls so impressed by the single-minded pursuit of Soviet objectives over the decades that they persuaded themselves to believe that the men leading the Soviet Union were invincible, and that preemptive surrender was our best way of dealing with their iron resolve? Serious Western observers ascribed, as Soviet propaganda had intended, special strength to the Soviet system on account of the performance of Soviet and East German athletes. "For athletes read Soviet institutions," we were told, "and you get the measure of Soviet socialism." East Germany was a special object of admiration. The success of the "German Democratic Republic," it was suggested, demonstrated that Marxism need not end up in Sovietism. In a West European advanced industrial environment, Marxist ideas—never meant to be applied to backward imperial Russia—could operate with remarkable efficiency. In dealing with East Germany, we were warned to respect the "ethics of responsibility" *(Verantwortungsethik);* the "ethics of political conviction" *(Gesinnungsethik)* were for the enemies of "socialism." And it was darkly hinted that East German per capita production had exceeded that of Great Britain.

Finally, there was a widespread belief on the Western Left, especially the Far Left, that the Soviet Union, embarrassing and difficult though it could be, nevertheless provided a political iron reserve of sorts for all "progressive" mankind. The mere fact of its existence, it was claimed, restrained the hands of "capitalism" and "imperialism" and furnished social democratic ideas with a certain robustness which they would otherwise have lacked.[18] The confidential conversations which occurred, at the height of the Cold War, between Neil Kinnock of the British Labour Party and the Soviet Embassy in London in an atmosphere of "Left-talking-to-Left" cast an interesting light on this syndrome. On one occasion, we learn from a Soviet Embassy memorandum, Kinnock compared the situation of the Labour Party vis-à-vis Margaret Thatcher's government to that of "the defenders of Stalingrad, with the Volga at their back, and nowhere to go."[19]

Appeasement was in the air. It stemmed from the shaken state of American morale after Vietnam; the misreading, in both the U.S. and Western Europe, of the character of Brezhnev's rule up to the invasion of Afghanistan; and in no small degree from Kissinger's misjudgement of what détente could and could not deliver. His Metternichian subtlety proved too subtle for Americans. The trap he had laid for the Soviets ended up consuming himself and his policy. The will to win the Cold War had, by the time Brezhnev gave way to Andropov, long evaporated; the will (such as it was) was to obfuscate issues, conjure up bridges between banks that were unbridgeable, and soothe public nerves. In any case, the Cold War was said to have ended—with the 1962 Cuban crisis, as some believed,[20] with détente and the "intertwining" of interests, in the perspective of others.

Let us recall, in fairness to policy executants, that our "enemy image" had been deliberately blurred by the periodic misconceptions or shortsightedness of our rulers. President Carter warned the West against the "inordinate fear of Communism"; senators Fulbright and Church warned against establishing any "linkage" between our relations with the Soviet Union and Soviet behaviour on the human rights front at home; and John Kenneth Galbraith and his friends earnestly advocated that capitalism and communism would spontaneously converge, with the resulting sum of human happiness owing as much to the virtues of the communist organization of society as to democracy, the free market, and capitalism.

Let us also recall that it was during the quarter-century preceding the collapse of communism that the German federal government courted and hosted Brezhnev with exceptional courtesy, that the murderous Ceausescu was elevated to the knighthood by the queen of England and awarded the Great Cross of the Legion of Honour by France.[21] It was of him and to him that President Carter said on the occasion of Ceausescu's American visit on April 17, 1978, "Our goals are the same, to have a just system of economics and politics. . . . We believe in enhancing human rights. We believe that we should enhance, as independent nations, the freedom of our own people." And it was about him that former president Nixon wrote in a letter of congratulations on Ceausescu's sixty-fifth birthday in January 1983 that he was one of the world's greatest leaders. It was during the same twenty-five years that Edward Gierek was hailed and assisted as the great Westernizing Polish reformer by the whole of Western Europe and America, and especially by Helmut Schmidt and the German federal government; that the legitimacy of the "German Democratic Republic" and the existence of a separate East German nationhood were recognized and eulogized, culminating, in September 1987, in Chancellor Helmut Kohl's celebration in the Palais Schaumburg of Erich Honecker as a friend and partner. On 29 July 1992, Chancellor Kohl secured the extradition of the same Erich Honecker from the Russian Federation on charges of war crimes.

The brush and the whitewash were, therefore, basic equipment in the tool kit of Western policy executants. One wonders what would have happened to their careers had they spoken but a fraction of those truths about the Soviet system with which they were, or ought to have been, privately acquainted. We shall probably never know because not many did, and those who did take a robust stand—for example David Funderburk, U.S. ambassador to Romania—retreated in desperation. Reagan was strong enough to rattle the Soviet Union but not strong enough to rattle the bureaucracy of the State Department.

* * *

But, the reader of these lines may well ask, if the situation was so bad, how did the outcome turn out to be so good? My answer to that question is twofold: The situation was not *all* bad, and the ending of the Cold War was not a unilateral Western triumph.

Our misjudgements of what was going on in the Soviet Union and the resulting rhetoric were matters of fundamental ideological bias only in a minority of cases, though these were important. Most of the "false consciousness" stemmed either from misplaced idealism (the activities of professional "peace" people) or wishful thinking, sometimes elevated to the level of national policy.

That "leverage" could be obtained vis-à-vis this or that Communist state by cosying up to some Communist leaders and keeping our distance from others, was an article of faith with virtually all Western governments. This was "differentiation," the carrot-and-stick approach, and I readily concede that it worked within narrow limits. But the price we paid in terms of lost moral stature was great. For example, the U.S. did manage to induce Ceausescu and his lieutenants to make or to promise to make certain concessions in the human rights field, in return for which Romania was granted or continued to enjoy most-favoured-nation status. It was hoped that by playing on Romania's economic needs, the U.S. would be and would be seen to be rewarding "independent" behaviour. But the facts as known to the people on the ground told a different story. Ceausescu pocketed the Western orders and exploited the encomia as honours rightly bestowed on a new Alexander the Great or Julius Caesar, both of whom he caused himself to be compared with in the Romanian media. But the Romanian nation and the minority nations under his rule suffered increasing violence at the hands of the megalomaniac, and their living standards plummeted as the years went by. Romania's much vaunted independence remained a matter of dispute—not so the sharp decline of respect for America in the eyes of the Romanian public.

Although many of our attitudes were mired in defeatism and reflected a gross overestimate of the power, cohesion, and indeed of the legitimacy of the Soviet and Soviet-sponsored governments, sane counsels on the whole prevailed. There was always enough sophistication and leadership around to identify Soviet power and the Soviet system as the principal threats to Western security and the main sources of subversion.

The cohesion of NATO and the ban on high-technology exports were maintained. True, the status quo was, formally at least, left undisturbed. Hungary and Czechoslovakia had not been fought over for fear of igniting world war, but certain initiatives were taken which proved of momentous importance. Jimmy Carter's human rights campaign, with the indomitable Zbigniew Brzezinski as Carter's right-hand man, struck a fundamental blow for liberty. So did the Helsinki round of conferences and declarations which, on the American side, Max Kampelman exploited to the hilt, preparing the way for the loosening, and then the disruption, of the satellite empire and eventually of the Soviet system itself.[22]

Farsighted Americans in the early 1950s promoted the establishment of Radio Free Europe and Radio Liberty and kept them going despite continuing vituperations from the Liberal Left; others, with CIA support, launched the Congress for Cultural Freedom, which soon proved itself to be one of the great counterforces to Stalinism and the international communist-front organisations. Seldom have public funds been more subtly used or to better effect. There were dedicated private organizations such as the Heritage Foundation under Edwin J. Feulner, which sensitised American opinion to the phony, subversive, and mendacious, and tried to equip policymakers with that extra "ideas-dimension" without which democracy flakes away and foreign policy is a mere tinkering with the mechanisms of power. There were American diplomatic representatives of the stamp of Jeane Kirkpatrick, Michael Novak, Vernon Walters, Elliot Abrams, and the constituencies they stood for who would not be defeated by Soviet and Soviet-inspired phrase-mongering in the United Nations and other international fora. There were trade union leaders of the stature of Lane Kirkland and Tom Kahn, who assisted the Solidarity movement in Poland at the hour of its greatest need. And there were men of the commitment of Frank Shakespeare who saw to it, at a time when Baltic independence was almost unmentionable in Western capitals, that a departmental reorganization between Radio Free Europe and Radio Liberty removed—at least in broadcasting terms—Estonia, Latvia, and Lithuania from the embrace of the Soviet Union, a step which put these countries squarely into "Europe," with far-reaching consequences. And there were Americans like Melvin J. Lasky, former editor of *Encounter* magazine, who turned the tables on the Soviet system with effects all the more lethal because he had himself come from a Left-inspired background. Misguided and downright preposterous initiatives, such as Helmut Sonnenfeldt's attempt to promote an "organic" relationship between the satellite states and Moscow as a necessary element of the balance of power (the Soviet side was said to be insecure and had to be reassured) were quickly repudiated or ignored as errors of judgement. That was indeed the least that could be said about them.

The wobbling of the American media establishment is harder to explain. Men and women who had, as members of the privileged fourth estate, special reasons to be loyal to America, turned in many instances against America. They distorted the true correlation of forces in the East-West relationship by their long and vicious concentration on the Watergate affair and their animus against Richard Nixon. Whatever wrongs may have been committed at Watergate in the American domestic perspective would not have much mattered on a larger canvas, had the Watergate scandal not undermined American prestige and weight in the world and distracted attention from the militancy and moral bankruptcy of the Soviet system. American self-laceration was an unexpected boon for the Soviet Empire and an invitation to expansion. It was under the impact of Watergate and Vietnam that Brezhnev and his colleagues decided that the U.S. was unprepared for yet another police action far from its shores, and invaded Afghanistan.

The American liberal media have much to answer for. Their precise role in weakening Western positions in the Cold War remains to be examined. American power and standing suffered setbacks which were wholly out of proportion with the events to which they were ascribed by a handful of journalists. It was not easy for the outside world to understand that the liberal press and television did not represent the whole of American public opinion, or frequently anything but a small section of it, and that on the Eastern and Western seaboards. Conclusions were drawn by friend and foe alike which made the U.S. appear a frivolous crusader, with no stomach for confronting the real issues of the world if American domestic preoccupations demanded otherwise. The disproportionate influence of internal issues and constituencies has for long debilitated the consistent conduct of American foreign policy. It still does.

* * *

Who, then, won the Cold War? The Soviet system collapsed principally under the weight of its own inhumanity and absurdities: its inability to secure for the population a decent and dignified life, its refusal to recognize the centrifugal force of national consciousness, the growing contradiction between rhetoric and performance, and the glaring discrepancy between the reality of Soviet life and life beyond the Soviet borders. But none of these things would have brought the system to its knees had there not been, in the person of Mikhail Gorbachev, a man at the helm since 1985 who thought (and thought very intelligently but not intelligently enough) that a thorough reform of the system could be set in train without threatening its very existence. But life is not as neat as that; there are certain wrongs and lies in history which are so contrary to human nature and so offensive to human dignity that they cannot be put right by tinkering. The first intimations of real freedom, and Gorbachev's often-expressed determination not to nip them in the bud, were enough to make those wrongs intensely felt to the point that they were not correctable within the limits of the system. Stalin and Gorbachev had this much in common: Without Stalin the Soviet system would not have taken root, without Gorbachev it could not have been uprooted. Neither paid any attention to the "impersonal" forces of history on which their rule officially rested. Then as now, voluntarism was triumphant; the "ineluctable will of history" lay in ruins. Both took the Soviet Union by the scruff of the neck and changed it, much for the worse in the first case, much for the better in the second.

But the collapse of the system was far from inevitable. Had it depended purely on the Western world, had a Gorbachev never arisen, had Gorbachev turned out to be a reformer at home but an empire conservative abroad in the mode of Khrushchev, had an unreformed Soviet system decided to develop a Soviet version of the Strategic Defense Initiative (SDI) regardless of the sacrifices, the Soviet Union could have gone on for many more years, threatening the world with further increments in Soviet power and perhaps a cataclysmic show-down. It is well to bear these things in mind when evaluating Gorbach-ev's services to peace and perhaps to human survival. As long as his brand of reform communism was in the running, we were understand-ably reluctant to support it, for the possibility could never be entirely excluded that it might succeed, leaving the world with a variant of communism that worked. But with that possibility gone, we owe it to history to acknowledge Gorbachev's great merit in bringing down the old without managing to put anything viable in its place in the com-munist/socialist genre.[23]

The Cold War, then, was won, in one important sense, by the Russians themselves—because they lost it. They lost their Soviet dimension, their millennarian Soviet militancy, their Soviet right to interfere in men's affairs everywhere in the world in the name of an unproven Utopia. They lost the Soviet knack to preach, threaten, and subvert, and to treat their own people as so many pebbles on the beach of which there was an inexhaustible supply. They lost their Soviet faith in the legitimacy of One Voice in the Kremlin, their Soviet belief in the superior good of the Collective and of the nothingness of the individual. It was, I am confident, in this sense that Boris Yeltsin took exception to President Bush's claim, in the President's 1992 State of the Union message, that America had "won the Cold War." "We all won it," Yeltsin observed, and I believe he was right.[24]

That said, it is nevertheless a point worth making that the Gorbachev revolution might not have ended in the liquidation of the Soviet system, or at the speed it did, had the Western side not done its best to hasten it along, and tentatively to shape it. Four broad factors made the untenability of Sovietism politically explosive, apart from the unquali-fiable Gorbachev factor. The first factor was Ronald Reagan's military buildup, which brought the Soviet system face-to-face with the di-lemma of either spending itself into bankruptcy if the Soviet Union were to match the American effort, or of not matching it and thus forfeiting the USSR's only claim to superpower status—its military might and preparedness. SDI in particular conjured up for the Soviet economy the prospect of so heavy an extra burden, that the Soviet leadership under Gorbachev was forced to surrender one by one Moscow's outposts in the colonial empire as well as its glacis in Eastern and Central Europe. In one important sense, *glasnost* and *perestroika* were Gorbachev's responses to this pressure, although there is a strong argument to be made that Gorbachev, Eduard Shevardnadze, Alexander Yakovlev, and other radical reformers had been intending to reduce or eliminate imperial overextension in any case, recognizing that the Soviet Union was no longer in a position to take on the entire capitalist world plus China without inviting self-destruction.

Much before the election of Ronald Reagan and the elevation of Mikhail Gorbachev, there was a growing realization among Soviet economists and social scientists, especially in research centres such as Novosibirsk, that the Soviet Union was in danger of becoming a social and economic backwater. Under Gorbachev, these apprehensions were openly articulated—indeed, they became elements of official thinking and *perestroika,* but the American military buildup gave them a new emphasis and helped them to assume dramatic proportions in the minds of the military leadership. All but the most ideologically dyed-in-the-wool marshals and generals could see that even military power was bound eventually to suffer if the pool of resources, and the technology on which it had to draw, were in uneven competition with those of the U.S., Japan, and Western Europe. It was the massive American effort, in combination with the technical superiority of Germany and Japan, the cohesion of NATO, and restlessness in the Central European domains of the Soviet Empire, that finally drove the reforming spirit irresistibly forward, and the Soviet system irresistibly into liquidation.

The second way in which the Soviet system had been ripening for collapse was by force of comparison. The mere existence of rich, free, and culturally permissive capitalistic countries, next door to the Soviet Union and its restive satellites, carried its own message. Some of the spirit of rebellion grew from nothing more combustible than geographic proximity. This was especially true of Western Europe, where wealthy and on the whole well-managed states such as Austria, Germany, Holland, and the Scandinavian countries offered daily and highly damaging standards for comparison. There was, above all, the spectacle of the European Community—rich, socially responsible, uniting and cultured—which became, despite the pinpricks and scepticism of the British, an object of wonder and envy for most East and Central Europeans precisely because they felt, but were not allowed to be, part of it. With *glasnost,* the abolition of jamming, growing economic links, cultural cross-fertilization, and international travel, it became no longer possible to isolate the Soviet system from the rest of the world. Stalin had been right, we can now clearly see, to segregate the system from the rest of humanity, for as soon as the Soviet model of society came into contact with the West, it withered and brought the empire down with it. In 1825, tsarist officers, who had seen Paris and the rest of Western Europe in the wake of Napoleon's retreat from Moscow, staged the "Decembrist" rebellion. Their distant successors, who had sampled the welfare and liberal temper of Vienna, Munich, Amsterdam, Paris, and London in the 1970s and 1980s, rebelled for reasons not wholly dissimilar. Showing Europe to the Russians has always been as fraught with danger for Russia as showing Russia to the Europeans.

Our third contribution to the fall of the Soviet system and ending the Cold War has been a deliberate policy of identification with the nations under Soviet tutelage. In the United States, Radio Free Europe and Radio Liberty were this policy's principal vehicles, and it would be churlish not to recognize that they performed their task with distinction. The $100–$200 million the American taxpayer was annually asked to devote to surrogate broadcasting was about the cheapest, and certainly the most effective, foreign-policy investment any American administration has yet made in peacetime. The Cold War was fought in terms of ideas, loyalties, and culture, and it was in those terms that the communist systems were systematically kept in a state of uncertainty and eventually destabilized. This was no subversion in the ordinary sense of the word; it drew its rationale from our nonrecognition, at the intellectual and moral levels, of the legitimacy of the extension, after World War II, of Soviet hegemony to Eastern and Central Europe, and of the brutal enforcement of monolithic rule in the Soviet Union itself. But more important than our nonrecognition was the nonrecognition of the legitimacy of Soviet power by the victim-nations themselves. It was in their name, in their interests, in the context of their religions, and of their national culture that our surrogate broadcasters spoke to them, because the victims could not speak for themselves. These broadcasters countered "newspeak," "crimethink," "prolefeed," and other Orwellian nightmares by pitting the true meaning of words and ideas against the homogenizing influence of Marxism-Leninism. They helped save Poles from being deprived of their history, Estonians of their culture, Ukrainians of their language, and the Russian nation from being identified with the claims and practices of communism. With self-liberation in 1989–91, the lifelines which Radio Free Europe and Radio Liberty had provided from the outside since the early 1950s became domestic life forces. They are now instrumental in shaping the mentality of almost four hundred million people at the behest and with the cooperation of their freely elected governments, including those of Ukraine and the Russian Federation.

Fourth, there was the uneven but significant persistence of religion, whether practised or just secretly felt, which proved, as so often in history, an insurmountable obstacle to the monolithic claims of dictatorship. "Was there ever a time when religion did not form some kind of covert opposition to the state? Its durability was an assertion that somewhere, somehow, in the hearts and minds of a section of the population communist indoctrination had failed."[25] There were heroic Baptists, Orthodox Christians, Roman Catholics, Greek Catholics, and Jews in Soviet camps and prisons, news of whose resistance, and often martyrdom, percolated through to the population and helped to sustain a spiritual frame of reference which the system, as well as the "official" churches, feared and tried to suppress.

From the Polish pope, who visited some of the Soviet-dominated countries, there emanated a message of perseverance, especially, but not only, for Catholics in Central Europe, Lithuania, and Ukraine. John Paul II's electrifying pontificate created a climate in which Christians found the strength not so much to oppose the communist system as to think away from it, creating a parallel culture and parallel forms of being and thinking. Such were "the pope's divisions" against which the Soviet system proved ultimately defenceless.

Appreciation of the pope's central role in the liberation of Eastern Europe came from no other person than Gorbachev himself three months after the Soviet president's resignation. Writing in the Italian daily *La Stampa* on 3 March 1992, he said, "What has happened in Eastern Europe in the last few years would not have been possible without this Pope, without the great role—including a political one—which John Paul II played in the events of the world. I remain convinced of the importance of the activities of Pope John Paul II in those years. . . . We are facing an extraordinary personality. I do not want to exaggerate, but I received a distinct impression as if this man radiated an energy which causes one to have a deep feeling of confidence in him."

The pope's tribute to Gorbachev's part in phasing out the Soviet system had been no less profound and made at a critical moment. On the second day of Gorbachev's captivity by the putschists in the Crimea (20 August 1991), the pope told a large gathering of Hungarians in Heroes' Square in Budapest: "I reflect with gratitude on my two encounters with President Gorbachev. I appreciated especially the sincere will by which he was guided, and the high inspiration which moved him to promote the rights and the dignity of Man.''[26]

* * *

The Cold War ended peacefully. Of the totalitarian systems we have known, the Soviet variant was the first to go without war or carnage, although it remains to be seen whether civil war can be avoided. There is much here to be marvelled at. Why were the satellites allowed to defect without protest?[27] Why did some latter-day Samson not pull down the pillars of the Kremlin and throw the Bomb at us? Why did the legions not march on Moscow and fire? Why did the keepers of the sacred books not flee to China to launch a "free Soviet Government"?

The constellation of governments and leaders in the national and international arena was uniquely favourable for a peaceful outcome. The Soviet Union itself was being chaperoned into radical reform in the only way possible: in the name of orthodoxy. Policies clearly inconsistent with Leninism were put on the statute book in the name of Leninism; and they were put there by a man who was, initially at least, above suspicion in the eyes of true believers because he owed his position to orthodox leaderships and had sprung from the bosom of the Party. This inviolability of Gorbachev and his reforms did not last, but while it lasted it set the stage for a disintegration that could be slowed but not reversed.

Ironically, the conditions which Lenin had written into his famous definition of how revolutions occur were faultlessly satisfied by the Gorbachev variant: There had to be a national crisis affecting both the exploited and the exploiters, and the ruling classes themselves had to have lost faith in the legitimacy of their rule.[28] The reforming process got bogged down precisely because Gorbachev could not persuade himself that the revolution he had started was a real revolution and had to be allowed to run its course. He was the first to use the word "revolution" in this most un-Leninist of contexts, and the last to realize that it was carrying him and the system to unwanted destinations.[29] But by the time this realization dawned on him, unreconstructed men in the leadership, sensing that Gorbachev was losing his grip and might not oppose them if they got the country quickly on their side, staged their coup, which then led to the final unravelling of the system and the empire. The spectacle was awe-inspiring, predictable, and predicted. Had the system enjoyed popular support, or even a modicum of residual legitimacy, it would not have disappeared with a mere whimper. Eyes remained dry from Brest to Vladivostok; only a handful of left-wing socialists in Western Europe and Marxists on the faculties of certain American universities felt that their loss was irreparable.

Everything was set for a peaceful denouement at the Western end of the international constellation, too. Ronald Reagan had put the Soviet Union under great indirect pressure, but he was no warmonger. Having pushed the Soviets into a corner, he, like Margaret Thatcher, embraced Gorbachev and worked for a bloodless change in the international balance of power. The Germans, under Helmut Kohl and Hans-Dietrich Genscher, had been gradualists almost (and understandably) by definition because they had the most to gain from the undisturbed progress of Gorbachevism; and in the Vatican, too, the Polish pope, with the revitalisation of a Christian Eastern and Central Europe at the centre of his attention, was more interested in a just and dignified world order than a bloody rout of atheism. Of the satellite countries, Hungary and Poland had a traditional stake in promoting the peaceful retreat of Soviet power, while among the hard-line regimes, only the Romanian dictatorship was prepared to put up a short fight to stop it. The *Götterdämmerung,* which so many feared, did not take place in Moscow; in the West there was no Clemenceau to wreak vengeance on the vanquished; and in Rome no Savonarola to demand the punishment of the godless.

The system expired and the empire fell apart because they had been drained of both legitimacy and power. Khrushchev's "secret" speech at the Twentieth Party Congress in 1956, which had been *the* seminal experience of Gorbachev and many of his colleagues, was finally coming to fruition. By the time the walls came down, even the leaders of the system failed to show any conviction that in them resided the will of history.[30] Such happy endings are rare in the successive activities of men. It would be a pity if a historian's natural reluctance to believe that there are "endings" in history prevented him from saying so. At two vital junctures, in the autumn of 1989 and in August 1991, a "war" was won, freedoms were restored, and countries reestablished without—save in Romania—a shot being fired in anger.

It all could have ended very differently. We had been working for "victory" but with one arm tied behind our backs, half-persuaded that it could not be done. Jean François Revel's 1983 forecast, *How Democracies Perish,*[31] turned out to be mercifully wrong, but it was a close-run thing. In the international failure stakes, it did seem at one time that the West might be overwhelmed by its own decadence before the Soviet system had time to succumb to *its* absurdities. Our governments had been staunchly consistent in showing their preparedness to live amicably with whoever was in power in the East—Brezhnev, Andropov, Chernenko, Jaruzelski, Kádár, Gottwald, Ceausescu, Honecker, Zhivkov. We were ready to go along with "feasible socialism" and follow a policy of "small steps" in the hope that it might, in time unspecified, perhaps lead to a less threatening and less inhumane order. But our governments never repudiated the Soviet abuse of the Yalta agreements, or challenged the legitimacy and territorial integrity of the world's last colonial empire; indeed we seemed to be endorsing both when we put our signatures to the 1975 Helsinki accords. We had the strength of lions, but spoke with the voices of lambs. In the end, it was our friends in Poland, Hungary, East Germany, Russia, Czechoslovakia, and Ukraine who ensured we did so no longer. It had always been their war because they had endured all the suffering; if anyone won it, they did.

August 1992

Chapter 1

End of an Era of Political Faiths

A Conversation with Sidney Hook

Idealism and Its Limits

URBAN   You have spent a long and famous life wrestling, in one way
or another, with the legacy of Marxism, and especially with the way in
which that legacy expresses itself in the Soviet system. I should
imagine that you would not have done so had you not yourself been
powerfully attracted to Marxism early in your career. Indeed, one of
the critics of your recent autobiography, *Out of Step: An Unquiet Life
in the XXth Century*,[1] asserts that your preoccupation with Marxism-
Leninism has been obsessive. Although he acknowledges that your
book, *The Hero in History: A Study in Limitation and Possibility*,[2] is a
notable contribution to the scholarly literature on the subject, he seems
unaware of or indifferent to an impressive corpus of your writings in
education and philosophy—impressive to a layman by the sheer weight
of bibliography. Nonetheless, the number of items in the area of
Marxism and allied fields suggests a deep and continuing absorption in
the subject manifested by comparatively few other philosophers. To
declare my own interest, some of my personal sympathies are with
you, because in my studies of human behaviour and history I find the

---

I wish to acknowledge Sidney Hook's generous cooperation in shaping our long
colloquies into the present document. Some of the work was done in letters and over
the telephone, his final suggestions for revisions reaching me after Sidney Hook's
death. (GRU)

1

motivating force of disillusion highly significant, and I suspect that your career may throw some light on that.

On the other hand, some of my sympathies are not with you, because you seem to focus your attention on problems of a practical, utilitarian character, and choose not to grapple with those more difficult, even scandalous problems which generate in the observer that sense of wonder at the "philosopher-magician"'s craft which Karl Popper decries, but which most students of philosophy delight in.[3] I am, basically, one of the latter. The pursuit of social justice is a pursuit I respect, but it leaves me feeling small and very much a pedestrian.

Have recent developments in the Soviet Union and East/Central Europe led you to reflect upon the relevance of your past concerns?

HOOK   Before responding to your statement, let me remind you that, in a sense, Plato's attempt to answer the question, "What is Justice?," opened up in systematic fashion perennial questions about knowledge, truth, and existence. My own view of philosophy does not regard it as an autonomous subject, as a rival or substitute for any of the scientific disciplines. Historically, philosophy has been many things, but under-lying all intellectual enterprises that are philosophical has been *the normative consideration of human values*. That to me is, and in some ways has always been, the philosopher's vocation.[4]

But, to return to your question: No, I do not regret the nature and extent of my original interest in Marxism, communism, and social problems although my greater intellectual delight has been in technical philosophical issues. For one thing, as I leave the scene I am still very much concerned about the future of the free and open society. I believe it is faced by multiple dangers, still among them unpredictable devel-opments in the Soviet Union and China. When I look back on the last forty years and recall the periodic indifference to, sometimes the explicit denial of, the truths about Communist totalitarianism in the intellectual circles I knew—despite the Moscow trials, the Nazi-Soviet Pact, World War II, Berlin in 1950 and 1953, Hungary in 1956, Prague in 1968, and the consequences of the victory of Hanoi in 1973—I believe my analyses and predictions were sounder than those of many academic pundits and politicians who influenced American policy. Perhaps this was a consequence of my studies of Marxism, Leninism, and all their varieties, together, of course, with my own limited involvement on the periphery of the political movements of the time.

But there is another aspect of your question that I want to address. I have never been able to liberate myself from a sense of guilt for my participation in a movement that had a tremendous influence on a large group of idealistic, remarkable human beings. In contradistinction to many of my friends, I still believe that communism is a sort of disease of idealism, and that one of the great pities of the Communist movement is that it has wrecked so many wonderful lives—not merely the lives of those it has physically destroyed, but the lives of those who became involved in this movement. Although it is so easy for people to draw an equation between Communists and Fascists, the Communists whom I've known were originally, on the whole, decent human beings who progressively lost their qualities of human decency the longer they remained in the movement. Usually this was a consequence of their practice first to deny and then to approve the systematic and ruthless destruction of elementary human rights in the Soviet Union and its satellites—actions that, considered from any moral dimension, were many times more offensive than the episodic violations of social justice against which they declaimed in the free cultures of the West.

URBAN   Do you in any way feel responsible for the perversion of this idealism?

HOOK   Recently, in reading about the large number of young British Oxbridge students who were inveigled into the communist movement, I wondered whether I may have been responsible by virtue of my first book, *Towards the Understanding of Karl Marx: A Revolutionary Interpretation*,[5] which had quite a vogue in England. I read with relief that Kim Philby, Guy Burgess, Donald Maclean, and others had been drawn to the movement long before they read my book. Nevertheless, I suffer from a sense of guilt that, unwittingly, I may have had some effect upon others, not only because of my books but because of my other writings on Marx and socialism. Although I was never an orthodox Marxist, rejected the dialectic, stressed the role of personality in history, and was more pluralistic than monistic in my social philosophy, I have often been told that I had made a more reasonable case for Marxism, especially in the years of the depression, than most other expositors. Although this attracted my readers to Marxism, most of them refused to go along subsequently with my political criticisms of the Soviet Union and the Communist movement.

But I will say that the manifest manner in which Stalin used the theory of "social fascism" to help Hitler come to power by splitting the German working class, as well as events in the Soviet Union like the Moscow trials, the purges and cultural terror, should have been enough to disillusion anybody who was genuinely idealistic. Although

I always opposed the theory of social fascism, it never dawned on me until Hitler came to power that the paralysis and destruction of social democracy was precisely what Stalin had in mind, since he anticipated that Hitler would go to war against the West and he would pick up the pieces. If social democracy died, communism would be the only alternative. "Nach Hitler kommen wir" was one of the Communist slogans. And then, retrospectively, I began to see that the twenty-one conditions for joining the Communist International, with its insistence on the destruction of "reformists of every colour and shade" (i.e., the Social Democrats in Western Europe), explains the emergence of Mussolini as well.

URBAN   Isn't that a rationalization *ex post facto,* though?

HOOK   I don't think it is, and these impressions gave rise to further reflections. The most painful years of my youth arose from the fact that as a very young Socialist I opposed the First World War and regarded it as a war between imperialist powers (I still believe that interpretation is justified). I was in consequence denounced as pro-German, as a traitor, and then as a Bolshevik. Many people today may not be aware that in 1916 Woodrow Wilson had been elected on a platform promising that he would keep the United States out of war. Most of the people in the community where I lived, which was made up of foreigners and Jewish immigrants, were much more sympathetic to Germany and Austria than to Tsarist Russia. Britain and France were unfamiliar countries to them. Most of them had come from either Austria or Russia, and their route of travel had been through Germany. They believed or had been told that the Kaiser was not as anti-Semitic as the Tsarists. I still recall their boasting of the number of famous German Jews who were accepted at the court of the Kaiser and their sympathetic words about the Emperor Francis Joseph of Austria, whom the Jews praised as someone who had protected them from anti-Semitic ethnic groups during the Austro-Hungarian Monarchy. This was *before* the United States entered the war.

When the United States got into the war, as if to compensate for their lack of martial spirit, everybody went gung ho, including the former isolationists and the various ethnic groups. I learnt the meaning of nationalist enthusiasm and what it could lead mobs to do. Some Socialists were lynched, and there was public mass violence, sometimes official lawlessness, against anyone whose patriotism was suspect. I don't think it ever got as bad in England as it did in the United States, even in the period of "hang-the-Kaiser" after the war. In the crescendo of violence in the United States, which came to a head after the Armistice, raids were made on Labour and Socialist groups. Many individuals were deported. I was caught in one of the raids, and although I was a native citizen, I was threatened with deportation. The incident had its amusing sides which I relate in my autobiography.

The irony of it is that although I was *called* pro-German (all Socialists were since we were anti-war), looking back at what resulted I ask myself on occasion, "what would have happened if there had been a negotiated peace?" I remember Lord Lansdowne's proposal to negotiate peace with Germany and that it was repudiated. What would have happened even if there had been a victory by Wilhelm and the Germans? What probably would have happened couldn't have been worse than what actually did happen. There would not have been Lenin, there would not have been Mussolini, and there would not have been Hitler. The irony of it! It makes one a little humble about predicting the course of history.

There is another thing I should mention in this connection which is often overlooked: the impact of the First World War on the sensitive youth of the time—the trench warfare, the pictures of the horrible fatalities, followed by the revelation that the British had done a wonderful propaganda job in persuading the American public that the German soldiers were guilty of terrible atrocities like cutting off the hands of Belgian children! I was in Germany in 1928 and 1929 and often spoke with former German soldiers. The thing that hurt them most was the memory of the accusation that they had been guilty of the kind of bestiality which at the time Americans assumed they were guilty of as a result of skillful British propaganda. This had a definite effect on the future in two ways: first, it made everybody strongly anti-war, and second, when the news began to trickle out about the horrors of Hitler's extermination camps, we were at the outset absolutely incredulous. Many said, well, we've been taken in once before.

The horrors of the First World War were so intense that a good deal of the attraction of the early Communist movement was its promise that it was going to bring wars to an end—that its triumph would mean no more war. The day following the Bolshevik seizure of power, Lenin and his Party issued their "Decree on Peace" with its demand that peace should be made "without annexations" and "without indemnities." This gave the Bolsheviks a hearing and a following in the socialist movements of the world. Only gradually did it become clear to us that although the Bolsheviks were against war, they were in favour of *another* sort of war, world civil war, the nature of which we did not grasp. And when we read the conditions for the affiliation of the Communist parties to the Comintern, we felt that although these conditions spoke to the necessity of smashing the bourgeois state and of armed insurrection, we thought these reflected the peculiarities of the Russian situation and didn't understand what they really involved, perhaps because we didn't realize what a revolution was in its concrete, practical effects.

URBAN   But the Bolsheviks, and Lenin in particular, always denied that they were pacifists. They made it very clear that war against "imperialism" was much to be approved and that violence and coercion were the natural instruments of revolution.

HOOK   For us it was primarily a question on the theoretical plane. We recognized of course that if there was to be a social revolution, at some point it was likely that violence would have to be used. The moral question was: How could we justify violence? We fell back on the view that if we didn't change the capitalist system, the result would be civil wars and eventually world war as in the First World War. So we rationalized our acceptance of the communist outlook, and said that even though communism involved some violence that we could morally not approve, it was, nevertheless, the lesser evil on the grounds that it might be the only way to prevent another world war. At that time we took for granted that the war would be at least as bad as the First World War, and much worse if there was widespread use of gas. There were sensational articles in the press in those days which predicted that the next world war would make the world uninhabitable because of the use of poison gas. I think it was Captain Liddell Hart in the thirties who warned about the unimaginable consequences that another world war would have.

There is a footnote in Karl Popper's *The Open Society and Its Enemies,* a book I admired despite some criticisms I had of it (among other things, Popper tried to portray Hegel as a racialist, which he was not), that comments on the justification of the use of defensive violence as a means of achieving a Socialist revolution on the grounds that the alternative seemed to be another war. Popper scoffed at that. He thought this was sheer rationalization; but I can assure you that many of us believed it.

We believed it because of the intensity of the anti-war propaganda of the twenties: "Nie wieder Krieg" was the slogan in the Germany of the twenties, and pacifist sentiment was universal in the thirties. The ghastly pictures of war in the trenches—the broken bodies and piles of corpses—had the widest circulation and a lingering effect. They explain in part the relief with which the capitulation to Hitler at Munich in 1938 was greeted even among anti-Nazis, and especially in England. Many have suppressed the memory of the eagerness with which they greeted Munich and their indifference to Hitler's earlier invasion of the Rhineland when a show of force could easily have defeated him. I mention this here only to stress how deep the memories of the First World War were, and to show why many Socialists balanced the possible costs of social revolution against the much greater costs of a war that seemed endemic to the economic conflicts of the great powers.

URBAN　Popper said, referring obliquely to yourself: "These Marxists do not, however, disclose the scientific basis of this estimate, or to speak more bluntly, of this utterly irresponsible piece of oracular pretence."[6]

HOOK　Popper was wrong—vulgar economism, but not oracular pretence or nonsense. I am not trying to mitigate the foolishness, the mistakenness of the analysis that the capitalist economies we knew would push the world into another war. There were certainly other causes of war, notably nationalism. And Marxists never took the terms "inevitably" and "determinism" literally. But it seems undeniable that the economic consequences of the Treaty of Versailles were among the economic causes of the Second World War. (Incidentally, the term capitalist was rarely used, and when it was, it was used only in radical circles. It was regarded in ordinary parlance almost as a subversive term. In the high school I attended the very fact that I used the word *capitalism* made me a suspect character.) All I'm trying to explain is that we did have scruples about revolution and met those scruples by pointing to what we thought would be a worse alternative: war.

URBAN　You were accepting what you would probably not be accepting today, namely that ends justify means, no matter how unpleasant those means might be. Weren't you, also, rejecting something that I would have thought you would have had great respect for as a Socialist philosopher—Kant's categorical imperative?: "Let your action be such that it can serve as a model of universal application"—or so I would summarize it for our present purposes.

HOOK　The formulation is inexact but even the exact formulation is inadequate. You can't derive an ethic on the basis of Kant's categorical imperative. What Kant was saying is: Your action is wrong if you cannot generalize the principle behind it without contradiction. He tries to derive from pure logic a specific ethic—and that is impossible! One can universalize the denial of any or all of the Ten Commandments without logical inconsistency.

But there was a much more powerful argument that we faced. It was the challenge of Tolstoy's pacifism that I found appealing, even at a time when I was strongly attracted to communism. Although Tolstoy offered the alternative of a persuasive pacifism, it broke down on the issue of evil done to others. He offered a wonderful defence of the Sermon on the Mount, about turning the other cheek and loving one's enemies. I thought there was a tremendous psychological insight in his view: If you personally could bring yourself to love your enemies, you would get rid of them because, if they were really convinced that you loved them, they couldn't really *be* your enemies. For obvious reasons this presupposes a common cultural community or tradition, some would say a common nature, for all humans.

To test Tolstoy's insight, I would sometimes ask students in my classes to imagine someone whom they regarded as their enemy. It's testimony to the naiveté and attractiveness of most American youth that usually the only hateful persons they could think of were Hitler or Stalin or Mussolini or a historical figure of the distant past. But that was not what I had in mind; I wanted them to think of individuals they personally knew and hated. They tried hard and finally they came up with someone they at least intensely disliked. I would then say to them: "Now imagine that you have acquired independent evidence of the devotion of this person to you—of his willingness to sacrifice himself on your behalf so that your initial doubt and even disgust at the idea that he could help you or even love you disappeared, and you were convinced that he was really devoted to you. Could you hate him?" Almost invariably they confessed that in those circumstances they could not hate the person involved, which confirmed Tolstoy's position. (By the way, the only ones who held out were some young women who would think of some very objectionable and persistent suitor. Even so these girls would say, "I couldn't hate him, but I would still dislike him.")

Now, here was the difficulty: if it is just yourself who is the object of evil treatment by an enemy, you can remain faithful to Tolstoy's philosophy by trying to win him over, if not by loving him, then by friendly actions, by not offering resistance and not using violence against him. But this philosophy breaks down when it comes to violence toward others. I can honour the man who, no matter how violently he is maltreated, lives by the Sermon on the Mount and loves and blesses his enemies. But if his enemies treated his children or wife in the same violent way, then I would say that he would have to be more than man, or less than man, to love his enemies. And if the *only* way he could save their lives or prevent their torture was by killing the evildoer, and he refused to do so, I would regard him, assuming he was sane, as hardly better than a man who ran away. That's where Tolstoy's philosophy breaks down. And it really broke down for Tolstoy, too, because occasionally, as I read him, he admits that there are certain situations in which he himself could hardly live up to his own position.

URBAN   Is Tolstoy's message that clear, though? In one of his letters (to Ernest Howard Crosby[7]) Tolstoy uses the same sort of example you have just mentioned. Is it a Christian's duty, he asks, to defend a defenceless child against his assailant by killing the assailant? And he answers, no, it is not. It is (he says) generally assumed when such a case is put that the reply should be: One should kill the assailant to save the child. But a Christian has no right to abandon God's law and do to the criminal as the criminal wishes to do to the child.

HOOK   Presumably Tolstoy would say the same thing if it were a question of saving the whole human race if a homicidal maniac threatened to detonate a battery of nuclear bombs. One can imagine even less extreme situations. If this is God's law, how does it differ from Satan's law? I put this crucial question to many followers of non-resistance, especially those whom I met in Asia—the Buddhists who make an absolute of it: "Suppose you saw an innocent person being killed, and the only way you could stop it would be by killing the attacker—what would you do?" Many of them would answer the way Tolstoy did: "I would let him kill me in order to stop him." I would respond: "But suppose that didn't work. Suppose the only way you could stop a man from killing a thousand innocent people was by killing him? Would you make the prohibition absolute? Wouldn't you kill him? If not, don't you become co-responsible for the deaths of the innocent victims?" I rarely got a clear answer.

In my book, *Philosophy and Public Policy*,[8] I give an account of a walk I took in India with one of its holy men, Vinobe Bhave, a follower of Gandhi. I put to him a variation on the same question that always arose in our youthful encounter with Tolstoy's philosophy of non-resistance and later with Gandhi's philosophy of passive resistance. When I defended the use of violence in situations where it was the only way to prevent a far greater evil than any resulting from our use of it, he replied, "In such a case I would find it in my heart to forgive you." It is obvious that where we are committed to plural values, as we all are except religious fanatics, we cannot make an absolute of any one value in our moral economy.

URBAN   In sum, as a young Marxist, you accepted a certain amount of evil because you had convinced yourself that it was in the service of a larger good.

HOOK   Yes, and I think most reflective people will make similar compromises, if you want to call them that, when they are defending freedom or any other ideal. At the time, we were ignorant of the real situation in the Soviet Union. We interpreted the ideals of communism as a more complete fulfillment of the ideals of the Enlightenment and liberalism. It meant carrying the torch of emancipation to all areas of life. Read Stephen Spender's *Forward from Liberalism* or Freda Utley's *The Dream We Lost*. Utley wrote: "In my mind Pericles's funeral oration, Shelley's and Swinburne's poems, Marx's and Lenin's writings, were all part and parcel of the same striving for the emancipation of mankind from oppression."[9] Neither she nor we read carefully most of Lenin's writings, and if we had, we might have recovered sooner from our illusions, not only about what the real situation was in the Soviet Union already in the early years, but about the fundamental indifference, indeed the hostility, of the Bolsheviks to the ideals of the Enlightenment.

"Alchemists to a Man"

URBAN   I should imagine that Marxism, and even Bolshevism in its early form, appealed to you because they offered fully rational answers to the rational analysis of human society. Inequality, social discrimination, bigotry, economic crises, poverty could all be done away with if we could only transfer the application of the dispassionate methods of science from inanimate things to human beings.

If that reading is correct, your disillusion in later years was due to the creeping realization that this rational design came to be mocked and defied by the Bolsheviks. You probably found that Stalinism perverted your image of a just society by superimposing on it the whims and crimes of despotism and the heavy burden of Russian political culture. What you were seeking was a free and permissive order. What you got was the hate oratory of Vishinsky at the Moscow show trials, the gulag, and the massacre of the peasants in the Ukraine. Am I misreading you?

HOOK   Yes, you are. It makes it sound as if we were idealistic cretins, and disregards the devastating impact of the "war to end all wars" on our traditional loyalties, and our burning resentments at the outrages to which some of us, and other essentially harmless persons who didn't support the war, were subjected. At the time of the October Revolution we had never even heard of its leaders, and when we learned about them, we were often critical of many of the things they did. When we justified their actions, we did so as a kind of "war necessity." Nobody I knew in the circles sympathetic to the Russian Revolution accepted Lenin's, or Stalin's, or any of their followers' authority in philosophy—with the exception of those who subsequently became members of the Party apparatus. There was admiration for Trotsky's literary style, but we didn't buy his defence of revolutionary terrorism or his replies to Bertrand Russell's *Bolshevism in Theory and Practice,* which was a remarkable book for its time.

Nor is it true, as your question suggests, that Marxism appealed to us primarily because it was a rational analysis of the social problems and a scientific reconstruction of society. We were not social engineers. Our *primary* motivation was ethical, as it is and was in all socialist movements. The most powerful considerations were moral. Like all Socialists, we took the idea of freedom, simply but seriously, for granted. We recognized that property was power, especially property in the means of production. Anyone who owned and controlled the means of production had power over the lives of individuals who had to live by them, whether it was property in land or mines or factories. We knew what effects a decision to close down a mill would have on the lives of people who worked in a one-industry town. We naively assumed that if the community operated a facility it would do so democratically.

But to return to your question, you must not overlook the fact that our disillusionment was a gradual process. What we thought we knew was often a mixture of ignorance and wishful thinking. The Bolsheviks were, from the very beginning, masters of propaganda. The criticisms voiced by the German Social Democrats fell on deaf ears, because we believed that if they had voted against war credits or called a general strike, the war could have been avoided. We were living in very confused times. We could detect deception in the periodic dispatches from Helsingfors which claimed that the Bolsheviks had been overthrown, but not the deceptions in the Bolshevik propaganda. When reports conflicted, as they almost always did, we gave the Bolsheviks the benefit of the doubt. We assumed that all the White Guard generals were killing Jews. Jews *were* being killed, but they were being killed by both sides. Some of us were so ignorant about Russia that we didn't know that in most of the regions where the White armies were operating there were hardly any Jews. But we swallowed stories like that uncritically. We never checked out the propaganda about the pogroms or about the heroic achievements of the Bolsheviks. We accepted all the noble proclamations and legislation broadcast by the Soviet regime as an earnest of its intentions as soon as the civil war was over.

URBAN   But you were not Socialists because you were Jews, were you?

HOOK   No, no. The Jews as a group and often as individuals were the victims of the revolution, not only because of their vocations but because they were the easy scapegoats of popular outrage. The American community in which we lived was largely Jewish. (I will come to that in a minute.)

The other thing that we were told was that the Bolsheviks had given land to the peasants and we understood that wherever the White Guards appeared they restored the rule of the feudal landlords and deprived the peasants of their land. We were outraged by this; we were all for the peasants, unaware that the Bolsheviks planned not only to deprive them of their land but forcibly drive them into collectives.

We weren't Zionists, we weren't Jewish nationalists. The reason we were so much concerned about the Russian Jews was that we lived in a largely Jewish community, many of whose members were related to the people Petlyura's troops were said to be killing.

So far I've been talking about a very small group of students and literary people in the twenties. The major turn towards an ill-considered, doctrinaire Marxism and sympathy for the Soviet Union came with the Depression, whose effects on the intellectuals were probably greater in the U.S. than elsewhere. It was *then* that the argument for a rationally planned society that would abolish unemployment and expand security became even more focal than the argument for freedom. The hard economic realities had less effect on sceptical faculties than on emotions. The nation was absolutely unprepared for the magnitude of the economic catastrophe.

When the Depression struck there was no unemployment insurance;

there were none of the safeguards that we now have both in the United States and Western Europe. The poverty and deprivation were quite real among groups that had never experienced them before. My book, *Towards the Understanding of Karl Marx,* was published during the "bank holiday" of 1933, the day on which Roosevelt closed the banks because there had been a panicky run on deposits. We were, and had been since 1932, in the grip of a fundamental crisis. That's when the Communist Party began to exercise a strong influence among the intellectuals. Not only that, but nobody had other solutions. I'm not speaking of the capitalists who were jumping out of windows, but the theorists who had no answers either. The country was in such a state of panic and bewilderment that if Roosevelt had socialized the economy in 1933, the country would have followed him. Nobody had any other point of view.

URBAN   But there had been a ten-year boom in the West between the end of the First World War and the Great Depression. Why didn't that affect you? Why didn't you say, "Although the capitalist world has pushed itself to the brink of disaster, lo and behold, it is staging a miraculous recovery! Capitalism works!"?

HOOK   When the boom was going on, it was only a minuscule group of young idealists—Norman Thomas and his Party—who took any interest in social questions; interestingly enough, the American labour movement was hostile to all forms of socialism. All they could see was that people were at work and there was relative prosperity. We, on the other hand, because we were idealists, were always aware of the pockets of inequality and poverty in U.S. society. We were aware of what we called the great waste of social resources. For example, we would notice that in one small block five different milk companies would be marketing milk during the time of prosperity and, not knowing too much about economics, we argued, "Wouldn't it be less wasteful if there were only one company serving that block and the other companies extended their work to other areas?" It seemed rational.

URBAN   How did that jibe with the NEP [New Economic Policy] period in the USSR? In the U.S. you were calling for a retreat from the market economy, while the Soviet Union was trying to rescue the system from economic collapse by *reviving* the market economy. Didn't that give you pause?

HOOK   The fine print of economic developments in the Soviet Union in this period was a matter of indifference to us. The only people who were aware of the NEP were little groups among Communists, and these began to quarrel amongst themselves in the same way the Soviet leaders were quarrelling. For example, Jay Lovestone's own group, which was in charge of the American Communist Party and was following Bukharin, began to expel Trotskyists as early as 1927 because it could smell what was happening in Moscow. So only a few of us were concerned with NEP, and then not very profoundly. I was, at the time of NEP, already immersed in professional philosophy and had other concerns. But I was puzzled as to what was going on in the USSR. More than anything, I was upset by what was happening to members of the opposition. They were being deprived of their freedom of speech, their right to medical treatment, and so on. I was especially moved by a letter from Adolf Joffe—the first principal armistice negotiator at Brest-Litovsk—who eventually committed suicide.

I was not an official member of the Communist Party, but I was close to it. I was reading Communist literature. The girl I married was a member of the Communist Party, and she used to bring home the literature so that I was reasonably aware of what was going on in Russia. I was sympathetic to the Trotskyists because they were victims of oppression, not suspecting the extent of their own fanaticism. It was only later—and this, of course, the Trotskyists never forgave me for reminding them of—that I realized that when the Mensheviks were tried in 1931, the Trotskyists not only approved of the frame-up, but attacked Stalin for not prosecuting them more vigorously! But I am jumping ahead of my story.

URBAN   You were saying, "Why have five suppliers of milk in a single block when one would be enough?" And you were apparently saying this at the same time as Lenin and Stalin were doing the opposite under NEP—giving every milk producer the right to sell his own milk.

HOOK   We didn't realize that. We thought that NEP was a way of making socialism more acceptable to peasants who would normally not want to enter into cooperatives. We had not yet reached the degree of economic sophistication to know that a farmer who is prepared to get up at midnight to take care of a cow he *owns* will not get up if he is just working for a kolkhoz. In fact, we didn't know much about economics. We learnt our economics by reading Marx's critique of capitalism as we thought it existed (tendencies towards monopolies, smaller firms being crowded out, though even these readings weren't true), but the other side didn't do a very good job of economics education either. Not only did I find very few Marxists who'd actually *read* Marx carefully the way I had—I found that very few had read any *other* book on economics. The recognition that one had to be educated in economics came much later. The kind of economics that were being taught in the textbooks—abstract theories of "marginal" utility and so on—didn't seem to have any application to what we were observing. Therefore, when the stock market crash came, no one paid any attention to the economists and they themselves couldn't explain why it was taking place. Every economist had seven different explanations, so we said, "What kind of a science is that?" But Marx *did* predict the collapse of capitalism, he did say that there would be overproduction and unemployment, and this gave us a firm footing.

Another thing that turned out to be true in Marx's prediction was his view that any attempt to introduce collectivism in an economy of scarcity in underdeveloped countries would lead to nothing but the socialization of poverty. That certainly was true. Marx and Engels never believed that one could start socialism in semi-feudal countries such as Russia or China, but to ensure that there was an escape clause in the theory, they observed that it was possible that *Russia* might skip some of the stages of history. Engels stated in 1885 that Russia provided one of the exceptional cases where it was possible for a handful of people to make a revolution. That, however, was on the assumption that the revolution in the advanced West European countries would come nevertheless—it never did.

So I think Marx was profoundly right in saying that you could never develop a socialist economy of affluence in backward countries that had not gone through the industrial and civil phases of development. What Marx was wrong about—and I realized that very soon—was that people who had revolution in their blood would make the attempt all the same, and that the consequences of that attempt would be disastrous. Unfortunately, Marx tended to be monistic in his view of history, although I tried to read him in such a way that an intelligent person could believe his theory. So I modified Marx's view to make it more pluralistic, but fundamentally it is monistic.

URBAN   You observe in one of your books (*Marx and the Marxists: The Ambiguous Legacy*[10]) apropos of the Soviet experience that any dictatorship that is prepared to be indifferent to questions of human cost and suffering *can* translate its ideas into reality: "We can make even a desert bloom into a garden if we are prepared to fertilize it with

human corpses and water it with rivers of blood."[11] But you also note
that Marx's ideas do not warrant such a procedure. Marx's "conception of man," you argue, "assumed that there were certain basic
human needs and moral values which would guide political action in a
civilized society, which would limit what human beings were prepared
to do to other human beings . . ."[12]

I'm inclined to question your optimism. If Marx's view of history
was, as you say, "monistic"—that is, false—then the system ruling in
its name *had* to be coercive because so much of that "monism"
required actions that ran counter to human decency and human nature.

HOOK Yes, but every system of the past, every revolution, has been
coercive, yet everyone admits that there has been some progress. I,
myself, had, of course, read a good deal about the history of the Jews
and their persecution and the terrible things that happened during the
Spanish Inquisition. Yet, like everyone else, we assumed that there
had been a certain progress and that we were standing on, so to speak,
a civilized basis. We may not have realized how thin the skin of culture
was that separated the animal and the human being. We believed that
the effects of culture and the ethos of the acculturated human being
could strengthen that separation. Our reading of history centered on
Pericles and the glories of Greece and of Rome, rather than on the
barbarities, the conquests, and the treatment of the slaves. We read
history selectively. Perhaps our faith might not have survived if we had
taken a more sober look at man's inhumanity to man, though we did
read Gibbon, and on occasion used to quote him, saying that history
was "little more than the register of the crimes, follies, and misfortunes
of mankind." But there was so much that we could find glory in that
we tended to ignore the dark spots and concentrated on those that
suggested light and reason.

URBAN Didn't Schopenhauer, whom I know you had studied, help
temper your optimism?

HOOK Schopenhauer was one of the thinkers I was examined in for
my doctorate. There were two things wrong with Schopenhauer. First,
his pessimism was very light-hearted. He didn't seem to take seriously
his own metaphysical doctrine. Second, he generalized this doctrine to
a point where not only was there deliberate evil where human beings
were involved, but the nature of *life* itself was evil so that you could
use Schopenhauer to justify not only ethical vegetarianism but mass
suicide. On his view it could be maintained that one had no right to

bite into a potato! That becomes absurd and ends up in a kind of spiritual Buddhism.

URBAN   But wouldn't that asceticism have been a nicely balancing influence to your activism as an impatient Marxist intellectual?

HOOK   No, it wouldn't because we also read what he wrote about other subjects, for example, women. He thought that women were inferior in every respect. We liked girls and concluded that something must be wrong with Schopenhauer. Perhaps he hated his mother or she was unkind to him. In any case, he didn't appeal to us. He was full of envy and vanity. He was spiteful toward Hegel and mean to everyone he regarded as his rival.

The philosopher whom we really admired because he had common sense, though we couldn't accept his point of view, was Spinoza—a Jew and an atheist, "the last of the medievals and the first of the moderns." Then there was [Ferdinand] Lassalle, who appealed to us because of his rhetoric, his fighting spirit, and gallantry.

What puzzles me even now is why Marx as a human being had such an impact on us. I think it was the story of his privations that appealed to us. We didn't know too much about his correspondence and his plain nastiness. We were bothered when we read him on the Jewish question, but we tried to interpret that as a sort of criticism of Jewish *capitalism,* although at the time he wrote it he was not yet a "Marxist." Looking back on my whole life, the thing that I would hold most against Marx is that when news of the pogroms against the Jews in Tsarist Russia reached him, he never wrote anything about them.

URBAN   In short, you and your friends were young idealists who believed, despite your philosophical education, and despite Kant's warning, that out of the crooked timber of humanity a straight thing *could,* after all, be made?[13]

HOOK   Yes, we did. But there is another point here that bothers me. I meet a great many radical people today—some of them former Socialists or Communists—who view intellectual and moral choices entirely in terms of cost-effectiveness. I find this a very simplified, not to say false, view of human affairs. For example, it is said of intellectuals who are drawn to Socialist and Communist movements that they are looking for an opportunity to increase their power and are not really motivated by genuine ideals. I am taken aback by that interpretation, because if what they say is true, then I must have been somebody who had been drawn to the movement to increase my power! Nothing could be further from the truth. In 1932, at the depth of the Depression, when I was an assistant professor of philosophy at New York University, I signed a statement endorsing the electoral programme of the Communist Party together with Edmund Wilson, Sherwood Anderson, Waldo Frank, John Dos Passos, and the cream of the crop of American intellectuals. This was, at the time, a great triumph for American Communism.

Did we act the way we did to increase our power? Of course not. Everybody expected me to *lose my job,* and Roger Baldwin, head of the American Civil Liberties Union, said to me, "It's a miracle that you have survived." The people who endorsed the Communist programme had more power *then* than they ever would have if the Communists had come to power. They would have been the first to be wiped out. They were perhaps misguided because they didn't recognize their own interest, but there was an element of idealism about their action, and it is wrong to deny it.

If you think of everything in terms of costs and benefits, you are practising a vulgar form of Benthamite utilitarianism. The notion that everyone acts always to further his own interest is in one sense a tautology, if an interest is defined as what gives satisfaction, and in another an absurdity if it involves a specific good, pleasure, power, profit, or any other particular interest. Cost-benefit considerations do not determine the way most people act, although they may guide the way *some* people act. The cost-benefit people argue that it is insanity to risk your life for causes and ideas that are of no obvious and immediate personal benefit to you, and if you nevertheless do, they judge that you're off your rocker. Well, maybe, but being off one's rocker in furthering a cause or concern for the other person is what a human being is about. I can only repeat: One of the worst things one can say about the communist movement is that it has destroyed so many human beings who, before they became engulfed by it, were decent persons.

URBAN   Toynbee described communism as Christianity gone awry and Jacques Maritain called it a Christian heresy. . .

HOOK   The cost-benefit people would say, "Of course the Christians sacrificed themselves, but they did so in the expectation of being rewarded." Toynbee and Maritain were devout Christians who believed in immortality, but the people I am talking about, well, they were often prepared to go to their deaths with no expectation of the felicities of either a Judaic or a Christian or especially a Muslim heaven!

URBAN   So the communism and socialism of your generation was a combination of science and idealism. Less charitable souls have called it scientism and fanaticism.

HOOK   They would be doubly mistaken. We were capable of learning, and our critics had their own illusions. Ours was an amalgam of idealism and a rational conception of man's place in history and of a better society. A purer idealism would have taken us into Buddhism or into some society for the prevention of cruelty to animals; or we could have gone to Africa as medical missionaries. But we didn't; we looked around and saw misery in the midst of plenty, and that ignited our moral indignation.

Apropos of fanaticism: A man whom I have always admired, although I disagreed with the strains of pacifism in his thinking, was Norman Thomas, because he had a wonderful sense of humour. You can't combine that with fanaticism. I have never met a person with a strong sense of humour who ever justified dictatorship. The two don't go together because humour is based upon the sense of incongruity and human imperfection. A fanatic will shut his eyes to everything except the one truth he wants to see triumph. (It is true, though, that there are some people who have been idealists and have gone through the mill; take, for example, Max Eastman, who wrote a great book on humour and the enjoyment of laughter.[14])

But coming back to your question: We *were* trying to use scientific methods and to apply them to the study of society. We didn't make the mistake of assuming that we could reduce everything to *physics,* but we did assume, rather naively, that if there were problems that could be solved in principle, then someday they *would* be solved. Perhaps we didn't recognize that there might be problems that could *not* be solved. Look what's going on in Northern Ireland!

URBAN   Did [Hippolyte] Taine's kind of positivism have an influence on you?

HOOK   No, we were acquainted with Taine but dismissed him as a geographic-determinist; he wrote about English literature in terms of England's physical and climatic characteristics. We thought this superficial and completely unimpressive.

We were more taken with [Ernest] Renan. I remember Renan's observation that the life of a scholar should be one of genteel poverty. We agreed with that although I now realize that, beyond a certain point, especially if you acquire a wife and children, scholarly privation has to have its limits. Maybe in the Middle Ages, to escape the horrors of the wars of the period, we would have found ourselves in monasteries engaged in study.

URBAN   This is what Norman Cohn says about your type of person in his book, *The Pursuit of the Millennium*.[15] He suggest that modern intellectual Communists and Socialists would have made good egalitarian clerics and purveyors of apocalyptic lore in the Middle Ages.

HOOK   Perhaps. That certainly would have been better than to be crusading knights butchering unbelievers or unruly common folk.

We would have all been *alchemists*—which is a very different thing. We were naturalists to a man; that's why people like Niebuhr, Tillich and Norman Thomas were uncomfortable with us. In our ignorance we subscribed to the Marxist theory that the belief in religion was a promise to the workers of an otherworldly happiness so that their earthly misery could be justified. We didn't realize the profundity of [Ludwig] Feuerbach's view of religion which Marx thought he had transcended by saying that religion was "the sigh of the oppressed creature . . . the opium of the people." Marx overlooked the fact that there was a personal, conciliatory role in religion which was of tremendous importance to the man in the street and had nothing to do with objective truth.

Cohn's attempt to make us into wandering missionaries is far-fetched. We would have been *heretical* scholars. We would have known enough to keep our mouths shut about denying immortality, but we would have taken very literally the Aristotelian view that the soul was the activity of the body and that when the body goes, the soul goes with it.

URBAN   Which would have got you into trouble. . .

HOOK   Well, Thomas Aquinas's works were burnt in Paris for similar reasons, yet his thought survived, modified to be sure.

URBAN   So, the spirit of the Enlightenment and the Socialist reform of society were two sides of the same coin for you—

HOOK   They went hand in hand, and I think that is really true for the whole Socialist movement, also for the early Fabian movement, as well as for John Stuart Mill and his followers.

URBAN   An austere, not to say forbidding, creed if there has ever been one—

HOOK   We certainly never developed an aesthetic sense by concentrating on the cultivation of our psyche as the Bloomsbury group did. We would have been repelled by people whose conception of the good life was cultivation of a pleasant frame of mind for the benefit of themselves. Some of us were rather shocked to discover that G.E. Moore, whom we admired as a human being and as a thinker, was a very close associate of the selfish sensualist, Lytton Strachey. And even the great Keynes, whom we admired because of his work on probability (we didn't know much about his writings on economics), fell from grace in our estimation when he confessed that he, too, was concerned with states of mind on the basis of G.E. Moore's *Principia Ethica*. But that was much later.

URBAN   You believed your radicalism required a certain personal austerity and perhaps asceticism. If so, you would have been consistent with much in the tradition of nineteenth century Russian revolutionary socialism, [Nikolai] Chernyshevsky, for example.

HOOK   We didn't demand asceticism—only ordinary sympathy with people in need and in trouble. We disliked selfishness because we knew that a man whose first thought was always of himself would not be much concerned with others. He might be moved to say "The poor beggar—let's help him because I can't stand the sight of him." But we didn't regard sympathy as a virtue; we just took it for granted. When human beings are in distress, we felt that one had a duty to help them even at some cost to oneself: that was our practical attitude. Nothing remarkable about that.

URBAN   Goethe wondered whether the man who accepted no family responsibilities but concentrated on the growth of his own mind and culture couldn't be making, in the long run, a greater contribution to the public good than the *paterfamilias* and fully integrated burgher.

HOOK   If Goethe said that, he was certainly wrong. We couldn't count on him to defend his family, or the city which made him and his cultured mind possible, against barbarism. My economist friends tell me that private vices can lead to public good, and they quote Adam Smith's observation to the effect that the best way of promoting the public interest is for everybody to lead a responsible life and pay his bills. It is certainly true that if we had to rely on the philanthropy of others to get our food and housing, we wouldn't get either; if, on the other hand, we can harness a man's self-interest to providing us with food and housing we are more likely to get them. That is said to justify private enterprise, and so it does.

Taken as an economic fact of life, that line of argument is acceptable, but when applied to other human relationships, it is not. I used to know Socialists who refused to give alms to individuals on the grounds that giving alms, if widespread, would uphold the capitalist system. This was a transparent kind of rationalization that really didn't fool anybody but themselves. *Society,* they said, had the responsibility to take care of the unfortunate! Agreed; but in the meantime, couldn't you and I spare something to help the needy? That, we thought, was the first human duty.

URBAN   Twice I have now heard you say that communism is a sort of "disease of idealism." "One of the great pities of the Communist movement," you have stated, "is that it has wrecked so many wonderful lives" (p. 3, present volume). I am a little concerned about the implications of that observation, for you seem to be hinting that the proper target of a young man's idealism is what one might call the Agenda of the Left. You seem to be implying that there is, in our time, no other agenda essential to the improvement of human life and worthy of our respect—certainly no "conservative" agenda.

I am sensitive to these implications because the ideas they contain are widespread even among people holding centrist views in Western Europe. I vividly recall the astonishment with which vaguely Social Democratic friends of mine looked upon the Hungarian Revolution in 1956. They were, of course, supporting it, but they were puzzled by its particular character. How was one to understand that people in 1956 would go to the barricades under national banners to promote national ideals? Was this some anachronistic replay of 1848? The revolution did not quite make sense within the progressivist framework.

Would you allow that there is an idealism concerned with national culture, the preservation of language, national homogeneity, and indeed national identity that a decent man might embrace even though he may, if he is unlucky or lacking judgement, be sometimes drawn into fanatical expressions of these things—in much the same way as a decent Socialist runs the risk of being pulled into the Communist movement if he hasn't got his wits about him?

Examples abound. To stick to Hungary, the declining birth rate and the large number of Hungarians living outside Hungary's present frontiers sustain a profound anxiety about the survival of the Hungarian nation and of Hungarian culture. It could assume accents of an intolerant nationalism—as it did, on occasion, in the past—but the good faith and idealism of those fearing for the future of their nation cannot be doubted. Nor can the good faith and idealism of many French men and women who see their civilization threatened by the influx of Muslim North Africans. The same goes for the Soviet Armenians who see the identity of their kinsmen in Nagorno-Karabakh threatened by a fast-growing population of Muslim Azeris, and for that majority of people in Britain who insist that British civilization is Christian and must remain so, even though their own retreat from Christianity is one of the most striking facts about British life today.

"National identity comes before democracy" is the way one American Zionist leader encapsulated Israel's problem not long ago. This may be an unduly provocative way of putting it, but isn't the question of national identity as a focus of loyalty and idealism still very much with us, and doesn't it deserve to be considered on a par with the social idealism of the Left?

HOOK   Whenever I have referred to a belief in communism as a disease of idealism, I have immediately added that those who remained in the Communist movement became transformed into hardened cynics or ruthless defenders of a corrupt and lying despotism in virtue of the practices they were required to defend. Those who retained a tincture of idealism or moral decency got out.

I find puzzling your reaction to what seems to me obviously true. First, I am speaking of the initial impulse, of the original appeal of communism, especially to the young, and not the state of mind of the veteran *apparatchik* who has rationalized the abandonment of his moral ideals as growth into a tough realism. Second, you seem to be falling into the fallacy of simple conversion. Because those drawn to communism are idealists, it by no means follows that all idealists are drawn to communism or that only Communists are idealists.

There are many varieties of idealism, all marked by a willingness to sacrifice oneself for a larger good, by actions that put oneself at risk and are not motivated by a desire for personal advantage, or greater power, or even safety. Examine the biographies of the numerous persons who have written their own version of *The God That Failed,* of those you yourself have written about as young Communists, and you will find that they thought they were furthering a cause that would fulfill the ideals of social justice, peace, freedom, and classlessness. Invariably these ideals had a universalist and communitarian dimension. All Socialist and Communist movements stressed their international character. This was particularly attractive after periods of ghastly war. Often the first signs of disillusionment among Communists developed when it was discovered that the interests of the Soviet Union were being given overriding importance by the Kremlin.

Call this idealism naive, Utopian, uncritical, even unintelligent. But it remained untapped by the other idealisms that centered on the preservation of national culture or language or redemption of territory or some kind of irredentism. It was not a question of having one's wits about oneself, but of history, the memory of past movements and the cluster of chauvinist associations that came with it.

Of course, today there are many idealisms that one can embrace with good faith, especially resistance to the oppressions of totalitarian despotisms. But I cannot agree that "national identity comes before democracy," or before political freedom. National identity may become a focus of loyalty and idealism for *strategic* purposes, but not merely to further the victory of, say, Vietnamese communism over Cambodian communism. The struggle for national identity should always be harnessed to a struggle for *political* freedom—as indeed it was in Hungary in 1956, no matter how some observers may have misread the character of the uprising. Only in that way can the struggle for national identity be morally preferable to what you call the social idealism of the Left.

Of Collective Guilt and the Gullibility of Intellectuals

URBAN   Let me try to induce you to speculate some more about the might-have-beens of our time. As we do not believe with Hegel that "what is, had to be," we can, in this free-roaming conversation, afford to ask, "Did everything in our century have to happen in the way it did happen?"

You said that a negotiated peace or German victory in the First World War might have forestalled Bolshevism, nazism, and fascism. But given the state of affairs that existed in Russia in the summer and autumn of 1917, could the Bolshevik *coup d'état* have been avoided?

HOOK   You are asking hypotheticals contrary to fact which "scientific" historians tend to reject as unworthy of their attention. I take a different view. In the natural sciences, hypotheticals have to be answered or else we must admit that we are ignorant. It may be asked, for example: "If this aeroplane were to fall from a height of 40,000 feet, at what velocity would it hit the ground?'' We can answer that question because we have all the relevant bits of information: the weight and load of the aircraft, its present speed, and so on. Or somebody may say to me: "This man committed suicide by swallowing all the pills in the vial. What would have happened if he had not swallowed the pills?" To that I must be able to answer, "If he hadn't, he would not have died in this way at this particular time," or else admit that I am, at present, ignorant of the cause of his death.

Now, the humanities, and history in particular, are not like that. There are too many variables both of the broadly physical and psychological kind involved to make definitive judgements possible. We can, nevertheless, risk some informed conjectures. These may throw light on our topic and may be interesting to make.

Despite my early Marxist orientation and the predilections I had for scientific enquiry and the search for causes, I have become acutely aware that the historical pattern of events that developed did not have to be. There is nothing that I can see that made the victory of the Bolsheviks in October 1917 inevitable or inescapable. Of course, given the events during the *days* preceding their coming to power, there may have been no other alternative. But Kerensky could have acted differently, and the Allies subsequently might have done things that would have made the Bolsheviks' rise to power and their retention of power much more unlikely.

Or take Lenin's return to Russia in the sealed train through Germany. This was, for the Germans, an astonishing, calculated gamble. We must give credit to the Kaiser's high command for their rare grasp of things geopolitical. I do not think any other military command would have been shrewd enough to count upon the possibility of liquidating one of their fronts by letting an unknown agitator get through to the enemy to break his morale. The Germans certainly had no expert knowledge of the situation of the revolutionary movement in Tsarist Russia. Yet Count von Brockdorff-Rantzau, the German ambassador in Copenhagen, told the Foreign Ministry as early as 2 April 1917: "We must now definitely try to create the utmost chaos in Russia . . . We must secretly do all we can to aggravate the contradictions between the moderate and the extreme parties, since we are extremely interested in the victory of the latter, for another upheaval will then . . . shake the Russian state to its foundations."[16] Lenin certainly did that. But if the Germans had not been high-risk players, Lenin's return would have been delayed or rendered impossible—in which case the Bolshevik *putsch* either would not have happened, or would have taken a different course, with much reduced staying power. After all, it is not often that ministerial dispatches from minor ambassadorial posts are so quickly acted upon. Sometimes they remain unimplemented or even unread for a long time.

Or take Japan's war strategy. Again, things didn't *have* to happen the way they did. After Pearl Harbor, because of the anti-Comintern pact with Germany and Italy, all of us expected that the Japanese would strike against the Soviet Union in Siberia. Who was to know that the Zen Buddhist military zealots were going to concentrate on the United States, the British, the French, and the Dutch? I know that the historian, Charles Beard, a good friend of mine, was convinced that Roosevelt had engineered it all. By denying the Japanese oil, he had precipitated the Japanese action and brought the U.S. into the war. It was a scandal that the United States slept at Pearl Harbor, but the amazing thing was that the Japanese decided to go south. They could probably have made enormous gains in Siberia and at the very least prevented Stalin from transferring his Siberian divisions from the Far East to Moscow. This would have cost the Soviet Union its capital and perhaps the war. But for the Japanese leadership, expansion to the south was more alluring, and Stalin was saved.

And then another event, which perhaps you can shed some light on, because I cannot. No historian has been able to explain to me why, after Pearl Harbor, the Germans declared war on the U.S. Hitler's general staff didn't approve of it. If Hitler hadn't declared war, American public opinion would not have stood for diverting most of our military resources to Britain instead of waging all-out war against Japan in the Pacific as the first priority. By the time the U.S. had won in the Pacific theatre of war, Hitler probably would have occupied the whole of Europe, including Britain. Fortunately for Britain, and ultimately for us, Hitler appears to have been guided by a sense of honour *vis-à-vis* his Far Eastern ally, and had a special hatred for Roosevelt, "the lame anti-Christ."

URBAN I can't answer your questions any better than you have done. We know from several sources (General Walter Warlimont's account is the one I have particularly in mind[17]) that the first priority of the Japanese was to establish their "New Order" in East Asia, although they realized that one day they would have to defeat the Soviet Union. It was apparently Ribbentrop who saw most clearly the need for a Japanese attack on Siberia, but, according to Warlimont, Hitler maintained that Germany could take care of Russia as long as the Japanese took care of the U.S. and helped to defeat England, which he regarded as the main enemy.

Why exactly Hitler declared war on the U.S., more or less, as you say, behind the backs of his generals (only Jodl and Keitel accompanied him to the Reichstag where the announcement was made on 11 December 1941) is not clear and does not appear to us to have been rational. No plans had been made. The armed forces were unprepared. I have no explanation other than what you have suggested: ideological loyalty and, above all, the hubris of a man obsessed with the prospect of world conquest. But many people in Hitler's entourage were deeply worried, as we know, for instance, from *Ciano's Diary*.[18]

HOOK   Well, given the character of Hitler, I suppose almost anything that he did can be attributed to his hubris. Yet even the Nazi movement did not have to go down the road it did. There were alternative possibilities of development within it.

There were groups and parties on the German far Right—for example Gregor and Otto Strasser's North German anti-capitalist group, to which, until mid-1926, Goebbels had also belonged—that were in many respects more radical than Hitler's NSDAP turned out to be, but were not always as fanatically anti-Semitic and warlike as Hitler was. They were, of course, all of them a nasty bunch, but I can imagine a strong right-wing movement, even a strong right-wing government, in post-Weimar Germany that would have been traditionally racist but would not have carried its anti-Semitism to the point of genocide. Moreover, something might have happened to Hitler in those stormy years in the 1920s and early 1930s, and the leadership might have passed to Goering or Roehm or Otto Strasser. I don't think Goering, for example, would have had the stomach for Belsen, Birkenau, and Auschwitz (although his record in 1933 as Prussian minister of the interior was cruel enough even by Nazi standards)—or a world war, for that matter. Don't forget that as late as mid-1932 Hindenburg ran successfully against Hitler, and many of the generals despised Hitler, even after he had done their bidding and purged the movement, in June 1934, of Roehm, Strasser, Schleicher, and many others. They looked upon him as an upstart, a guttersnipe and a demagogue. It didn't have to happen the way it did. There is some evidence that by the time the semicretinous Hindenburg had called Hitler to organize the government, the Nazi movement had passed the highpoint of its popular support.

URBAN   Goebbels reserved his greatest hatred to the end for plutocrats and "high society," and expressed admiration for the communist type of leadership. So did Hitler. Talking to a conference of *Reichslei-ter* and *Gauleiter* in May 1943, Hitler said it had been easy enough for the German forces to knock out the "bourgeois states" because "they were quite inferior to us in upbringing and attitude." Stalin's Soviet Union, however, was a very different matter. In the East, he observed, "we met an opponent who also sponsors an ideology, even though a wrong one."[19] "Stalin, too, must command our unconditional respect," Hitler said on another occasion. "In his own way, he is a hell of a fellow! He knows his models, Genghiz Khan and the others, very well. . . ."[20] The respect for ideology was mutual. After the partition of Poland, Molotov protested that the ideology of Hitlerism "cannot be destroyed by force."[21]

HOOK   Even on the question of decapitating the Red Army, Hitler and Stalin were of the same mind—but not for the reasons one might think today. Hitler believed and said that the execution of Tuchachevsky and the cream of the Red Army leadership was a cleansing process that strengthened the discipline and fighting power of the Soviet forces. Revelations made in the USSR under Gorbachev support an opposing conclusion—but then, Hitler hated his generals for their alleged defeatism and was not averse to bloodbaths of his own.

However, this may be—and at the risk of sidetracking ourselves into a discussion subsidiary to our main theme—I must add some words here about "collective guilt." Hitler's fanatical hatred of the Jews as a "race," and the unspeakable crimes he and the men under his command committed against the Jews, are as infamous as they are well-known. They could not even be covered by the insane rationalization of "collective guilt," because the Jews were innocent victims, guilty of no crimes whatsoever against those who had vowed to exterminate them. About the crimes of the Nazis there could be no rational doubt. But were the German people as a whole collectively guilty of the Nazi crimes? This became a troublesome question after 1945. The whole concept of collective guilt has been selectively applied in human affairs.

There is, of course, a national *collective responsibility* for permitting a regime to come to power or approving of a power capable of such transcendent evils. In a sense every nation has a collective responsibility for some acts of its past—otherwise treaties, currencies and national debts would have no *prima facie* binding obligation on those who come after us. But that is different from *collective guilt* for specific crimes committed. The two concepts are often confused, with the result that those who condemned *all* Germans overlooked the German victims of Nazi terror as well as those who disapproved of the Nazis but were not courageous enough to risk the fatal consequences of overt opposition. It is unfair to embrace them, or present-day Germans, in the notion of collective guilt. Guilt seems to me personal and a matter of degree.

Belief in collective guilt is wrong no matter who holds it and why. I was taken aback to discover that some admirable human beings, such as Einstein and Erwin Panofsky, and other eminent German Jews, accepted this doctrine of German collective guilt. I do not see how, as rational human beings, they could have done so. To some extent, because of the unconscious influence of the doctrine which was quite strong after the war, some prominent German Jews, and other refugees in the U.S., became for a period quite hostile to American foreign policy in Europe as too friendly to the Germans and too hostile to the Soviet Union.

During the famous Waldorf "peace" conference, indirectly inspired by the Communist Party and the Kremlin in 1949, held at the Waldorf Astoria Hotel in New York, Einstein, Panofsky, and other prominent German Jews rallied to its support. We were unsuccessful in our efforts to persuade them to dissociate themselves from this organized propaganda effort on behalf of Soviet foreign policy. Only years later, after my exchanges with Einstein, did I realize why they had done it. At one point Einstein gave it away when he said to me, "You Americans are much too sentimental and naive about the Germans." I got the impression that what he was really saying was, "Only the Russians know how to treat them."

Mind you, these people had no use for communism, and were terribly distressed at what the Soviet Communists were doing in the world of art and science, but when it came to foreign policy, to my astonishment I would hear them say that the United States was a greater threat to world peace than the Soviet Union! Here was Rudolf Carnap—a distinguished philosopher who had found a fresh home in the U.S., and for whom I had rallied support to protect his job at the University of Chicago when he thought (mistakenly as it turned out) that he was under attack from Robert Hutchins and Mortimer Adler— signing the Stockholm Peace Pledge that was directed against the U.S. I exchanged some sharp letters with him. (The most outstanding of the group of Berlin and Viennese philosophers who politically knew what was what, and never went into any of the peace movements, was Hans Reichenbach, leader of the logical empiricist group in Berlin.)

What was behind all this? Most of these German and Austrian Jews justifiably believed that they had become an integral part of German culture and that they had been repudiated in a way that went to the very roots of their being. Most of them were not Zionists: their Jewish identity was weak and their dislike and disdain of Polish and Russian Jews apparent. Their acculturation only a century or so after the Enlightenment and Napoleon was remarkable. They were making very great contributions in the fields of science, medicine, and the arts, and were going to make more. They felt, as Heinrich Heine and the "forty-eighters" had felt before them, that they were Germans every whit as good as the other Germans. Suddenly they had been brutally disinherited. The intense resentment all this generated could not be assuaged easily.

URBAN I do not want us to go into your exchanges with Einstein because these constitute, by now, a famous chapter in contemporary intellectual history. Let me just say that I, too, found Einstein's intemperate reaction to his German background and his lack of political judgement surprising. If a man of his scientific eminence cannot rise above the needs of personal resentment and spurious generalizations, who can?

HOOK The feelings of these emigré scientists were natural. After all they were only human beings. It was their political judgement that was questionable. And this is largely explicable by the fact that from field to field, there is no transference of training. A man can excel in one field of learning by his intellectual sophistication and yet remain naive and innocent in his daily commerce with his fellow creatures and the world of politics. Linus Pauling, the famous scientist and Nobel Prize winner for his theory of bonding in chemistry (he is on the campus here [Stanford University]), once made the observation over the radio that Sidney Hook was pathological about the Russians and about communism. My response in effect was to say to him: Since you are a scientist and you believe in the peacefulness of the Soviet system, why not judge by the record of Soviet behaviour? This was in the early fifties, years before Hungary and Czechoslovakia, but I have seen no evidence that he has altered his political judgement.

When scientists make forays into politics they often fall victim to the assumption that the Kremlin will react to events the same way they themselves would. The normal inclination of a scientist, when he reads a report, is to give it credence, and this is how many scientists behave when they discover the "social problem." Let me give you a simple example from my own experience. It has to do with the famous physicist Percy Bridgeman, who received the Nobel Prize for his experiments on the conductivity of metals at very low temperatures. It turned out that one of his assistants, or someone he knew who was a member of a group engaged in classified research, had been accused of being a member of the Communist Party. There was some newspaper publicity and other unpleasantness. A year or two after that incident, at a conference on determinism which I convoked and he participated in, I asked him, "By the way, whatever happened to the chap who was accused of being a security risk in that project?" "Oh, that scandal," he replied, "he was not a member of the Communist Party at all." I said, "How did you know?" Bridgeman replied, "I *asked* him and he denied it!"

It didn't even enter Bridgeman's mind that a scientific co-worker could systematically lie to him, or that deception at every level was traditional Communist policy whenever it was deemed necessary for the cause. Yet he was a very keen scientist who showed a good deal of methodological sophistication in his work. But he had never paid much attention to politics and communism. Now, nobody was surprised when Paul Robeson became a Communist fellow traveller or Ezra Pound, the poet, went off the deep end broadcasting fascist propaganda from Italy; but one would, theoretically, expect scientists to have a greater respect than others for rationality and evidence. Yet, as I say, scientists do not automatically transfer their training to other fields. Some first-hand experience with the subject matter of politics or some reading or study is necessary. In its absence one would expect scientifically trained minds to suspend judgement about controversial matters. Many scientists have refused to do so.

URBAN   Some of us who have been watching totalitarian systems over the past half-century have often run into the following optimistic argument: In the modern world there could be no such thing as a compartmentalization of knowledge or of the spirit of enquiry. A man asked to show initiative in his scientific research, or in translating the results of science into economically useful procedures, could not be expected to wear blinkers when it came to discussing the merits and demerits of nazism or Stalinism. There was, it was alleged, only a single kind of intelligence. Applied in one field it would spill over into others. Hence, totalitarian systems would either have to remain or become scientifically and economically backward, or else they would be destroyed by the spirit of modern science and technology. Modern society, it was said, could not be half slave and half free any more than modern man could.

The evidence we have confirms what you are saying—that there is, in effect, little or no cross-fertilization. In Hitler's Germany the scientists and technologists—notably the physicists—were perhaps the most meretricious estate in the realm. The von Brauns served Hitler, but then they also served Stalin and American rocket research. Their devotion to scientific enquiry did not induce them to ask too many uncomfortable questions about the applications of the results of their enquiry. In Stalin's Russia, the rapid industrialization of the country was due to the massive and, with all its grave faults, successful application of science and technology. The Soviet hydrogen weapon and the Sputniks came into being under totalitarian conditions. With the sole exception of Andrei Sakharov, the scientific and technological establishments were careful not to allow their critical faculties to complicate their lives outside the research institutes and laboratories. If they had doubts about the concentration camps and the gulags, they took care not to voice them. Perhaps the most bizarre chapter in this sad affair was written by those incarcerated Soviet inventors and technologists whom, early in the war, Stalin restored to a semblance of liberty *within* the prison regime, provided they resumed their research in support of the system. And they did.

What we are, then, both saying is that training is not education, and that a man of great intelligence in one field can be a great fool in another—hardly a new conclusion in the history of human thought.

HOOK   It may not be new but it is supremely important because it helps us to arm ourselves against certain contingencies, in the face of which we would otherwise be defenceless. Totalitarianism and scientific inventiveness can, up to a point, go together. That is, incidentally, why Gorbachev may be right in his assumption that the spirit of his kind of *glasnost* will not wreck the Soviet system. What is much more difficult to understand is how and why some men of outstanding scientific intelligence in our own free societies should suspend their critical faculties when confronted with the claims and practices of communism. But it is a fact. Some are taken in again and again.

The subject is vast and we can only nibble at its edges. McCarthy and stupid reactionaries who indiscriminately hurled false charges of communism were a boon to the Kremlin. But even before McCarthy appeared, ignorance of the history, theory, and practice of communism led many intelligent persons of good will astray.

During the Spanish Civil War, certain Communist agencies were collecting funds in the U.S. allegedly in aid of Loyalist Spanish refugees of all political persuasions. We soon discovered that some of these funds were being diverted to Communist political purposes. Naturally we sought to expose these practices and put a stop to them. One of the leaders of a medical aid group was the distinguished medical scientist, Walter Cannon, the author of *The Wisdom of the Body*. I wrote to him of the shady Communist practices in the refugee and medical aid organizations. We had evidence from a Brooklyn dental surgeon who had just returned from the scene that admissions to one of the hospitals were being controlled by Robert Minor, an official of the American Communist Party, then in Spain.

Cannon, a man of great integrity, would never have sanctioned Communist duplicity, but he seemed to think I was protesting any cooperation with the Communist Party. In effect he replied to me: "All right, I grant that there are Communists in our organization, but the fact that Communists follow the same objective I do doesn't make it impossible for me to work with them. What is wrong if I, working for peace and public health, cooperate with Communists who are also for peace and public health?"

Again and again, those of us who were trying to expose the deceptive activities of the Communists would encounter this outwardly reasonable objection. So I said to Cannon and the others: "Very well—you are in favour of peace and public health and you will work with anybody. But tell me, Professor Cannon, the Nazi-American Bund under Fritz Kuhn also proclaims that he and his members are for peace now, and they are. If they approached you to work with them for peace, would you?" And I would go on: "Supposing you were working with a group to further public health and you discovered that there was an active Communist group within it. Wouldn't you be surprised if some Friday night, when very few people came to your meeting, a resolution were introduced condemning American foreign policy? It is not red-baiting but simple prudence, when one works with Communists, *even in a good cause,* to look very carefully at who is secretary and who are the executive officers, because your ostensibly philanthropic peace or health committees may take political actions that sooner or later will embarrass you and compromise your cause."

Well, that message got through only after the Nazi-Soviet pact, when all the multiple peace organizations in labour, liberal, and church circles in which Communist Party factions were active gradually began to support Stalin's "peace policy" in Poland, the Baltic states, and even in Finland. A whole cluster of organizations that had clamoured for "collective security" and for active measures to stop Hitler began to assert that democratic England was no better than Nazi Germany.

The message got through to that generation. I still recall the anger and bitterness of Roger Baldwin, who had used variations of Dr. Cannon's argument to justify coalition politics with Communists. The events that followed the Hitler-Stalin pact cured him. But the generations that followed Baldwin remained vulnerable to the same uncritical approach, particularly in the recurrent peace movements launched by the Kremlin to further its foreign policy of the moment.

More than once these days, Hegel's famous observation has come to mind: The only thing that we learn from history is that human beings do not learn from history.[22] This is a paradoxical statement and cannot, of course, be taken literally. It cannot be true whenever we say that we learn by trial and error—we do gather experience by trying things out and making mistakes. That is the meaning of the inductive principle. It is not a fireproof principle (no inductive statement ever is), but we could not survive without relying on it. Sometimes we do learn the truth about important matters soon enough to make a difference— sometimes, alas, too late!

If Trotsky Had Made It

URBAN   Can we go back to the "hypotheticals" and ask, "What would have happened if in 1914 the German and French Socialists had lived up to their resolutions and refused their governments war credits, and voted against the war?"

To this day, the working man's enthusiasm for the First World War, and the Socialist parties' endorsement of that enthusiasm, are among the sorest points in the Socialist conscience. Talking to György Lukács two weeks after the Soviet occupation of Czechoslovakia (7 September 1968), I asked him for his view of the suppression of the Prague reform movement. He said, "This is the greatest disaster that has befallen the Communist movement since the German Social Democrats approved the Kaiser's war credits in 1914. That was the end of the first dream of the socialist brotherhood of men."[23]

HOOK   The Social Democrats had said that they would respond to a declaration of war by a general strike. If the general strike had been internationally observed there would have been a postponement of the war. But if, for example, the French had gone on general strike and the Germans had not, then the Germans would have walked in and ended the war. It would have been a short war. If *all* Socialists had gone on strike, it may be that the Russian hordes would have rolled over into Germany, because the Russian Socialists were not strong enough to paralyze the tsar's war machine. Now, if *that* had happened, I have no doubt that the German forces would have put up a great fight (one could not withhold admiration from them for their technology and the skills that enabled them to take on virtually the entire world). But the tsar's armies had almost inexhaustible manpower and, bearing in mind that they survived the awesome losses they had suffered at Tannenberg and the Masurian Lakes at the hands of Hindenburg and Ludendorff, I would venture the guess that they would eventually have overwhelmed a Germany weakened by a general strike. This, too, would have made for a shortish and relatively light war.

URBAN   But would it have forestalled the "stab in the back" legend in Germany? The stabbers would have been the Social Democrats who rendered Germany prostrate or crippled with their "sabotage" of the national interest—a charge not dissimilar to the one that was actually levelled at them after November 1918.

HOOK   It would not have made much difference to the "stab in the back" myth, but a short war need not have produced a Hitler. And the Imperial Army would have been clearly defeated in the field. Nothing was preordained to happen the way it did. If Jaurès had not been assassinated on the eve of the war, he might have rallied the French Socialists to turn against the war, and if the German Social Democrats had gone along with Eduard Bernstein—well, the war, as I say, might never have taken place or would have ended in the rapid victory of one side or the other. The slaughter of many millions of young men and the degradation of European civilization would not have occurred.

And yet, and yet—one need not be a Marxist to say that in 1914 a war of one kind or another was probable. There were conflicts and animosities of all sorts waiting to be turned into a *casus belli*. There was the Franco-German crisis over Morocco, which the Germans had engineered to provoke the French, the Anglo-German naval competition, the annexation by Austria of Bosnia and Herzegovina and the offence this caused in Serbia and St. Petersburg, and others. None of the major powers imagined that a war could last more than a few weeks or months. All nursed claims and grievances against their neighbours.

None thought that the satisfaction of these grievances would push the world into disaster.

So I answer your question in the way I would answer the question: "What would have happened if Columbus's ship had foundered at sea and he hadn't discovered America?" Nothing much would have happened; America would have been discovered by others, as indeed she was repeatedly "discovered" after Columbus. In the decade before the assassination of the Archduke Franz Ferdinand, war in Europe was in the cards. The only question was when and where it would break out, unless a way could be found to resolve the basic conflicts, the national resentment and grievances. Perhaps if there had been a more realistic awareness of the nature and cost of modern war, it might have had a moderating effect.

URBAN   Presumably you were just as deeply disturbed by the triumph of nationalism as Lukács was? One didn't have to be a Marxist to hope that the unprecedented prosperity, technological interdependence, and cultural internationalism that characterized Europe on the eve of the First World War would get the better of nationalistic ambitions, whether in the streets or the chancelleries of Europe—

HOOK   Yes, I was. Two major things dealt a death blow to Marxism. The first was, of course, the growing prosperity of Western society and especially of the working class; the second was the intensity and pervasiveness of nationalism. Who would have expected that the workers, who, according to Marx, did not have a fatherland, would develop such strong nationalism in every European country and go to the trenches and kill one another with gusto? This came as a great surprise to me. The pictures of the mass enthusiasm for the war are still shocking today. I have never been satisfied with any explanation of its strength, especially with its emergence in the United States some fifty-odd years after our Civil War, the bloodiest human conflict up to that time in human history.

Worse, nationalism has now spread and become, as it were, decentralized. From the now happily extinct jealousy between Germans and Frenchmen, we have advanced backwards to a state of affairs where Serbs hate the Croatians, the Flemish the Vallons, the Republican Irish both the Ulstermen and the English, and even in that model of "internationalistic" coexistence, the Soviet Union, the Armenians have their knives out for the Azeris, the Azeris for the Armenians, and most nationalities for the Russians. In our naiveté as Socialists we thought the time would come when nations would disappear and only classes would count. How innocent and absurd we were! Absurd, because when we spoke of class war, we had no notion that it could be worse than national war, more total.

It took me a long time to understand why the Russian tsar decided to go to war on behalf of Serbia: When Gavrilo Princip's bullet killed the Archduke Franz Ferdinand, didn't the tsar realize that Princip and his friends would just as well have killed royalty *anywhere?* One would have expected him to feel a certain kinship with the victim. Not so. Nationalism in high places proved immeasurably stronger than the threat of the assassin's bomb, as indeed nationalism in lower places proved stronger than the threat of national blood-letting—and this in a country that had just been through the Russo-Japanese war and had direct experience, at Port Arthur, of the horrors of modern warfare.

URBAN   What if the 1919 peace treaties—especially the Treaty of Versailles—had been more tolerant of the self-respect and interests of the defeated nations?

HOOK   I had not yet achieved mature consciousness when I realized that if the Allies had made the concessions to the Weimar Republic that they subsequently were to make to Hitler, they might have so mitigated the weight of shame and the burden of poverty and unemployment, that the rise of Nazism would have been slowed down and perhaps prevented.

Although, as a very young Socialist, I was, as I said, critical of Woodrow Wilson for having taken us into the war, once Wilson developed his Fourteen Points for the future peace of Europe, it seemed to me his plan was a reasonable basis on which to conclude the war. Indeed, as I was later to discover, it seemed to be a hopeful basis even in the eyes of our then-enemies. Some of the Germans I met in the late 1920s claimed that they had not fought hard to the bitter end because they expected Wilson's Fourteen Points to be put into practice—that there would be no indemnities, reparations, or annexations. If so, then the Germans had their own innocents, since the post-war plans of the German high command reflected no weakening of its aggressive militarism.

Of course, at Versailles, Wilson's plan was torn to pieces by Clemenceau with the aid of Lloyd George. If Wilson, with his enormous prestige and America's unimpaired power to support him, had turned his back on the revenge-seeking French and walked out of the conference chamber, and if, therefore, there had been no Versailles Treaty with its infamous clause that made Germany *solely* responsible for the war, I do not think that Hitler would have won Germany, because Hitler came to power largely on the tide of the nationalism that developed over what the Germans called the Versailles *Diktat*. And that, in truth, was what it was. It was the one thing on which there was unanimity.

Everybody, with the exception of the French, was aware that Germany had received a raw deal. But Wilson failed the test of history. He did not have the courage of his convictions.

Wilson's weakness was compounded by the weakness of the German Social Democrats. They should never have signed the Versailles Treaty. By so doing they were handing Hindenburg, Ludendorff, and the whole German nationalist Right an excellent excuse for creating the legend that the German fighting man had never been defeated, but "stabbed in the back" by scheming politicians, unpatriotic Socialists, and effete intellectuals. Hitler was to be the beneficiary of those sentiments.

Then—to jump ahead a few years in our search for the "might have beens"—there was a *good* Anschluss to be had if the opportunity had been seized *before* Hitler came to power. Throughout the 1920s and up to their suppression in 1934, the Socialists were a strong force in Austria and a leading force in Vienna. After the dissolution of the Habsburg Empire, the Austrian Germans were casting about for an identity and a role for themselves in the middle of Europe. Were they Austrians? Were they Germans? Many of them, led by the Socialists, were eager for an Anschluss with Weimar Germany. Speaking with the wisdom of hindsight, we can now see that this might have been a good thing for both Austria and Germany—and the peace of Europe. It didn't happen, but it could have happened.

URBAN   To go on pursuing the unfashionable subjunctive mood in our story: What if Lenin had not died in 1924 but lived to be 65 to 70? Would the Soviet Union have avoided Stalinism, the forced collectivization of agriculture, the purges?

May I suggest that we limit ourselves to two related types of reasoning? The first, which originates, on the official plane at least, with Khrushchev, holds that, but for the criminal personality of Stalin, none of the "errors" of Stalinism would have occurred. This highly un-Marxist analysis has been reinforced and given popular currency under Gorbachev. One of Gorbachev's closest advisers, the outspoken Fyodor Burlatsky, put it in this way:

> Had Lenin lived for another 10 or 20 years, would the country have undergone the grim ordeals that befell it in 1937 and 1938? Never! . . . .

What would have happened had the 13th Party Congress followed Lenin's direct instructions and relieved Stalin of his duties as General Secretary of the Party Central Committee? There can be no doubt that our path would have been easier, more humane and much more effective.[24]

The second kind of approach asks whether Stalinism was a necessary or just a possible outcome of Leninism, and the answer that I personally hold to be most convincing comes from Leonard Schapiro:

All the elements which characterize Stalin's system of rules are to be found, at least in embryonic form, in Lenin's political practice. . . . It may be that Stalin was an 'improbable' development of Leninism. . . . But once the opportunity presented itself, "Leninism" contained all the elements for him [Stalin] to use for his purposes and for indulging the base elements in his character—there was not the remotest safeguard built into the system against the rise of a despot of this kind.[25]

The crucial question that will soon have to be asked under Gorbachev is whether the *system* can be rendered fireproof against despotism, and if so, at what risk to the assured rule of "socialism."

So, would Lenin, if he had lived longer, have given Soviet Communism a totally different complexion and left the world a different legacy?

HOOK There are so many contingencies involved that all I can offer are some informal guesses. First, as I read Leonard Schapiro, he is *not* saying that Stalinism is a "necessary" outcome of Leninism, and that if Lenin had lived, something comparable to Stalinism would have evolved. Second, had Lenin lived, Trotsky would probably have lived, too, but as a Jew he could hardly have become Number One. Both Lenin and Trotsky were much more intelligent than Stalin. Both were as capable of resorting to extreme measures as Stalin was if they deemed it necessary to preserve themselves in power. At one time Lenin advised shooting every tenth worker at random to overcome labour indiscipline, and Trotsky's behaviour at Kronstadt is well known. When the Mensheviks charged that NEP was introducing elements of capitalism into the Soviet Union, Lenin wrote indignantly, "And they complain that we shoot them for saying such things!"

Both Lenin and Trotsky were aware that "the leaden rump" of the bureaucracy was producing severe distortions in the Soviet economy, but they would never have permitted any other group, socialist or not, to come to power, because they still banked on the Marxist dogma of the inescapable collapse of capitalism and the Revolution in the West. They probably would have made a concerted move with the powerful

German Communist Party in the depths of the Depression, and have militarily intervened in 1936 (first with Polish marshal Józef Piłsudski and then against him) when Hitler marched into the Rhineland. World war would probably have followed civil war, whose outcome would have determined the fate of all Europe, including the Soviet Union, if the red armies had been defeated.

Lenin and Trotsky were more truly internationalist than Stalin. Lenin was always prepared to sacrifice huge areas of Russia to hold on to power. Had he lived, he would easily have come to terms with China in an attempt to establish a world socialist economy.

The programme of agricultural collectivism would probably have proceeded more slowly under Lenin and Trotsky than it did under Stalin, not out of human concern, but purely on the basis of domestic cost-benefit considerations. Gorbachev in the USSR and Deng in China are today more Leninist than Marxist. The economic disaster of trying to introduce socialism into such backward countries has impelled them, with the help of the capitalist West, to try anything that will enable them, after so many decades, to feed their own peoples.

Elements of free enterprise have therefore been introduced. How far they will succeed is an open question. If Marx is right, these economic changes will be reflected in political demands that will threaten the monopoly of political power of the Communist Party. If there is substantial danger to this monopoly, Gorbachev's policies may be reversed. Soviet apologists in the West will then attribute Gorbachev's defeat to the failure of the West to cooperate with him. Beyond this it is too risky to speculate. Nothing is fated but not all options are equally probable. There are too many variables involved.

URBAN   What if Stalin had never made it to the top post, but Trotsky had?

HOOK   Although I was, because of the treatment Trotsky had received at the hands of Stalin, in sympathy with Trotsky at the human level, I had written as early as 1935 that Trotskyism was "Stalinism manqué." I had come to that conclusion because I had opportunities to observe that the Trotskyist groups were prepared to act organizationally in exactly the same way as the Stalinist groups. They acted like genuine Leninists—fixed and sacred dogma, Machiavellian practice, and all.

On matters of policy, Trotsky was almost invariably more radical than Stalin, but there was a flaw, a strange capriciousness and unpredictability in his character. He was often asked, "How was it that you let Stalin come to power?" He didn't have a convincing answer.

Somehow he did not master the rules of the power struggle. For example, he did not go to Lenin's funeral, and, although he was the darling of the Red Army and a bit of a Napoleon in his own right, he always talked about the threat of Bonapartism. Side by side with his great oratorical skills and his sense of himself as a world historical figure was in him a certain diffidence about his own power. He could have played a Napoleonic role under the pretext of preventing a Thermidor and Bonapartism.

URBAN   What if Trotsky *had* come to power?

HOOK   Well, in that case Europe would have faced a full-scale civil war, but I am convinced that the Communists in Western and Central Europe would have lost even under Trotsky. Trotsky would have provoked revolutions in Germany, France, Italy—in every country that had an organizable band of idealists and malcontents he could have harnessed to his purposes—and there would have been bloody civil war. But I believe the West European Communists would have been defeated and so, most probably, would the Russian Communists themselves under Trotsky's leadership. The repercussions of a West European defeat could not have been limited to Western Europe. Lenin and Trotsky had frequently stated that the Bolshevik Revolution could not endure long if Western Europe did not follow suit. But from their point of view the reverse was equally true: the defeat of communism in Western Europe would have probably spelt its defeat in Russia, too. Neither of them believed that socialism as Marx conceived it could flourish or survive in one country. In the absence of a revolution in the West, everything that developed in the Soviet Union was an improvisation. It also showed that there were more possible variations in history than were conceived of in the Marxist schema.

URBAN   You are saying that it would have been in the general European interest if Germany, France, and other West European countries had experienced brief, prophylactic Communist revolutions similar to those that erupted in Bavaria and Hungary. The collapse of these would have made the Bolshevik Revolution in Russia equally short-lived.

HOOK   This is quite speculative; probably, yes, *if* Trotsky had taken and remained in power in the Soviet Union, and *if* the Red Army, which would have been involved, had been thoroughly defeated. Stalin was too cautious to run risks of the kind Trotsky seemed prepared to take. Why do I hold this view of Trotsky? Because, brilliant as he was,

Trotsky was a prisoner of Marxist dogma. John Dewey once referred to him as a first-rate mind frozen in Marxist dogma. He believed that misery would necessarily create the consciousness and the will on the part of the proletariat that would carry it to victory, and he believed this regardless of other conditions. Evidence: an article he wrote from Mexico in the magazine *Liberty* in 1936. In it he analyzed the situation in the U.S. and predicted revolution! Trotsky showed no awareness of traditions, history, and actual empirical realities. He reasoned in politics like a geometrician. He could do that much better than Stalin, who mumbled his dogma as he blundered, intent on holding on to what he had, without taking risks, no matter what. Hence "socialism in one country" regardless of what "socialism" turned out to be, a gulag economy, and a strong army.

URBAN   Your relationship with Trotsky was ambivalent. You helped to establish the Dewey Commission although Trotsky and his disciples were quite critical of you. You argued with Trotsky and defended him against the charges of the Moscow show trials. You had a certain sympathy for Trotsky because he was hunted, but you were impatient with his tyrannical nature and his blinkers.

HOOK   Well, democracy became of greater importance to Trotsky and his followers after he had lost power. Its attractiveness didn't last long. But let me say here before we lose the point that the Dewey Commission was not just about Trotsky, but about the truth of the Moscow trials and, in effect, about the legitimacy of the Bolshevik Revolution itself.

I am told I am an overly sentimental man by some unfriendly critics, and sometimes am disproportionately affected by small incidents in much larger tragedies. I never got over the news that when Tuchachevsky was shot, his twelve-year-old daughter hanged herself—nobody would take her in in Stalin's Russia. In Trotsky's case, too, it was a relatively minor aspect of his persecution that had a profound effect on me. On 23 May 1940, that Mexican thug the painter [David] Siqueiros and his accomplices attempted, at the NKVD's behest, to assassinate Trotsky. They broke into his study and swept his bedroom with submachine gun fire, leaving incendiary bombs and a large high explosive behind them. Trotsky and his wife escaped with slight wounds, but his ten-year-old grandson was more seriously injured. When I first heard about all this, although I knew that Trotsky's life was in danger (three months later, on 20 August 1940, he was assassinated by Ramon Mercader), I was indignant—and I wept, literally wept, at the fate of his grandson. It was the same emotion I had experienced when I heard about the suicide of Tuchachevsky's young daughter—the shame and the pity of innocent blood being shed.

But then, almost immediately, I said to myself shamefacedly, "Remember how many children and grandchildren and innocent adults *Trotsky* killed or ordered to be executed—why didn't you cry about *them?*" Well, such are the weaknesses of the human psyche. Trotsky's grandson and Tuchachevsky's daughter met their fate right before our eyes. Their tragedy became graphic and symbolic, whereas the slaughters Trotsky had been responsible for were hidden in history books and in statistics. None of which reduces Trotsky's responsibility.

URBAN   I respect the candid way in which you describe these matters, yet I am a little disappointed. After the defeat of Hitler and the death of Stalin I heard it repeatedly stated by friends in both Britain and the U.S., "Ah, the horrors of the gulag and of the Nazi concentration camps didn't really make an impression on us because the figures were too large and the misdeeds too outrageous." And the sequel to that observation was to say in later years: "But Anne Frank's diary and Solzhenitsyn's great work on the gulag—now those have brought it all home to us."

People who held such views were guilty, in my eyes, of intellectual parochialism and an inability to make the imaginative leap from statistical figures to live human beings and suffering. Yet, here I have a similar admission from an outstanding intellectual whose courage and imagination I admire.

HOOK   I regret disappointing you, but here I believe it is not I who am revealing parochialism. I doubt that you or anyone else can make an immediate imaginative leap from the vast statistics of war, crime, rape, poverty, and oppression to the bleeding and agonized victims the numbers refer to. Life would be a nightmare if you were so constituted.

At times what is dramatically imagined enables us to get a realizing sense of what we only abstractly know. "If we were all seated at the same table, no one would go hungry." I forget who said it, but it is profoundly true. In a sense we are all seated at the same table, but sometimes the imagination is necessary to bring the faces beyond our vision into focus. Perhaps the cultivation of the imagination, especially where human beings are involved, should become one of the primary educational arts.

Another illustration comes to mind. Long before I took the field against Lillian Hellman, a fanatical Communist fellow traveller who also endorsed the Moscow trials, I had seen or read her play *The Watch on the Rhine,* written before but produced after the Ribbentrop-Molotov pact. I was struck by the words of one of her protagonists, organizing help for refugees: "And what about the children?" I was outraged to the point of hysteria. "Wasn't she aware of all the children wandering the streets of the Soviet cities and villages or living in camps because Stalin's terror had left them parentless and destitute?" Of course she wasn't. She denied the terror and the terrible truth, as so many at that time did, because it would have shaken her faith had she actually seen concrete evidence of it. Of course, no one has a universal perspective. It is the individual drama and detail that gives the cognitive meaning of the fact a force that may affect our behaviour and sometimes reorient our understanding. There is no escaping this truth about human psychology. I take no credit for the incidents mentioned. They may just have been an attack of nerves.

URBAN   All three cases you have mentioned concern children. This is, if I may say so, an admirable trait, but I often think it is too easy to love the innocent and much more difficult to love and to forgive their parents. Yet, the peace of the world demands the latter more than the former.

HOOK   It does, and I hope I have not been completely remiss in recognizing it. It is for others to judge that aspect of my life, rather than myself.

URBAN   Did you know Trotsky?

HOOK   No, I had some correspondence with him. According to one of his secretaries, van Heijenoort, there were two persons in the U.S. the mention of whose names drove Trotsky up the wall. One was James Burnham and the other Sidney Hook—Hook apparently more than Burnham, and the reason is quite comic. Trotsky was convinced that he lost his following in the U.S.—a following split between James Cannon's orthodox group and Burnham's—because they did not understand the theory of the dialectic! And why did they not understand it? Because Hook had published an article attacking Engels's view of the dialectic in the *Marxist Quarterly,* which infected Burnham, who infected [Max] Shachtman and others. Hence, Trotsky would say in his typically graphic way, "You see, from a theoretical scratch of that kind it is only one small step to political gangrene."

URBAN   Wasn't that rather flattering for you? You must have demolished the dialectic pretty effectively.

HOOK   No, it was rather an indication of the utter dogmatism of Trotsky and of his belief that the theory of the dialectic had practical applications, whereas it is easily demonstrable that, with a little ingenuity, one can square the theory of the dialectic with anything one wants to believe. But Trotsky thought Marxism equalled the dialectic, and if one abandoned it, before long one would become a revisionist, then a Social Democrat, and end up as a counterrevolutionary.

If the destiny of nations were unaffected by this kind of scholasticism, one might well say that Trotsky's attitude was good for a laugh and nothing else. But, as we know from Gibbon, the lives of men and nations often depend on what appear to us to have been trivia, but were by no means trivia in the imagination of earlier times. The early Christian controversy about the consubstantiality of the Father and the Son—whether Homoousion or Homoiousion was the right way of denoting it, and whether consubstantiality meant the shared substance or the likeness of the Father and Son—is one celebrated example. People who dismiss or make fun of Communist theory in radical movements today as so much theology like to say, "Oh well, they are like the Christians, some of whom believe one gets reborn by sprinkling, others by dipping," not realizing that sometimes these important theological differences conceal policy differences that can decide, and did decide, the fate of large numbers.

URBAN   The glib journalists' and hurried parliamentarians' dismissal of the ideological element of Soviet rule—they can seldom afford reading difficult books—is very much in evidence on both sides of the Atlantic today. Isn't this one of the most effective barriers to the public understanding of totalitarianism?

HOOK   Yes, it is. Reading and digesting books is an effort, and there is a type of person who does not like to believe that people are really guided by ideas, because *he* is not. There is little you can do about them. The *causes* of ideas in personal and historical life is a very difficult and complex question, but the *effects* of ideas on human behaviour can more readily be established. Sometimes the effects are fatal.

URBAN   What was your correspondence with Trotsky about?

HOOK   I had written an essay on Marxist method to which he wrote a reply. Then we exchanged letters. My approach, even in my salad days as a Marxist was that the Marxist study of society could correct itself by the use of its own methods of empirical investigation. This meant perpetual revisionism, which ruled out Marxist orthodoxy. From Trotsky's point of view, the trouble with my approach was this: If Hook was going to use scientific methods to test social theories, then he was duty-bound to accept any conclusion resulting from it. Why call it Marxism? Trotsky was dimly aware that there was a danger of stressing Marxism as a *method* rather than as a *programme*.

Let me add that György Lukács, on other grounds, had come to a similar conclusion. Whether he was ever aware of what I had written, I do not know. In any case, I had very little respect for Lukács, and that for at least two reasons. First, I heard from people who knew him in Moscow at the time of Stalin's great wave of terror that he was a "finger-man"—that he owed his life in part to his willingness to denounce and betray other Hungarian Communists. Second, he is on record with a judgement that is despicable. He is said to have opined, after a mild critique of "existing socialism": "In the end, however, I want to make it clear that I believe that the worst Communist regime is better than the best capitalist regime." I have never forgiven him for this piece of untruthfulness and demagogy.

The Lure of Ideology

URBAN   Suppose we were able to cast our eyes back upon our time, with the wisdom of hindsight, a few hundred years from now, after nuclear wars and ecological disasters have done their work and knocked some sense into the warring tribes of mankind—wouldn't we look upon the contests of ideologies and nationalisms of the twentieth century with incredulity? Wouldn't we be inclined to relegate fascism, communism and nazism to minor chapters in the history books, as so much evidence of the myopia of an age that went on playing childish games when the erosion of the biosphere of our planet and nuclear profligacy were about to deprive humanity of the very basis of its existence?

One factor that accounts for Mikhail Gorbachev's popularity in the West appears to be his recognition of global problems of this kind. He has what *our* politicians haven't: a transnational "peace" agenda based on a transnational philosophy. This has earned him a great deal of criticism from Stalinist quarters in the Soviet Union ("Does the international working class no longer oppose world capital as embodied in its state and political organs?" Nina Andreyeva asked[26]), but has by no means stopped him.

Can you, as a leading protagonist in the war of ideologies of our age, place the focus of your thinking, say, three centuries ahead of our time and agree with those who claim, as it were *sub specie aeternitatis,* that the battles of this blood-soaked century will appear to future historians as a gigantic irrelevance to the real problems of mankind?

HOOK   Three hundred years from now our survivors, if they *were* willing to recognize some kind of consanguinity with us, would probably refer to this period as the era of the wars of political faiths. I do not think that they would look at it so narrowly as to distinguish the Nazi political faith from other expressions of totalitarian political faiths; they would regard our time as a time of struggle between the political theology of totalitarianism on one hand and democratic open societies on the other.

But there are more things in the future than we can anticipate. We cannot tell whether, when the fires of theological faiths are extinguished, there will not emerge new kinds of nationalist goals, for example, in Africa, or whether, if the Chinese don't settle their population problem, there won't be fierce wars for survival in Asia and between Europe and Asia. A few years ago, in an idle moment, when I was trying to encourage Chinese opposition to the Soviet Union in order to weaken the aggressive impulses of the Kremlin, I asked myself what would happen if the West educated and armed a billion bright Chinese whose fundamental values were very different from our own. And I thought: "Who knows, maybe a time will come when the Soviets will approach us and say, 'For our joint safety, we have to unite against this new wave from the East. They have tremendous numbers; they can lose hundreds of people for every one of our own and still survive.' " I remember Mao Zedong's remark that he was prepared to lose 300 million in a conflict with the West. So I said to myself, "Let's not encourage them prematurely."

Three hundred years of calendar time doesn't amount to very much in history. Wouldn't there be other issues almost of equal importance challenging that mode of life which today we identify with England and the United States, without defining it too precisely? All I am prepared to say is: If this liberal, humane outlook on the world were destroyed, it would be a matter of complete indifference to me who my descendants were, just as now I don't care who my ancestors, the tree-dwelling animals of the past, were.

So, to meet your question head on, I hope a time will come when the genuinely united democratic nations of the world will look back

upon this period and say, "Just as we transcended the wars of religion
that lasted a couple of centuries, so we have transcended the wars of
political theology which lasted a whole century, and ended in a nuclear
explosion of such devastation that we are now going to sit down and
live, if not according to the Sermon on the Mount, like Christians, at
least like tolerant civilized human beings under a Parliament of Mankind that offers the hope of a new age."

Now, if you asked me about the probability of this happening at the
present time, with an eye on what's developing in Africa and elsewhere, I would say it's not very high. Even if the Soviet Union were
to return to the comity of nations of the era before 1914, the Ayatollah
Khomeini might carry all of Asia Minor and North Africa with him.
The world would then enter another era of fanaticism with characteristics we can only vaguely imagine. We live in a world of plural
conflicts. I have been accused of seeing only the conflict between the
Soviets and the West. That is not true. I am aware of what is happening
in China and in Iran, but I do think all these fanaticisms could have
been avoided if our statesmen had understood, in time, both the nature
of communism and the nature of the other totalitarian doctrines.

URBAN   Let me assume, in common with many students of history,
that, within the short span of three or four thousand years, human
nature is constant. If so, wouldn't a universal peace under a "Parliament of Mankind" extinguish those springs of idealism in the souls of
men that have led to our greatest achievements in art and culture, but
have also led to suicidal wars and totalitarian fanaticism? In other
words, if entertaining holistic credos and fierce idealisms is an unalter-
able need of the human psyche, where will these idealistic passions go
if and when mankind can no longer afford to give them quarter?

HOOK   I was interested in that opening phrase of yours—that you
believed in the constancy of human nature. One of the permanent
insights in Marx, which derives from Hegel, is his historical approach
to the concept of nature. I believe with Marx that human nature is
modifiable, but it is very difficult to modify it. We have seen human
beings change their eating habits from cannibal civilizations to the
exquisite cuisine of the French—human beings possessing the same
human nature. So I would say, "Human nature is anything human
beings can be induced to do." As I read the record, there is nothing
you can't get human beings to do, or prevent them from doing, if the
pressures of the environment are strong enough.

I don't know whether I should say this in public since it can be easily misunderstood or distorted. What the Germans did to the Jews seemed to be a violation of human nature: the Beethoven- and Mozart-loving Germans, and the Goethe- and Schiller-loving Germans supported a regime that organized the genocide of Jews—even though individual Germans did not countenance what happened. I know that this sounds quirky and even offensive (and I dare not say it to my friends), but I believe any people in the world, when roused to a fury of nationalistic resentment, and convinced that some individuals or group is responsible for their continued and extreme misfortunes, can be led to do or countenance the same things the Germans did.

I am mindful of various incidents in the Old Testament and of what happened to the Jews in Spain when they were driven out at the time of the Inquisition. There *have* been *autos-da-fé* in other countries, if not on such a vast scale as in our century. Most of my Jewish friends throw their hands up in horror and say, "How can you make a comparison between incidents of past brutality and the Holocaust?" It has become something of such unutterable horror to them that one is not permitted to compare anything with it, even though to call it the greatest crime in human history is already to compare it. I can't go along with that. I believe that if conditions in the U.S. were ever to become as bad psychologically and economically as they were in Germany in the 1920s and 1930s, systematic racial persecution might break out. It could happen to the blacks, but it could happen to the Jews, too, or any targeted group. Listening to how some redneck Ku Kluxers talk, or to [Louis] Farrakhan's panegyrics to Hitler and his defamation of the Hebrew religion, one is shocked into fear that unimaginably evil programmes could find agents to carry them out.

URBAN   But is there really any ground for such feverish fantasies? Was the American Civil War fought in vain? Has the American civil rights movement not altered the political climate?

HOOK   Where human relations are concerned, war rarely determines anything except which side is the stronger. The Holocaust was an unimaginable fantasy to the most persecuted people of the world.

To diverge for a moment: It may strike you as odd, but I have considerable documentation which will establish in the mind of any objective person that a handful of militant blacks on some U.S. campuses determine what is to be taught in many areas, how it is to be taught, and by whom; and if their demands (they never say "requests"—it's always "demands") are not met, they occupy the administrative offices until they are gently persuaded to leave—not by the police, but by the trembling accents of the administrators. I can't believe that anything like this would occur in England, and it certainly wouldn't happen in many areas of the United States.

These blacks have become militant because they realise that they are dealing with a lot of timid, cowardly whites—liberals who are fearful of the consequences of talking back. Actually, there is more suppressed bitterness and anti-racial feeling amongst both blacks and whites since the desegregation decision[27] than there was before it.

The fundamental reason is this: The liberals are trying to atone (they can never *really* atone) for the sin of slavery. The American colonists should have hanged the slavers when they first appeared off the coast, even though slavery as an institution was universal at the time. But they didn't, and so U.S. society is now trying to compensate the blacks for their sufferings by offering them equal opportunity, or rather greater opportunity. Unfortunately, some blacks, especially those who have improved their lot, are not as eager to extend these opportunities as they are to get revenge or receive special dispensations. That's why there may be a lot of trouble in the future. The blacks may go too far and some whites may react.

Many of my liberal friends, however, are prepared to yield and concede everything in order to avoid an escalation that may result in open racial conflict. This is wrong, because it is almost certain to provoke it.

URBAN   Can you see a solution?

HOOK   There are no easy solutions to the problem that becomes more acute with every passing year. It won't go away by ignoring it or refusing to talk about it, or, as is currently observable on the academic scene, yielding to false cries of racism by militant black students and compromising principles of fairness and academic integrity in hopes of placating black demagogues and their white ritualistic liberal allies. Such behaviour plays into the hands of genuine racists, both white and black.

URBAN   But compared with how the Russian, the Estonian, the Polish, and all the other peoples of the Soviet empire lost more and more of their rights in the 1930s, 1940s, 1950s, and arguably later too, isn't it true that the lot of the American blacks has been one of amazing progress and emancipation?

HOOK   Despite what some demagogues say, the improvement of the political, social and economic status of American blacks since the defeat of nazism and fascism in World War II has been more impressive than of any other oppressed people in history in a comparable time frame. Roy Wilkins and Bayard Rustin were foremost among the few black leaders to see and say this. The United States has still far to go to achieve the objectives of Martin Luther King, the approach to which is threatened by the words and actions of both white racists and blacks who persistently make false charges of racism.

But to return to the theme of human nature, when I was a boy living in Brooklyn, one day on the way to the Pratt Library from the slum in which we lived, I ran into a race riot. It was very frightening. I huddled in a doorway and watched blacks attack any white and whites attack any black. The *Brooklyn Daily Eagle* never carried that story for fear of inciting passions, yet the riots following the assassination of Martin Luther King and others could not be avoided. So you ask me to make predictions on the basis of human nature! Who knows, anything is possible. I cannot make any reliable predictions about the future of human behaviour on the basis of *human* nature itself, for all of its expressions reflect historical and cultural forces of varying intensity.

URBAN   When I suggested that, in one broadly accepted reading, human nature is constant, I was merely trying to stress that in every age and in every society we find a fairly constant "balance of the passions." In one guise or another there will always be "ideological" absolutists; there will always be appeasers for appeasement's sake, appeasers who just want to save their bacon, power holders whose passion is power, born iconoclasts whose passion is deflating authority, born romantics and people an innate classical disposition, and so on. It was this distribution of psychological types that I was trying to describe as "constant," and I was wondering where the "absolutists" would go in a sanitised world 300 years on. They cannot all become English football hooligans.

HOOK   I would agree with you only to the extent that the *biological* aspects of human nature are given. Man is a singing animal, he is a laughing animal, he is a jealous animal, he is a fighting animal. But what he fights for, what he sings, what he prays for—all that varies according to culture. Some people say that even biology is affected by culture. In his early writings, Marx goes so far as to maintain that how people *see* and *hear* is culturally determined. Just recently somebody made a reputation by maintaining that *seeing,* too, is a sort of cultural phenomenon, that you are taught what to look for in such a way as to affect your powers of vision. I am sceptical of that, although prepared to admit that genetic engineering may do the work that uncontrolled mutation took thousands of generations to achieve.

Dialectical materialists tend to believe that somehow or other, if you change the class structure of society, you will end up changing the biological aspects of man too. They believe that if you modify the social environment sufficiently then, in time, there will be some hereditary response. But this is obvious nonsense. I recall the case of [August] Weissman, the German geneticist, who cut off the tails of mice for ninety generations; yet all the mice were born with tails. I remember saying to my professor of genetics at City College of New York, "Why do you have to perform an operation on ninety generations of mice? The history of the Jews and Muslims shows that circumcision has gone on for hundreds of generations and yet it has to be performed again and again." Until quite recently, the influence of Lamarck was still strong, not only on people like [Trofim] Lysenko in the Soviet Union, but in the West too. The need to believe that acquired characteristics would turn out to be hereditary was for many years part of the liberal credo.

URBAN   Don't you fear the impoverishment of the human experience if our world turned itself into a super-Switzerland? Can we want to bring about a state of affairs in which *War and Peace* could not be written because there would be no war, or the *St. Matthew Passion* could not be composed because no one would respond to the type of dedication and sacrifice that underlies the Gospels? (I never tire of quoting Goethe's words: "Wer nie sein Brot mit tränen ass . . . Der kennt euch nicht, ihr himmlischen Mächte."[28])

HOOK   I certainly believe that is a possibility. The greatest essay I have yet read along those lines—much profounder than some of Freud's works—is William James's *The Moral Equivalent of War*.[29] James was the most insightful psychologist who ever lived, even though he had an undue sympathy for the intellectual underworld which made him listen to cranks; but he had profound vision. *The Moral Equivalent of War* was an attempt to harness man's warlike instincts to the elimination of injustice and other perils to the common good. He thought that the satisfactions we get from martial victory could be realised in the satisfactions of "road-building and tunnel-making," or solving difficult problems. There is great truth in that. I don't know how far it would go, but I'm willing to try it.

URBAN   Do you think we can purge the human experience of its martial elements and yet retain some of those passions that make for "high" culture?

William James concedes that even in his own warless Utopia, "We must make new energies and hardihoods continue the manliness to which the military mind so faithfully clings. Martial virtues must be the enduring cement; intrepidity, contempt of softness, surrender of private interest, obedience to command, must still remain the rock upon which states are built."[30]

Several decades later, Stalin's regimentation of both Soviet youth and the Soviet economy, and Hitler's *Kraft durch Freude* movement, were inspired by similar considerations—though I doubt whether either Stalin or Hitler made a study of what William James had written on the subject in 1910. Sustaining the "martial virtues" seems to me common sense—or a common vice, depending on one's personal philosophy and the kind of society in which the martial virtues are practiced.

HOOK   This is a bit far-fetched. William James's "moral equivalent of war" was envisaged to be a *substitute*—not a *preparation*—for war. I never accepted the theory that war is a blessing in disguise. In Germany and elsewhere it was widely believed, both before and after the First World War, that war brought out the best in human beings, that it was an intellectual fertilizer, that it led to discoveries and had a positive effect on civilization. Georg Friedrich Nicolai's book *Die Biologie des Krieges*[31] was one of the flagships of this theory. My view is that we can find other stimuli without bloodletting. I can imagine the feeling of glory that a knight had when he beheaded some horseman who was trying to do the same to him. It's something of the feeling I have when I have just devastated an apologist for totalitarianism in a book review! Demolishing a man in a piece of writing is a fairly civilized way of exchanging blows, yet even there I have often been rebuked for writing too severely and not thinking of the feelings of the poor fellow whose book I was criticising. That often made me uncomfortable, especially when it aroused sympathy for my victim.

URBAN   But doesn't some blood have to be drawn? Nietzsche observed, "Write in blood." He didn't say: Write in red ink. You have yourself described one of man's tragic dilemmas in the following words: "If we have played it safe and made our existence apparently secure, the fascinating life of adventure and experience can never be ours. . . . If we have scorned to put down roots . . . we have thrust

from ourselves the warmth of sustained affection and comforting
regularities which can best heal the bruised spirit.''[32]

HOOK   I was speaking in that passage of individual choice of possible
careers. All my knowledge of literature tells me that you need not
write in blood. The appeal of Faust, for example, doesn't depend on
anything martial. Rather is it a superb invocation of the eternal
disparity between human ambition and human capacity. This has,
incidentally, assumed a fresh dimension in our own day—and here I
must digress once again for a moment.

The unhappiest people I know are no longer people who suffer from
material want, but those whose ambition outruns their talent. When I
was young, during the depths of the Depression, I knew people who
were hungry, people who wondered how they were going to pay their
rent. Today most of the people I know are much wealthier than I am
and they live in grander homes, but very few of them are happy—in
fact some of them are *very* unhappy. And what are they unhappy
about? Usually they are unhappy about an unfortunate love affair, or a
son or a daughter who has gone astray or been crippled in an accident.
Others have been bereft by the death of a loved one and not yet made
their peace with the irreversible.

But unhappiest of all are my academic colleagues whose ambitions
far exceed their capacities and who have before them models of
achievement that constitute almost a permanent rebuke to them. Some
of them overcome this feeling by becoming tribunes of the people.
They are the ones who sound off about the rights of the faculties, who
always say that faculty morale is terrible, who are always in the
forefront of academic unrest, demanding improvements in conditions
that are already comfortable. They are *not* the people who are making
the greatest contributions to the fields of science and art. If one
compares their academic output, it is usually way below par of the
average, which is not very high.

In the universities of the United States one can take fifteen years to
write a book and one can live on one's reputation for scholarship for
another fifteen years. By the time the second fifteen years are over,
one is close to retirement! Over the years, our intellectual standards
have deteriorated. Maybe they have deteriorated because there are so
many of us. We have, in the U.S., some 15,000 philosophers! I can't
imagine there could be, in our country, 15,000 "lovers of wisdom"—
that all of them could be really wise. The reason why, until recently,
the English philosophers were often first rate was because there were

so few of them. They were the cream of a select few, whereas in American universities everyone is called *and* chosen; they *call* themselves and their *colleagues* choose them.

URBAN Let me take the question of uniformity on broader ground. Opponents of European unification argue that the standardization of the European economy, a uniform transport system, a single system of weights and measures, standardized taxation, etc., would iron out those fruitful differences between Europeans of different languages and traditions that have created the sparkling variety in our culture— that a homogenized culture would result. This is the kind of thing I have in mind when I say to you, "Wouldn't an overall peace, induced by the threat of environmental extinction, mean the peace of the graveyard in the domain of culture?"

HOOK I don't believe that for a moment. The main justification I see for a United Europe is that it would create, for example, a united traffic rule system so that wherever you go you'll find the same traffic rules— including England. But I can't imagine that the cultural differences would disappear. There is an element of spontaneity in people that will keep those differences alive. But it is by no means obvious that even a unified currency system, a transport system, or a legal system can be achieved. I recall the remark made to me by Frode Jacobsen, once the leader of the Danish Resistance and a sensible man in that he was aware of the Soviet threat, but who eventually became a foolish and sentimental pacifist. In one of his rational moments he said to me that he despaired of European unification because "our attempt to unify Scandinavia runs into so many difficulties—I can't imagine that we will have fewer difficulties with uniting Europe!"

The Scandinavian countries illustrate what I have in mind. I think as a group they are probably more unified than any other area in Europe, and yet, when I go to Denmark I meet a different kind of a person from the people I meet in Sweden or Norway. In Denmark I get the impression of an easy-going Scandinavia, the equivalent of what Vienna used to be—decent people but unwilling to take even necessary risks. I go to Norway and I feel that I'm among Norsemen—upright and straightforward individuals. When I go to Sweden, I get the impression of fat, hypocritical, bourgeois types. I may be influenced too much by historical events, because, after all, Sweden was neutral and gave access to Hitler's troops, and it is now Sweden that is in the forefront of aiding every Third World dictatorship, provided it opposes the United States. I sometimes wonder why the Swedes are that way but not the Norwegians—whether the Swedes have really emancipated themselves from a sense of guilt about their attitude in the Second World War. Of course, they talk about having helped the Jews, etc., but they don't compare with the Norwegians who fought. Even my good friend, Gunnar Myrdal, who wrote a book about the American dilemma, contrasted the American credo with the absence of a similar credo in Sweden. This was at a time close to the end of the Second World War, and Myrdal must have been very unhappy that the Swedes took the neutral stance they did. But he was morally much more admirable and consistent than Olaf Palme, who contributed so much to the victory of the barbarous North Vietnamese Stalinists whose regime surpassed in terror and horror the acts of the South Vietnamese defending their national freedom.

URBAN   Clearly, you don't think that a more standardized environment would deprive us of those creative tensions which some of us feel we need if we want to avoid the castration of our intellectual and spiritual life?

HOOK   What puzzles me is why anyone should believe that it would. Look at France, which is certainly a highly centralized country. What strikes me there, once you leave Paris, is the difference between the various regions.

Let me, while we're on the subject of France, make some tangential observations. In the early postwar years, I found it very difficult to meet a Frenchman who wasn't contemptuous of Americans. I used to say that Paris was such a lovely city that the present generation of Frenchmen didn't deserve it. After experiencing a great deal of French irrationality, I ended up feeling that the only thing logical about French thinking was the Paris subway system, where everything was laid out perfectly.

The French were and are highly chauvinistic, except for their Communists. They voted against the European Defence Community, promoting, in effect, the rearmament of the German Federal Republic. I think the Americans were much too generous to the French after the war. The French largely collaborated with Nazi Germany after their defeat, and they have never forgiven us for that. In 1948–49 my wife and I were in France and we went round the country, especially Normandy and other places the Germans had occupied. We stayed in French farmhouses and were curious to learn about the behaviour of the German soldiers during their occupation. Everywhere we went we were told that German behaviour had been "très correct." The local population—at least those we spoke to—had no complaints. I have, of course, no doubt that those heroic elements who had come into contact with the Gestapo would have told us a very different story. But they were comparatively few. They constituted the heart of the resistance together with the Jews, and after Hitler invaded the Soviet Union, the members of the Communist Party were Soviet, not French, patriots.

Also, in France, the Germans were on their best behaviour. They showed a different profile in Poland and Russia. But all that is by the way.

URBAN   To come back to our story: You don't think that suffering is a vital stimulus for our spiritual culture?

HOOK   I would be prepared to forego the beauties of all of Solzhenitsyn's novels if there had not been a gulag. *War and Peace* is a little more complicated because the horrors of the Napoleonic war were spread out and didn't affect the general population so much. At the same time, the camp literature has opened the eyes of the world to the real nature of the Soviet system in a way nothing else could. Part of the intensity of my anti-Communist passion has been fuelled by reading the revelations of people who suffered in Soviet concentration camps. It began, even before my complete emancipation from the vestiges of Marxism-Leninism, when I read V.V. Chernavin's book, *I Speak for the Silent: Prisoners of the Soviet*,[33] which is an account of Chernavin's and his wife's escape from the northern camps through Finland. I didn't really know how to interpret that book, but then I read Anton Ciliga's *The Russian Enigma*.[34] I saw how the Soviets were treating people who were their comrades. Then there were three other books that made a great impression on me: the Austrian physicist Alexander Weissberg-Cybulski's *Hexensabbat*,[35] Margarete Buber-Neumann's *Als Gefangene bei Stalin und Hitler*,[36] and Elinor Lipper's *Elf Jahre in Sowietischen Gefängnissen*.[37] I wept when I read them, and I must tell you that I was looking for revenge as a result.

Then came Solzhenitsyn's shattering volumes about the gulag. My wife complained that I would just groan as I read them, and when I put these volumes down I felt I had lived through a nightmare—a nightmare that is still with me. From that day on, when I ask myself, "If I had power, how would I punish the people who had engaged in all these tortures?," the only thing I can think is putting them on the moon with nothing to read but Solzhenitsyn's *Gulag Archipelago*. Perhaps this is naive on my part, but I believe that reading those volumes would be punishment enough for the perpetrators, unless they were complete monsters.

And yet, and yet, I would be prepared to forego all these works of art that came out of human suffering and misery, if the suffering and misery had not occurred in the first place. Perhaps I'm a Philistine or just suffering from weak nerves.

URBAN   Whichever it is, you are in good company. Some years ago I discussed a similar question with Salvador de Madariaga and he told me almost exactly what you have.

HOOK   Well, Madariaga always surprised me. A Spaniard with commonsense—there are very few of those! A good many of the Spaniards I know are Don Quixote types. A man whom I can't abide (I hope I'm not doing him an injustice) is Miguel de Unamuno, author of *Tragic Sense of Life*.[38] For him the tragic sense of life is that he is not immortal. The conceit of the man to complain that he doesn't live forever!

URBAN   Isn't this a matter of personal inclination, though? Unamuno cannot tolerate the finiteness of the human adventure and the finality of death. You, on the other hand, if I read you correctly, see man's tragic dilemma in the conflicts between one good and another, and one right and another. Unamuno is what one might call *jenseitsorientiert*, whereas I would describe your sense of the tragic as *diesseitsorientiert*. Aren't these just two different but complementary approaches to understanding the human condition? I would not want to invoke Unamuno's philosophy in planning the future of my children, any more than I would want to be offered the verities of pragmatism on my deathbed.

HOOK   Well, Unamuno's hunger for immortality is so strong that he rejects not only the finiteness of life but also intelligence and reason as the chief enemies of life. "The very essence of tragedy," he tells us, "is the combat of life with reason." And since the Inquisitor is concerned with the eternal life of his victim's soul, the potential victim must defend the Inquisitor's place in society and regard him as far superior to the merchant who merely ministers to his needs.

I embrace what one might call the pragmatic approach to the human tragedy. I think it is more serious and more heroic than any other approach because it does not conceive of tragedy as a preordained doom, but as one in which the plot to some extent depends on us. It is an attempt to make it possible for men to live in a world of inescapable tragedy without lamentation, defiance, or make-believe. It focuses its analysis on the problems of society in order to reduce the costs of tragedy. It sees in men something which is at once more wonderful and more terrible than anything else in the universe, namely, the power to make themselves and the world around them better or worse.

Looking back, therefore, at our time from an imaginary observation platform some 300 years from now, as you suggested at the beginning of this conversation, I would say that the meaning of our century is the need to think through the problems of freedom and survival afresh. I hold the view that our alternatives are not limited to surrender and the extinction of freedom on the one hand, and war and the danger of human extermination, on the other. There are alternatives to be explored—all tragic in their costs, but not equally extreme. The very willingness to go down fighting in defence of freedom may be the greatest force for peace when facing an opponent who makes a fetish of historical survival. The best way of saving one's life is sometimes to be prepared to lose it.

A Question of Allegiance

URBAN   In March 1933 you saw Earl Browder, leader of the U.S. Communist Party, at his request. What he asked you was to spy for the Communist Party and the Soviet Union. You were shocked and did not comply, but what were the psychological and political circumstances that emboldened Browder to ask you in the first place? You were, after all, not a member of the Communist Party, and had been taken to task by American Communists, not least by Browder himself, for your "revisionism."

HOOK   When Browder asked me "to spy" for the Communist Party and the Soviet Union he did not, of course, put it in such a crude fashion or in words as plain and simple as that. I was asked to engage in an "extension of organized labour activity," to counter a disinformation campaign organized against the American working class by a *positive* educational campaign through newspapers and magazines, and to pass on news about weapons that could be used in a war that would destroy civilization, a war that would start, of course, with a crusade against the USSR.

If Browder were taxed at the time to say that he was trying to recruit an espionage agent, he would have responded that he was just giving "an honest liberal," someone who preferred to be a sincere friend of the Soviet Union, an opportunity to live up to his responsibilities. To a hostile critic Browder probably would have said that Hitler had come to power and anything that worked against Hitler and the Nazis and for the defence of the Soviet Union could, *a priori,* not be against the true interests of the United States.

Remember, Browder was a very shrewd and experienced recruiter for the NKVD, and until he had wrapped someone up in irretrievably compromising ties he would never be so explicit as to put himself in a position where an untried neophyte and possible defector could have him at his mercy. One slip by Browder would be enough for his superiors to send him into oblivion.

URBAN   When you refused Browder's offer, did he find a replacement?

HOOK   I have reason to believe that the "arrangement" I turned down was undertaken by a very high-society lady and social worker à la Beatrice Webb, of impeccable antecedents, one of the Daughters of the American Revolution, Mary Van Kleek, who, I am convinced, was a secret member of the Communist Party and a friend of the Dewey family. She almost betrayed her hand in her desperate attempt to persuade Dewey not to go to Mexico to chair the Trotsky hearings.[39]

URBAN   Were you aware that other members of the U.S. left-wing intelligentsia (Whittaker Chambers for example) were about to perform, or were actually performing, the same kind of service, on the basis of the same rationale Browder was articulating to you?

HOOK   I happened to be aware, because of a number of oversights by lesser Communist Party officials, that an underground apparatus was in operation. So I surmised very quickly what was involved; what Browder asked was too much for me.

It may surprise you but I am convinced that there were at the time quite a number of fanatical Soviet sympathizers who were not prepared to risk their status or reputation by being members of the Communist Party, but who would have been most willing to accept the sort of offer Browder made to me, not realizing what they were letting themselves in for until it was too late. To this day, very few people are aware of the intensity of the psychological and moral chaos produced by the Depression, and all this happened at the depths of the Great Depression. Further, one must bear in mind the impact on totally disordered minds among the *literati*—on the bleeding hearts, pacifists and do-gooders—of the fears of Hitler and fascism (everyone assumed when Hitler came to power that war with Russia would soon break out). At the same time, we were exposed to a remarkably organized lying propaganda about the great triumphs of the Soviet Union's Five-Year Plans, the absence of unemployment, excellent social services, and so on. It is a sad commentary on human credulity, but it would hardly be an exaggeration to say that merely by reading inflated accounts of the dangers of war and equally inflated accounts of the remarkable achievements of the Soviet Union, a considerable number of people became emotional sympathizers with Soviet Communism. In time, they developed a scepticism towards any critical attacks and warnings about the Kremlin, and became willing consumers of propaganda emanating from Moscow.

You must also remember that the mentality I am talking about was centered in New York, which was, because of its closeness to Europe, polyglot population, and intense political consciousness and factionalism, not representative of other regions of the U.S.

URBAN   Browder must have looked upon you as a man of the Enlightenment, which you frequently said you were, and he must have assumed that for a man of the Enlightenment there were loyalties more profound than those of "King and Country." Why should a man of the Enlightenment feel that disloyalty to a system he regarded as unjust and wicked *was* disloyalty? As you have hinted, he could have assumed that one did not have to be a Communist in order to serve Soviet interests with a clean conscience.

HOOK   A man of the Enlightenment does believe in loyalty to "King and Country," but not to *any* king, and he does not believe in "my Country, right or wrong." To a man of the Enlightenment, the ideals of freedom and human welfare transcend all other ideals. If he were convinced that disloyalty to a wicked king and a wicked country would further the prospects of true freedom and true human welfare, he would maintain that he was still being loyal to the ideals of the Enlightenment if he violated the laws of the wicked king and country. A rough analogy: Imagine a person who is both a pious Christian and a patriot. The pious Christian has a revelation that the Second Coming is at hand. But to make the return of Christ possible with all its promise, he must violate the sacred laws of the king or country— whether they are good or bad. He would not consider himself immoral or unworthy in sight of the Lord if he did what was necessary for the

Second Coming. That is the most charitable interpretation that can be given to the treasonable activities of the fanatical Communist.

URBAN   Before the age of nationalism it was generally accepted that the crowned heads of Europe owed allegiance to a supranational source of legitimacy—Christianity and Rome. The fact that there were, from time to time, corrupt popes, was not supposed to weaken the crowned heads' loyalty, although it did, and we know with what consequences. Nevertheless, the idea that certain principles of faith and conduct transcend national cultures and loyalties was universally accepted for many centuries. If communism is a "secular religion" (as Richard Lowenthal holds), doesn't the supranational loyalty principle flow from it quite naturally even if, from time to time, communism is headed by a corrupt or erring leader such as Stalin?

What I am saying is: Browder was behaving naturally, and so were all those U.S. Communists or sympathisers who did his bidding. It is Sidney Hook's (highly honourable) refusal that has to be explained.

HOOK   Communism is indeed "a secular religion," but, as with all religions, there are various degrees of intensity and intelligence with which the secular faith is accepted. The fact that an individual pope is demonstrably corrupt may not affect the fundamental loyalty of believers in Catholic dogma, even in the dogma of infallibility, but a succession of such popes, or a succession of dubious actions of the Church, gradually undermines religious belief. One may compare the Communist Party to the Jesuits, actually to the discredit of the Communist Party, because only recently has the Communist Party disavowed one of its "criminal" leaders, and this only when he was dead. But, unless I am mistaken, the Jesuit order has very often, and certainly recently, worked against the power of the reigning pope.

URBAN   In your memoirs you depict the kind of reasoning that made it natural for U.S. Communists and their sympathisers to engage in espionage for the Soviet Union. You talk about "total sacrifice" and "highest fidelity" to the Soviet cause. How general was the acceptance of this rationale among American Communists and their sympathisers? Were you yourself at any time tempted to follow suit? Were Stalin's despotism and the Moscow show trials your only reasons for not falling in line?

HOOK   At no time, even in my salad days as a "revolutionary Marxist," was I a true believer capable of accepting everything the Soviet Union or Communism would do for the sake of "the health and survival of the Revolution." Remember, I had *publicly* criticised not only Marx and Engels for obvious mistakes and for fundamental errors in their theory of historical materialism, but Lenin himself. Actually, in the eyes of the Russians the latter was the unforgivable offence, but the bitter factional struggles among the leaders of the American Communist Party blinded these leaders to the significance of deviations from approved Moscow thinking in all fields outside the purely *political* sector.

I was considered a target and a "catch" by Browder because I was regarded as the best instrument for bringing that "honest liberal," John Dewey, onto the cultural periphery of the Communist movement. At that time Dewey was quite properly regarded as the leading intellectual figure in the United States. He had returned from an officially sponsored visit to the Soviet Union (where he had been regaled with visions of carefully organized Potemkin village exhibits on education and culture) with a generally sympathetic report. He was aware of and did make mention of the terrible human costs of these great social advances (on paper), and said that he was glad that the Revolution had taken place in Russia rather than in the United States. Dewey's subsequent writings and reports on the Soviet Union, for which I can, with undue modesty, claim some credit, made up, I think, for some of the shortcomings of his earlier report.

URBAN   You quote Browder as having said to you:

> Sometimes it is an advantage to be able to say that one is not a Party member. You would be surprised to learn the names of some persons whose application for membership we have declined. We are not asking you to be a member of the Party, and we would reject your membership. . . . But nonetheless, I am persuaded that, despite theoretical differences, you, like us, regard the existence and the defence of the Soviet Union as the hope of a Socialist World. You would get no reward except the satisfaction of serving the only cause that can resist fascism.[40]

This is probably the classic formula under which Klaus Fuchs, Bruno Pontecorvo, George Blake, Kim Philby, Guy Burgess, Donald Maclean, and others operated—although some of these men were, at one time or another, members of the Party.

Were you aware at the time that espionage work of one kind or another was being carried out by sympathisers? Was the pursuit of information work for the benefit of the Soviet Union a subject of discussion among sympathisers? Did the question of conflicting loyalties arise?

HOOK   It is difficult to answer the series of questions you ask with complete accuracy because I cannot now clearly distinguish between what I definitely knew then, in 1933, and the effects on my awareness of revelations that have poured out in the 55 years since then, but I did definitely know that some acquaintances of mine had disappeared from public life and were in the underground. In fact, I described in my memoirs a couple whom I met in Berlin in 1928 and 1929 whose case illustrates my point. They broke discipline by revealing the truth to me and I gathered from them that there were others who did similar work. Whittaker Chambers's activities were generally known, not only among his friends and comrades in the Communist Party, but also among individuals who had been expelled from the Communist Party and were active in the Lovestone and Trotskyite groups. In fact, I used to be regaled with stories, many of them embroidered or imaginary, by Felix Morrow and Max Shachtman about Chambers's exploits. One thing is certain and was confirmed to me by Walter Krivitsky in 1939, namely, that all the operatives in the underground were ideologically motivated; indeed, in the eyes of their Moscow controllers, *too much* so; because of the very intensity of their faith and willingness to sacrifice their careers and lives, they sometimes sat in judgement on the Kremlin's political line. That was one of the reasons, I was told, why these idealists were *compelled* to take money even when personally they didn't need it or had other ways of getting it. The Kremlin did not want them to feel holy and unselfish.

Later on, the Kremlin must have abandoned its reliance on ideological agents for the kind that could be bought. It is truly amazing to discover how many Americans have been "bought"—offspring of members of the FBI and of ordinary patriotic families included. The question of conflicting loyalties, so far as I can surmise, never became focal in the minds of the ideological agents. They would probably have answered that they were being loyal to the best interests and best traditions of the United States as they conceived these. I think they would have despised other Americans who became spies for the Soviet Union for *money* on the obvious ground that if they could be bought for X amount of dollars, then they could be rebought for $X + 1$ dollars. Interestingly enough, the Communists never recognized the force of idealism in those who fought against them. They never took note of the selfless dedication of some FBI agents who were frequently serving, in the cause of uncovering Communist subversion, in more dangerous posts than soldiers do for the sake of their country.

URBAN   You write in your memoirs:

Of course, most members of the Communist Party were inspired, perhaps foolishly, by the purest ideological motives and had nothing to do with underground activities. Thus it was unfortunate when, years later, the revelations of Chambers and Elizabeth Bentley about the covert penetration of high government positions by Party members led hysterical conservatives to attribute collective guilt to anyone identified as a Communist.[41]

One is, of course, against every kind of political hysteria and witch-hunt, but your use of the words *collective guilt* strikes me as curious.

I would have thought the attribution of collective guilt meant, for example, the persecution of blacks because they were blacks, of "kulaks as a class" because they were kulaks, that is to say, the persecution of people who have no choice of belonging or not belonging to the group to which guilt is ascribed. But Communists are not of that kind. Every Communist, when he joins the Party, makes a deliberate choice of subscribing to the tenets and obligations of Party membership. It would, therefore, seem to me that while the application of collective guilt to blacks and kulaks is wholly unjust and repulsive, the application of collective guilt to Communists is not, because they have freely chosen to embrace a creed that implies and frequently demands disloyalty to the law.

So while it is, for a civilized man, certainly distasteful to express suspicion about the security qualifications of every Communist *qua* Communist, isn't it something communism itself has foisted on us and we cannot evade?

HOOK   Of course, if individuals who joined the Communist Party because they were snared by the Party's activities in a strike, or for a specific issue in a neighborhood, a rent campaign or whatnot, knew what they were letting themselves in for, or if they could be encouraged to think critically about what they read in the Communist press, the Communist parties would lose large parts of their membership at once. (It is calculated that Communist Party membership in the United States ran into several millions, but very few people remained for any length of time. The Communist Party lost half its membership after the Nazi-Soviet pact, and large numbers on other occasions.)

Anyone who is or was recently a member of the Communist Party should be considered a security risk for any post in government and other areas involving national security. That goes without saying. And if there is any history, no matter how far back, of such affiliation, such a person must be vetted carefully. What was incredible about the

British security system was that a man's membership in the Communist Party at any time was regarded as irrelevant. This went for Fuchs and Pontecorvo and others as well. The trouble with American security was not that the U.S. *did* have a security system which was indispensable, in my view, when the truth about the Soviet penetration of government services in Canada, the United States, Britain, and other countries became known, but *how* that security system operated. Too many of the individuals who were assessing the degree of risk were political innocents who could not distinguish between Socialists and Communists and regarded anyone who believed in the government ownership of railroads or in rent control as suspect. There is a point to the well-known story of the police breaking up an illegal Communist meeting at Union Square and a man pleading with a policeman who had collared him, "But, officer, I am an anti-Communist." To which the policeman, presumably Irish, replies, "I don't care what kind of a Communist you are," as he hurls him into the paddy wagon.

The operating maxim of any security system should be that anyone who owes a superior allegiance to a foreign government is disqualified to serve his own. Until recently, anyone who was a member of the Communist Party in the United States was in effect giving allegiance to a foreign government.

URBAN   Do you think the Soviet Union in its present heretical and nonmilitant state is still able to attract the allegiance of the potential Philbys and Fuchses amongst us? Would they be willing to run great risks and make personal sacrifices for a system that seeks, by its own admission, to write off the international class struggle, that feels itself to be interdependent with the West, that is changing its offensive military doctrine to a defensive one and is seeking to present itself to the world as nonconspiratorial?

HOOK   The answer to this is no. Those who in the past would have been willing to serve the Soviet Union would no longer do so. They and other like-minded revolutionists agree today only on one thing: Abandoned and betrayed by the Kremlin, by Peking, by Hanoi, and by Havana, they are all and only anti-American. Anything that will bring down this country in anarchy and chaos, in spite of all the sweet talk of Utopia, is what they desire.

So far, *glasnost* is limited. I have seen no let-up in the disinformation activities of the KGB. They obviously deal only with people who will not only sell their country for money but their souls too. Their only fear is of buying the services of a double agent. I am still not convinced that the Soviet Union under Gorbachev is willing to become a sincere member of the concert of civilized nations. Things may have developed beyond the possibility of restoring a Stalinist regime, but to me so long as the Berlin Wall stands, the Cold War is not over. Judging by the sudden turns which the Kremlin is able to make in foreign policy, they must be counting on the limitless credulity of the editors of the *New York Times* and the *Washington Post,* of uninformed American public servants, fear of Germany, and anti-American sentiment in Europe.

One final word. I get the impression that I have not yet succeeded in answering the questions which puzzle you. Why should Browder have propositioned me? Didn't that presuppose a degree of shared political outlook hard to reconcile with my other statements? These, I presume, are the questions bothering you. You must remember that I was among the thirty or forty "distinguished," so-called intellectuals who in 1932, as a kind of protest against the platforms of the Democratic and Republican parties, which called merely for balancing the budget, supported the electoral ticket of the Communist Party—Foster and Ford. I was the only exposed person among them in the sense that I had an official university post. Everyone, including myself, expected me to be dismissed from my job at the end of the year. This was in line with what had happened in the past even when professors supported mildly liberal or progressive causes. At the same time, shortly after the electoral campaign, I came under fierce attack by the Kremlin through all of its outlets as a Social Fascist or worse, because of my criticism of Lenin and of dialectical materialism, and because of my semi-Trotskyist sympathies. The English *Labour Monthly* carried some articles by a Hungarian Communist in Moscow by the name of László Rudas under the title, "The Fascism of Sidney Hook." This was a little later, but at the time Browder had been warned about how dangerous a man I was.

From Browder's point of view, since he anticipated that I would be dismissed from the university and was *publicly* regarded as an enemy by the Communist movement, I would have made a wonderful "agent of influence" for the Kremlin's cause, since no one would have suspected me of hidden sympathies once I had been denounced as a Fascist and Social Fascist in Communist publications.

The real question one should ask is: Why was I so foolhardy and rash to come out openly with the idea that only the Communists would resist the rise of Hitler to power? This is a complex question involved with the devastating medical history and tragedies of my family which I discovered had taken place when I returned from my stay abroad. I had a very deep sense of guilt that they had suffered and I had not, since the news was concealed from me while I was abroad. I can imagine that psychoanalytical explanations might suggest that I was trying to punish myself, expecting as I did to incur the wrath of the powers that be, etc. But I have never put any stock in psychoanalysis, although I confess that despite its scientific failings I myself sometimes make use of it.

I don't know how much time I have left. Half the time I feel I shall leave the world with a sense of relief, half the time I feel I shall leave the world with a sense of regret that I can no longer be on the firing line.

1987–1988

Chapter 2

Aftermaths of Empire

A Conversation with Hugh Trevor-Roper (Lord Dacre)

If Hitler Had Won

URBAN These are intriguing times for the student of modern dictatorships. For the first time in history, a totalitarian party and state have shown themselves, without defeat in war, to be bankrupt in fact if not in rhetoric. "The dictatorship of the proletariat" is moribund, not only by the standards of its Western critics, but by those, too, by which it has itself chosen to be judged. The immensity of this fact has yet to be fully understood by our public opinion. How did it all come about, seeing that the system has always claimed to have privileged access to "the logic of history" and indeed to be its foremost representative? Was the "logic" a mere mirage, or were its vicars in the Kremlin in profound error?

But the questions raised at the Soviet end of the Soviet-Russian enigma are not the only ones that puzzle an historian—those at the Russian end of it are just as disturbing. We have scant experience of Russia without an autocracy or a world-mission . . . and the Soviet empire is in the process of losing both. Should we hasten the disintegration because it works for freedom . . . or slow it because it works for instability?

TREVOR-ROPER No revolutionary ideology preserves its full content for long. The essential unit in historical change is "the generation"; and the generation that has been through an ideological battle or crusade, building an empire on a revolutionary basis, has a different attitude towards the world from that of the next generation, which

69

takes it for granted. Historically, all revolutions lose their ideological content in measurable time—sometimes quite soon, sometimes in one generation, sometimes in two. It doesn't, therefore, surprise me that the Russian Revolution should have lost its ideological content now that we are out of the generation which participated in it.

You ask what will happen when an empire based on an ideological revolution loses its ideological content. It becomes mechanical, is my answer; or it ritualises its ideology, or it adjusts it, because ideologies are very elastic and they can be adapted to all kinds of circumstances. We have seen this in every such empire. If Hitler had won his war, the next generation would have gone through a similar experience. Hitler claimed that the system he had established would last for 1,000 years, but who believes that? A completely different generation would not have had the will, or the energy, or the finance to maintain the empire of brutal conquest which he had planned and begun to set up.

So the evaporation of Soviet ideological commitment does not surprise me. The difficulty is forecasting what form the revolutionary ideology will take in the next generation.

URBAN   The history of Christianity suggests a parallel. The founders of the faith are followed by schoolmen, administrators and interpreters. They lose touch with the basic inspiration and concern themselves with institutionalisation and discipline. Is it not remarkable, though, that despite institutionalisation, and many vicissitudes, Christianity has kept its basic message and its basic appeal virtually intact? Mightn't the ideological appeal of communism, too, survive the exit of the Soviet system?

TREVOR-ROPER   It might. When I said that ideologies are elastic, that is what I meant. They can adjust themselves, they can acquire a new or modified content. The revised ideology can spring from a hitherto neglected or "misinterpreted" source within the movement. Within communism we have Eurocommunism, which is different from Marxism-Leninism; and it's not impossible that Marxism—which has already produced a variety of heresies—should produce more, and that one of these heresies will replace the original faith and will be institutionalised. That's exactly what has happened in Christianity: what were once heresies became the source, within the old Christian envelope, of a new dynamism. It happens again and again.

URBAN   It has been said that Marxism itself is a Christian heresy: "Christianity gone awry," as one historian put it.

TREVOR-ROPER   A Christian heresy or a Jewish heresy—Christianity itself being, of course, a Jewish heresy. If Hitler had won his war (and one has to remember that he very nearly did—there were occasions when it was really a fluke that he didn't), Marxism would have collapsed and its political base in Stalinist Russia would have disappeared. An established nazism could then have bred its own National-Socialist heresies. A Nazi empire in the heartland of Europe, including the Ukraine and Russia, would eventually have assumed features of a functioning, bureaucratic state which most people would have accepted because it was a reality. But I'm saying all this to point to a mere possibility. I am chary of prophesying because not a single ideology in history has ever been predicted.

URBAN   You said National Socialism would have spawned its own heresy. Can you imagine an enlightened, rational, post-Hitlerian Nazi leader, a kind of "National Socialist" Gorbachev, saying this sort of thing after Germany had won the war and Hitler was dead?:

> We're sorry about the Jews and the concentration camps. . . . These things were a gross abuse of National Socialism. . . . Adolf Hitler and his anti-Party clique alone were responsible. . . . But here now is our own interpretation of the true meaning of National Socialism, a nazism 'with a human face,' a Euro-nazism. . . . We are going to 'restructure' our relations with the nations who have come under our rule in the *Reich*, rehabilitate the victims of Auschwitz and Buchenwald, abolish the *Reich* Ministry of Propaganda, reduce our armed forces, and have peace with our neighbours. . . .

Would Margaret Thatcher or Ronald Reagan have run happy summit meetings with such a National Socialist leader in the way they have done with Gorbachev? Would President Mitterrand have befriended such a second-generation Nazi?

TREVOR-ROPER   Yes, I can conceive the possibility. There was a side of nazism which carried an appeal outside Germany, especially as long as Germany seemed to be winning. It helped to create the international divisions of the *Waffen-SS*. There were several of these: the Grenadier division "Charlemagne," composed of Frenchmen; the Grenadier division "Landstorm" of Dutch volunteers; the 1st and 2nd Grenadier divisions of Russians (later made part of General Vlasov's army); two Latvian Grenadier divisions; an Estonian Grenadier division; the Grenadier division "Langemark" of Flemish Belgian volunteers; the Grenadier division "Wallonie" of Belgian Walloon volunteers, and so on.
These people believed in nazism, and I have no doubt that if Hitler

had won, the brutal face of Hitlerism would afterwards have been exchanged for nazism with a more human face. German nazism would have been "de-Hitlerised" rather as Soviet Communism has been "de-Stalinised", and the crimes of the revolutionary first stage of National Socialism would have been deplored and explained in much the same way as Stalin's great purges are now deplored and explained in the Soviet Union.

After all, why did nazism succeed? In one respect it succeeded because the old German historical philosophy—the philosophy of "the German mission"—was grafted on to it. It was men like the Secretary of State Ernst von Weizsäcker, father of the present president of the Federal Republic, who provided the sort of explanation that would have been used by sophisticated Euro-Nazis in a post-Hitlerian Nazi empire.

Ernst von Weizsäcker was an old imperialist who disliked nazism but served it because his eyes were fixed on the German mission and because he did not attach too much importance to the means that were to be used to attain it. Weizsäcker senior served the Nazis, in my opinion, in a pretty disreputable way . . .

URBAN   Which Franz Schönhuber, current leader of the right-wing Republicans, is now mischievously exploiting to attack the Bundespräsident Richard von Weizsäcker himself, as well as the entire West German establishment . . .

TREVOR-ROPER   Naturally, I deplore Schönhuber's smear tactics—guilt by association is an old Stalinist/Nazi method. However this may be, Weizsäcker senior was responsible for the diplomatic arrangements with Hitler's so-called allies—Bulgaria, Hungary, Romania, Slovakia—for the transfer of their Jews to the extermination camps. We have this amply documented. Weizsäcker signed the correspondence. He knew perfectly well what euphemisms like "transfer to the East" and "resettlement in the East" really meant, and what the Nazi *apparat* was doing. There was one occasion when Ulrich von Hassell, who was a real resister in the Foreign Ministry and who thought he was on good terms with Weizsäcker (they spoke "the same language"), was summoned by Weizsäcker and chided for his insufficient appreciation of the historical achievements of nazism. Weizsäcker said, "Great historical changes cannot be carried out without a certain amount of crime. . . ." In other words, the crime was purely incidental; you disown the crime and welcome the great historical changes which were inseparable from it.

If Hitler had won, the Weizsäcker class would have said just that. It would have felt guilty about the unfortunate crimes which had accompanied nazism, but it would have claimed, "Nazism nevertheless presented us with an empire which the Kaiser had vainly sought in 1914–18. Now we have succeeded, and succeeded through the genius of one man. We dissociate ourselves from Hitler's crimes but we recognise that they were historically inseparable from German's rise to greatness."

Yes, I can see that as a realistic development if Hitler had won the war.

URBAN   The sort of thing that is now being said about Stalin by many people in the Soviet Union . . . But do you think our own politicians might have extended the same friendly welcome to a "de-Hitlerising," "restructuring" Nazi leader as they are now extending to the de-Stalinising Gorbachev?

TREVOR-ROPER   I would rather not mention particular politicians, because it is unfair to give hypothetical answers about what they would have done. But I can see that there would have been politicians who would have extended such a welcome. After all, they could have argued as follows: "We are only continuing the policy of the appeasers of the 1930s, who were honourable men, and whom the events have proved right. They didn't like nazism any more than we do, but they recognised that it was there, and that they had to deal with it. 'We can't remake the world to our own specification,' they said. 'We've got to face the world as it is. Hitler is supported by the entire German people; we must negotiate with him'. . ." The same reasoning would have applied even more forcefully if we had suffered defeat and faced a de-Hitlerising Nazi leader.

Just before the war there was a book written by Sir Arthur Bryant— a respectable, patriotic, historical writer—called *Unfinished Victory* (published, rather interestingly, in 1940). It was pro-Hitler and in favour of appeasement. It wasn't merely in favour of yielding to superior force; Arthur Bryant felt that Germany had been wronged and humiliated by the Versailles Treaty, especially by the French, and that the rise of a strong man was inevitable. He believed that Hitler offered Germany a version of socialism without the Marxist gloss. He invited us to respect "the rude Cromwellian vigour" of Hitler's speeches and the single-minded dedication of the Nazi state, even though he looked upon Hitler as a megalomaniac and despot.

URBAN   Before we go on from the German theme, the late Sidney
Hook, the distinguished American philosopher, recently said to me:

> "Looking back at what resulted, I say to myself on occasions: What
> would have happened if there had been a negotiated peace [in World War
> I]? I remember Lord Lansdowne's proposal to negotiate peace with
> Germany and that it was repudiated. What would have happened even if
> there had been a victory by Wilhelm and the Germans? What probably
> would have happened couldn't have been worse than what actually did
> happen. There would not have been Lenin; there would not have been
> Mussolini and there would not have been Hitler. The irony of it! It makes
> one a little humble about predicting the course of history. (present
> volume, Ch. 1)

Would you agree with Sidney Hook, on the basis of what you have
just told me, that in one generation a victorious Wilhelmian Germany
would have lost its triumphalism and roughness (assuming that it was
going to be rough and triumphalist in the first place) exactly as
Hitlerism would have lost its revolutionary savagery, and Soviet Communism is in the process of losing it now? I would have thought a
victorious Wilhelmian Germany would have been an incomparably
lighter burden for the rest of Europe to bear, and much more open to
self-reform, than either Bolshevism or nazism.

TREVOR-ROPER   I have heard Hook's argument before—but never
from an historian. It is, I believe, a false argument. The short answer I
would give would be to refer to Fritz Fischer's great work *Griff nach
der Weltmacht* (1961), in which he extracts from beneath layers of
falsification and whitewash the consistent war aims of the Kaiser's
government in World War I. They were, *mutatis mutandis,* very similar
to those of Hitler, although they did not have the same racialist
inspiration. Fischer argues that had they been achieved they would
have sown a harvest of hatred which would have led to enormous
convulsions within a generation.

In fact Germany was defeated and produced nazism. But suppose
we and the French had suffered defeat? That would have prevented the
rise of German nazism. But then what about the defeated countries,
France and England? The French in particular had very reactionary
right-wing forces which would have reacted to defeat in French nazi
fashion. We would have come face to face with nazism whatever
happened, most probably in France, and elsewhere too.

It is too easy to imagine that if the Kaiser had won, history would
have stopped—that all the European monarchs would have kept their

thrones, that the aristocracies and hierarchies would have been pre-served in aspic, and the rise of parvenu dictators would have been put off indefinitely. It is easy to imagine this, but it is nonsense. History moves on. If Wilhelmian Germany had won the war, the European society that existed before 1914 would not have survived intact any more than it survived Imperial Germany's defeat. It was the war, not the Allied victory, which caused the social upheavals that followed.

Slaves and Masters

URBAN   The nazification of a defeated Western Europe is an intriguing idea. Do you really mean "nazism", or would it perhaps be more accurate to say that a defeated France and Britain would have become irredentist powers of the authoritarian kind we know from earlier examples? *Revanche*-seeking France before 1914 was certainly not a monument to human reason or wisdom. But can we compare it with nazism?

TREVOR-ROPER   A form of nazism *could* have arisen in Western Europe. The Germans, after a victorious war, would have imposed crippling reparations on France and Britain. We had a foretaste of that in the Franco-Prussian War of 1870 and the indemnities the French were made to pay. It has been argued that the Versailles Treaty and the naval blockade which went on for some time after the Armistice were in large part responsible for the economic, social, and indeed physical devastation of Germany and the subsequent rise of Hitler. There is some truth in that. But it is frequently forgotten that in Germany World War I was financed in the expectation of gigantic indemnities. There was practically no war tax. The war was run on loans which were going to be repaid out of reparations exacted from France, Britain, and Russia, as they had been exacted from France in 1870.

But, of course, 1870 was a successful *Blitzkrieg*. It was over in no time at all, which provided a fatal example for generations of German politicians to come. They were all misled into believing that the next war would be similar. But it was not. World War I went on for four bitter years. The loss of life and treasure was incalculable. So, if Germany had won, a defeated France and Britain would have been made to pay huge indemnities; and the imposition of such indemnities would, in my opinion, have produced in France and England social consequences such as led, in Germany, to nazism.

Let it not be forgotten that, despite the brutal language Clemenceau employed at the peace negotiations in Paris, Germany was treated rather leniently in terms of territory. Its losses were relatively small. Except for Alsace-Lorraine, bits of territory in the East, the Polish corridor, etc., Germany was left intact. A similar policy *vis-à-vis* France and Britain would have been most unlikely if Germany had won. Imperial Germany's war aims—as we now know from the documents—included the takeover of the French iron and steel industries, the acquisition of large territorial and economic assets, and other far-reaching measures of an expansionist kind. There was to be an entirely new order in Europe, which would have been not so very different from the one Hitler tried to establish, except for the racist philosophy.

URBAN   So, in answer to Sidney Hook's point, you are saying that nazism of one sort or another was bound to occur on the loser's side in post-World War I Europe. But what about Russia? Would Stalinism have arisen if the Germans under the Kaiser had won the war? Bolshevism had already arisen, thanks partly to the good offices of the Kaiser's government who provided Lenin and his entourage with a sealed train, guaranteeing their safe passage through Germany. Wouldn't the severe conditions of Brest-Litovsk have been made even more punishing if the German *Reich* had triumphed in the West as well as in the East?

TREVOR-ROPER   The Germans did, indeed, impose an extremely tough treaty on the Bolsheviks which Lenin had great difficulty in persuading his Party to accept. Russia was being deprived of its Ukrainian food basket, a third of its European territory, three-quarters of its coal and iron industry, and so on. The rump of Russia that remained was under internal attack and was hovering on the brink of economic collapse. If Germany had won in the West as well, I doubt whether the Kaiser's government would have tolerated the rule of the Bolshevik rabble on the territory of its enfeebled eastern neighbour. It would have regarded the threat of chaos and anarchy coming from Moscow as a threat to the *Reich* and the established order of Europe—as indeed it turned out to be, for in 1918 and 1919 there were Communist coups, or attempted coups, in Berlin, Munich, Hamburg, and a host of other major German cities, as also in Hungary.

A victorious Germany would have stamped out open communism, but I have no doubt that communism would eventually have survived as a radical underground heresy. If Lenin and Leninism had, by some miracle, nevertheless survived, then our hypotheses multiply at such a rate that any speculation becomes meaningless.

URBAN How would you answer the second part of my question . . . the future of Russia without a mission, whether a mission of Tsarism, of a particularly pristine Russo-Christianity, of Pan-Slavism, or of Communist ideology? Russia has, by the testimony of many of her writers, always felt unworthy of her true self without a message transcending the narrow interests of the Russian people. For example, Mikhail Petrovich Pogodin had this to say about Russia's "manifest destiny" in the 1830s:

> Who dares to pretend that the goal of humanity has been achieved or kept in sight by any of the states of Europe? In one country we see more knowledge, in another more production, more comfort, in a third more welfare, but where is the 'sacred good'? . . . It is the Golden Calf, the mammon, to which without exception all Europe pays homage. Should there not be a higher level of a new European civilisation, of Christian civilisation? America, on which our contemporaries have pinned their hopes for a time, has meanwhile clearly revealed the vices of her illegitimate birth. She is no state, but rather a trading company. . . . Oh Russia, oh my Fatherland! . . . You, you are chosen to consummate, to crown the development of humanity, to embody all the various human achievements . . . in one great synthesis, to bring to harmony the ancient and modern civilisations, to reconcile heart with reason, to establish true justice and peace.[1]

TREVOR-ROPER You can have a residue of power which has outlived its original doctrinal impulse. Whether you can have one which has *totally* outlived such an impulse, I'm not sure; but in the case of Soviet Communism I cannot imagine that it would be totally extinct. I have suggested that there would be some kind of heresy, or that it would be adapted rather as you suggested in the case of the evolution of Christianity—which was, after all, originally a religion of the outcasts but was later adapted to be the state religion of the autocratic Byzantine Empire and of medieval feudal Europe. Ideologies are elastic. I do not envisage the possibility of the total evaporation of communism in Russia or in China, but I do think it will lose its revolutionary impetus, as Christianity did.

The Empire could be maintained without a paramount ideology, although it would probably have to be a reduced empire. Let us not forget that much of the Russian Empire was formed independently of communism, by naked conquest, in the 19th century—before Marx, or in total ignorance of Marx. Much of it was and is Muslim, and cannot have been conquered either in the name of Christianity or of Pan-Slavism. The tsars used brute force or the threat of force, and populated the empty spaces with Russian settlers. The same process could go on even after the expiry of a central doctrine, provided that Moscow's will to rule was unimpaired.

URBAN   But whether it *can* remain unimpaired under contemporary conditions, which demand philosophical justification—that, it would seem to me, is the crucial question. And the truths that have come to light under Gorbachev's reformism appear to be undermining that philosophical justification. In the name of *what* can the Kremlin now justify the preservation of the Soviet Empire, seeing that for virtually the whole of Soviet history, after the death of Lenin, it has been ruled by fools and criminals, and has not only failed to catch up with the civilised world, but been so badly left behind that, in the late 1980s, it cannot even properly feed and house its population? The Soviet rulers' "mandate of heaven" is by now surely exhausted.

TREVOR-ROPER   Well, I rate doctrinal legitimation less highly than you do. The Kremlin could go on ruling by the exercise of its mere residual power, which is still formidable.

Think of Islam. In its first generation after the Prophet, Islam was a radical, crusading, expansionist movement. Almost all the great conquests were carried out very quickly, in that one generation. Then it was gradually institutionalised and became the state religion of various khalifates and monarchies which acquired great wealth and lived in great splendour. The austere, fundamentalist impetus all but evaporated, but the Islamic institutions remained intact and became centres of power, periodically reinvigorated by fundamentalist revival. With the Ottoman Turks, Muslim militancy revived and the Ottoman Empire became a great power threatening all Europe.

In the last twenty years or so we have witnessed an astonishing recrudescence of Muslim fundamentalism under the auspices of the Shi'ite branch of Islam. It is true that the Ottoman state survived into the 20th century, in part at least, because there was a stalemate in the European balance of power, but the relevant fact is that it did survive at a time when it was ideologically empty of content. Ultimately, of course, it collapsed; but I don't see why the Soviet Empire should not be able to have a long afterlife, with nothing but the sheer power of a great state to keep it going.

In applying these parallels to Soviet Russia, we are, incidentally, generalising from a very narrow base because we are assuming that Gorbachev will last, and this is making a large assumption. He may or may not; and even if he does, the liberalising Gorbachev may, under certain conditions, turn into a repressive Gorbachev. There are, indeed, signs that he may already have started going down that road. The fate of Kerensky and Khrushchev are reminders of the fragility of liberalising change in Russian politics. And there were liberal tsars—but not for long.

The Recognition of Shock

URBAN   Hugh Seton-Watson once said to me, apropos of British and French reactions to imperial decline, that France remained France even after the loss of the French overseas possessions, but Britain had been so closely identified with the Empire that the loss of it produced a profound loss of self-confidence and the relative decline of the 1960s and 1970s. Britain without the Empire was only half a nation. Assuming that we accept his analysis, would the loss of the Soviet Empire generate an analogous disorientation in the Russian people?

TREVOR-ROPER   The loss of an empire always produces psychological consequences. You *could* say that when we lost America in the 18th century, we were only marginally concerned; English politics went on as before. But no, there was a great *crise de conscience* which it took some time to overcome. When the Spaniards lost their empire in Europe they went into a period of introversion, and again when they lost their empire in America. If the Russians were to lose their control of Eastern Europe, I don't think that would have quite so much of an effect, because they have only controlled Eastern Europe since 1945; but if nationalism were to stake out claims in White Russia and the Ukraine, as it is doing in the Baltic states, that could have a traumatic impact on the Russian psyche and might generate a profound intellectual and political turbulence.

URBAN   What form might this take?

TREVOR-ROPER   What often happens historically is that after the first major defeat, if a people doesn't accept that defeat and is capable of reasserting itself, it embraces an extreme form of nationalism. Seldom is an imperialist drive finally defeated at the first check. The next generation—the sons of the original imperialists—tends to react against the crusading spirit, the heroism and the sacrifices that were extracted from the people by their fathers. They say no to imperialism. They are like the sons of self-made millionaires who renounce the entrepreneurial spirit of their fathers. "Of course," they say, "we could spend our whole lives making money as our fathers did, but to what end? The purpose of life is living. Let us sit back and enjoy what we've inherited." The generation after that—the grandsons—tries again.

We can see a similar pattern in the history of empires—the tremendous effort of the Spaniards in the 16th century and the check in the next generation. In the generation of the reign of Philip III, imperialist expansionism stopped and the Spanish ruling class relaxed and enjoyed their gains. But in the generation after that, the generation of the *grandsons,* the imperial drive was resumed and Spain had another try. And that was the last time. After the second defeat, imperialism expires.

Look at French history: there we see the immense effort of the revolutionary and Napoleonic period, the conquest of Europe followed by a period of stagnation and relaxation. But then, in 1848, imperialism reasserts itself. We can observe the same in German history: after the revolutionary unification of Germany under Bismarck, we see the drive to world power under William II, culminating in World War I. That drive is checked and the mood of the Weimar Republic is anti-war and anti-army; but then the *grandsons* come along, providing the energy and "idealism" (if one may use that phrase) for a second attempt, under Hitler; and the second attempt was final, as it was in other cases too. I'm not frightened of the Germans now.

URBAN   How would your periodisation fit the Soviet case? I suppose it might, if we said that the great period of energetic statebuilding and imperial expansionism comprised the whole stretch of Soviet history from 1917 to the death of Brezhnev, and that the ingratitude of the "sons" seeking a more settled life and the enjoyment of consumer goods started only with Gorbachev—which would leave us with the prospect of another Soviet try by the "grandsons" of Stalin . . .

TREVOR-ROPER   We have, in the case of Russia, no valid case for comparison. The Soviet Union did not have its Napoleonic period of aggressive expansion. Russia was, after all, *attacked* in 1941 and fought a defensive war, even though that defensive war produced the effect of enlarging the Empire. We must be wary of too much generalisation. What we can safely say is that under Brezhnev the Soviet Union acquired, by subtle or less subtle imperialistic means, a maritime

Empire—largely because, in the wake of Vietnam, the Americans were unwilling to stand up to them. But this has proved to be an imperial over-stretch which the Soviet economy could not sustain. Hence the Gorbachev retrenchment. Whether the next Russian generation will summon the energy for another try at imperialism is a matter of conjecture.

URBAN   To return to my question: Do you foresee the type of intellectual-political crisis gripping the Russian political class after the loss of the Empire as gripped Austria after the collapse of the House of Habsburg, or Britain in the 1960s and 1970s? Would there be a crisis of self-confidence, a tendency to say "Russia has lost an empire and has not yet found a role," as Dean Acheson remarked about Britain in 1962 (causing at the time great—though to my mind unwarranted—offence to the British political élite)?

TREVOR-ROPER   One can make long-term predictions on a geopolitical and perhaps economic base, but one cannot make safe predictions on the base of human responses. The standard instance for me is the prediction by Alexis de Tocqueville, and indeed by many other less known writers, in the early and middle 19th century, that the great powers of the future would be Russia and America. That could be predicted because in the age of railway-building and generally increased communications it was becoming clear that the mobilisation of great land masses was going to be possible, whereas hitherto it had been impossible. That prediction came true.

Another instance is the geopolitical predictions of Sir Halford Mackinder, published in 1919. He predicted that whoever controlled what he called "the Heartland," which was Central and Eastern Europe, would control the whole world. But when he applied that prediction, he said that the controlling power of the world would be Tsarist Russia. He has been proved right in forecasting that it would be Russia—that's how it has worked out—but it's not Tsarist Russia. The human response, the political response, cannot be foreseen.

Hitler set great store by Mackinder's geopolitics as interpreted by Mackinder's German disciple, Karl Haushofer. He aimed to conquer "the Heartland" because from here he thought he could control the rest of the world. His natural rival for that control was Russia. It was Russia, with her own huge land armies, land ambitions, and geopolitical outlook that had to be defeated before Germany could become "the Citadel of the World Empire."

I give these general instances to show that, although one can make a general prophecy, one can get the details wrong—and the detail, after all, can be rather important. In Hitler's case, the detail was whether the Germans or the Russians would be the ruling power. That struggle was fought out, and it was touch-and-go how it would end. But the geopolitical prophecy retained its validity.

URBAN   I respect your reluctance to engage in what you clearly feel is idle speculation, but as historians are seldom appreciated by the general public unless they can tell us from their experience of the past what the future is most likely to hold, let me press you slightly on the point of imperial hangover.

I do not think many people were worried after the fall of Austria-Hungary, or the French, Dutch or British empires, that the metropolitan country would, in some post-imperial tantrum, start attacking its neighbours or dropping nuclear bombs on its former colonies. Austria, Britain, France, and Holland threatened no one and were feared by no one, although they did suffer from a post-colonial shock.

May not Russia be different? Russia has been an aspirant to greatness and world respect both under the tsars and under the Bolsheviks. In the last three decades she achieved, militarily at least, her coveted rendezvous with history, but failed to do so in any other respect. She may now have to contemplate the loss of this or that of her peripheral republics as well as her maritime influence. Will she take the hammer-blows of history with the same relative composure as the Austrians, the Dutch, and the British did? Isn't there, as historians tell us, a dark streak in the Russian character that inclines to anarchy and is more easily controlled when Russia is engaged in some large enterprise such as "building socialism," or making the world safe for it, than when Russia has no consecrated purpose?

TREVOR-ROPER   I draw back timidly when historical deductions are made from "the soul of the people." I realise that it can be done and that it has been done, but I don't like it, because it is a most uncertain base from which to argue. I regard the future as full of unpredictable possibilities. I can remember prophecies which seemed rational but proved to be wrong, and other cases where nobody had prophesied what actually happened. Short-term forecasts are certainly most perilous. In 1900, who would have forecast anything that happened in the 20th century—the demise of monarchies and empires . . . the rise of fascism, Bolshevism, nazism, and Maoism . . . the massacre of the Jews, Armenians, and Cambodians . . . the recrudescence of Muslim fundamentalism?

There is a remark of George Grote, the 19th century historian of Greece, which sticks in my mind. Talking of the forms of government in ancient Greece, he says that if Sparta had not existed no one would have thought that such a form of government was a possibility. It is indeed unique. It had no predecessor, and there has been no replica of it since. If Aristotle had projected it as a possible form of government, it would have been regarded as impractical and totally Utopian. And yet it existed and endured.

Humanity has the capacity for more numerous forms of political organisation than anyone can safely prophesy. Who would have predicted Hitler's "Final Solution"? There was, to be sure, anti-Semitism in Germany, but there was a great deal more in France, Russia, and Poland. Who would have thought the German totalitarians would decide to exterminate a whole people?

URBAN   But would you be prepared to accept that national stereotypes do contain some truth, or else they would not be stereotypes? I am not suggesting that they apply to all people all the time, but I would have thought it is fairly obvious that, for example, French, German, and Russian political culture is more idea-oriented and more deductive than English or American political thinking, which is on the whole more inductive, practical, and even utilitarian. Would this, as well as the testimony of Russian and German history, not imply that the Russian and German people are more at home in the world when they have an ideological compass to guide them than when they have none? The question that interests me is: Now that the ideological battery of communism is clearly exhausted, what will take its place? Who or what will fill the vacuum in the life of the Russian nation?

TREVOR-ROPER   You press me where I am least willing to be pressed. I reluct against the suggestion that there are national proclivities embedded in particular people. I get round this problem by persuading myself that these so-called national peculiarities are by-products of social organisation (and that, I suppose, is a form of Marxism).

I go to Germany a certain amount now. The present generation of Germans is exempt from nazism. They seem to me Europeans in a way they were not before the terrible experience of Hitler, the war, the defeat and total destruction of their political system cleared away a lot of Germany's ideological foundations. When I was young and went to Germany, I found I deeply disliked the Germans' mentality. I refused to go there after a time because I found the attitude of the people I met so disagreeable. But now I positively enjoy going to Germany. There has been a profound change in German attitudes. This fortifies my scepticism about the permanence of national characteristics.

URBAN   But aren't some national characteristics more obvious and permanent than others? Political and cultural pluralism on German-speaking territories is an old and famous phenomenon: It is Hitler who has to be explained rather than the return of Germany to the spirit of the Peace of Augsburg.

In Russia, however, the tradition of tolerance and pluralism is extremely thin, while the tradition of autocracy is strong and continuous. To say of the Germans that they are born to be ruled by despots would obviously be wrong, but it is not so wrong to say that in Russia tolerance, and indeed support, of despotism of one sort or another is a national characteristic. Allow me to cite some evidence.

The Marquis de Custine, writing from Russia in 1839, quotes an excerpt from the correspondence of the Baron von Herberstein (Ambassador of the Emperor Maximilian to the court of Tsar Vassili Ivanovich) to the effect that in Russia the will of the tsar is accepted as the will of God and blindly obeyed. Custine observes:

> This letter written more than three centuries ago paints the Russians of the time absolutely as I see the Russians of today. Like Maximilian's ambassador, I still ask myself whether it is the character of the nation that has made the autocrat or the autocrat who has made the Russian character. . . . It seems to me, however, that the influence is reciprocal—the Russian government would never have been established anywhere other than in Russia, nor would the Russians have become what they are under a different government. . . . It can be said of the Russians, great and small—they are intoxicated with slavery.[2]

But it would be unfair to stop with Custine. This is what General Walter Bedell Smith (who served as U.S. ambassador to Stalin's Russia from 1946 to 1949) wrote about Custine's book in 1951:

> The analogy between Russia of 1839 and the Soviet Union today is so striking that one must pinch himself to recall that Custine was writing more than a hundred years ago. . . . Custine's reflections on this strange society . . . led him to dire forebodings. . . . "Russia sees Europe as a prey which our dissensions will sooner or later deliver up to her; she foments anarchy among us in the hope of profiting by a corruption she promotes because it is favourable to her views." Did we think this was a Communist idea?[3]

Doesn't all this suggest that for four centuries (the 1550s to the 1950s), and arguably longer, there was a remarkable continuity in Russian political attitudes, and that it would be foolhardy for us to believe that the demise of the inspiration of communism can fundamentally change what 400 years could not?

If, then, we discount the present period of relaxation as out of character, what form is the Russian reaction to the loss of empire most likely to take? A reversion to Ivan the Terrible, Peter the Great, Slavophilism . . . some combination of these?

TREVOR-ROPER   Who can say? It could be any of these things—or something else quite unpredictable. Loss of empire can lead to various responses: recession, introversion, isolationism, or, on the other hand, aggression, internal or external "adventurism." Short of catastrophic defeat, such as the Germans suffered in 1918 and 1945, which drastically limits the options, the response depends on internal politics: who, or what party, captures power.

At present I would not expect a Russian Napoleon or a reincarnate Ivan the Terrible; the circumstances are not right for them. Nor do I foresee an appeal to Pan-Slavism. What other Slavs would heed such an appeal now? The Poles? The Czechs? The Yugoslavs? To all these Soviet Russia is the oppressor—not, as it could claim to be in the 19th century (though not to the Poles), the champion of oppressed Slav nations.

A more probable response is the capture of power by the hardliners, a reimposition of the brutal authority which at present seems to be relaxed; but this will not solve the problems which such authority, in the past, has created. Of course there could be "adventurism," an attempt to escape from insoluble problems by diversionary aggression. It was a Russian statesman who, in 1904, recommended "a short, successful war" as a cure for internal unrest. It was not a success. But I do not really think that that is likely now, especially after the failure in Afghanistan. What problem would be solved even by a successful *Blitzkrieg* in Europe? It would only create far greater problems for the victor.

But, anyway, I do not accept your premise. If there is a consistent national character, I believe it is formed by historical experience: Russian historical experience is not merely one of slavish submission to tyranny; it is also one of patience, caution, tenacity in defence, readiness to retreat, rather than aggression, boldness in attack. This is radically different from the character formed by the Prussian experience, which was an experience of brilliantly successful, lightning aggression—though, now that such aggression has failed so disastrously (and twice), that tradition is, I believe, dead.

Of Bridges and Walls

URBAN   If the Soviet Empire is now beginning to weaken along its ethnic faultlines, is the parallel with Austria-Hungary our nearest appropriate model for comparison? The disintegration of Austria-Hungary removed stability from the centre of Europe, and indeed destabilised the whole of Europe. Would the disintegration of the Soviet Empire act likewise? Does the Western world, therefore, have a tacit (if unmentionable) interest in keeping the red flag flying?

TREVOR-ROPER   Imperial power is a great stabiliser. We would not have the present troubles in Northern Ireland, or in Israel, or in South Africa—the three insoluble problems of our time—if imperial power, in this case British imperial power, still controlled those areas. Imperial power can take the sting out of nationalism by removing the element of insecurity. People know where they are as parts of an empire. *Pax Romana* kept the peace because of the overwhelming power of Rome. I certainly agree, therefore, with the statement that the decomposition of empires does create problems for world peace and world order.

Whether empires should be preserved for that reason is a matter of balance. We all know that the decomposition of Austria-Hungary created great uncertainty in Central Europe. The Ottoman Empire was preserved for some time because of its convenience for the Western powers—left to itself, it would have disintegrated much earlier than it did. Some powers were interested in its disintegration, others in its preservation. We in Britain were largely responsible for it being preserved; but, in the end, we helped the process which broke it up, as we also helped the process that broke up the Habsburg Empire. Whether one supports an imperial power once it has stopped being a menace to mankind and is properly civilised, or whether one backs the nationalist movements that can break it up, is a matter of national and international politics—of present politics. One cannot give a general answer.

URBAN   But hasn't "present politics" many faces? One of them is the world's ecological interdependence, on which our survival depends. This surely demands world government; but, short of that, an American "empire," a Soviet "empire," a European "empire" are the nearest things we can have to some form of ecological stability, or at least the hope of it. Similarly, in the nuclear age, world peace is an indispensable condition of human survival. That, again, would seem to be better protected by large universal states, "empires," than by so many wholly independent nations, each going its own selfish way. Or would it?

TREVOR-ROPER Oh, I think it would, but the concept of empire has to be refined to make sense. The fact is that one kind of "empire," economic empire, already exists everywhere in the world. We are so economically interdependent that although we may please ourselves with the illusion that Ireland or some Latin American republic is independent, in fact, their independence is limited, because in economic terms they are not masters of their own fate. This applies to every country.

So there is already an economic empire in place in the world and there ought to be, as you suggest, an ecological one, too, if we are not to pollute ourselves out of existence. So I see a double layer of relationships: There should be economic and ecological cooperation under the rules of one imperium, but one should avoid, as far as possible, making it political. Of course, economic and ecological cooperation is bound to impinge on politics; but as we do not want to inflame nationalism and create opportunities for, say, Islamic fundamentalism, we must not allow the unavoidable "imperialism" of economic and ecological necessity to be converted into political imperialism.

URBAN You are making a fine distinction, one which people gripped by the spirit of independence have always found hard to understand. I doubt whether, for example, a Kosovo Albanian could be swayed to accept the Serbian domination of his province on the argument that he is economically better off under Yugoslav rule than he would be outside it, either as a citizen of an independent country or one of Albania.

But it seems to me that Soviet imperialism also presents us with a specifically Russian problem. In the British, French, Dutch, Belgian, Spanish, and Portuguese empires, the cultural superiority of the metropolitan country was on the whole accepted and often admired and indeed emulated by the colonial population. The prestige of the Soviet Empire is different. In the "Outer Empire"—that is to say, in, for example, Poland, Hungary, and Czechoslovakia—no one would be remotely prepared to recognise that Russian cultural superiority exists, much less that it could excuse the colonialism of the metropolitan nation. On the contrary, Poles, Hungarians, and Czechs would stress their own cultural superiority over all things Russian. But even within the "Inner Empire", Georgians, Armenians, Moldavians, and *a for-*

tiori the Baltic nations feel, for a variety of reasons (some more legitimate than others), that Russian culture and Russian standards of behaviour are inferior to their own and are not to be respected.

What I'm saying is that the acceptance of British and French cultural superiority has given British and French institutions—and the English and French (and also the Dutch) language—a kind of charmed afterlife in the former colonies. The cultural and technological "imperialism" of the West tacitly continues. I can foresee nothing analogous happening in the Soviet Union. The disintegration of the Soviet Empire is bound to be more drastic precisely because respect for the culture of the metropolitan nation does not exist.

TREVOR-ROPER   I wonder. Without wanting to go back to the Greeks' attitude to the Romans, let me just say that subjective judgements of cultural superiority and inferiority have not been uniformly decisive in shaping the impact of nations and empires. Sticking to modern times, the Rhineland Germans regarded Prussia as being backward, uncultured and Philistine; but they yielded to Prussian power because they realised that it was necessary to create that envelope of German nationalism which they needed.

In the case of Austria-Hungary, the superiority of German culture and government institutions was, openly or implicitly, well recognised by all, even the Hungarians. That empire nevertheless fell apart, partly at least because the various nations under Habsburg rule wanted to be politically independent, and looked upon their cultural underdevelopment (in so far as they admitted it) as something which would quickly be overcome. That some Austrian and Hungarian *K. und K.* [imperial and royal] institutions nevertheless survived in the successor states is a fact.

But it is, to my mind, equally possible that Russian institutions and cultural values might survive the winding down of the Soviet Empire in countries such as Georgia, Armenia, and Uzbekistan. A residual post-Soviet *Russian* cultural imperialism is just as possible as the survival of English and French culture and institutions in many parts of the former British and French Empire, even though Georgians, Armenians, and Uzbeks would be loath to admit that they have, or ever had, anything to learn from the Russians.

URBAN   I suppose what we are saying is that neither economic underdevelopment nor cultural underdevelopment has a decisive influence on shaping national attitudes. When the chips are down, national sentiment, the call of tradition, feuds, and irredentism—that is to say, irrational, visceral factors—tend to determine the amount of peace we can have among nations.

TREVOR-ROPER   Yes, and all the more important in an economically and ecologically interdependent world to keep those irrational factors within limits.

URBAN   Left to themselves, nations seem to have a curious order of priorities: independence first, prosperity second, internal freedom and democracy only third.

TREVOR-ROPER   What I'm saying is that the order of priorities has, in effect, already been eroded because no country can, in the 1990s, consider itself to be fully sovereign or independent. The sovereignty and independence of all of us is now highly qualified sovereignty and independence.

URBAN   If you were President Bush or Margaret Thatcher, and had to deal with the question of the desirability, or undesirability, of promoting the disintegration of the Soviet Empire at one of your cabinet meetings, how would you advise your colleagues? Would you say to them:

> Like it or not, we've got to help Gorbachev to keep the red flag flying, because the alternatives to the Soviet Empire would be so much more terrible: chaos in the Balkans and Central Europe, the reopening of the whole German question, of the quarrel over the Polish frontiers, the erosion of NATO and so on. . . .

TREVOR-ROPER   This is precisely what we said about the Ottoman Empire in the 19th century. Our liberals and romantics were all on the side of the nationalist movements, arguing that the Bulgars, Greeks, and Macedonians must be free and Ottoman oppression must vanish. But in Tory establishment circles your argument was used. It was said, "If we listened to our liberals and romantics we would be injecting disorder into Europe and upsetting the balance of power. So long as the containing envelope of Ottoman imperialism can be sustained, we sustain it. It is better than the alternatives."

But then it transpired at the end of the century that it could no longer be sustained, because the [Ottoman] Empire was facing internal collapse. So, politics being the art of the possible, we decided not to sustain it and to back the disgruntled nations and nationalities.

URBAN   Egon Bahr, the German Social Democratic Party's chief foreign policy adviser, said on German television recently that it is not only the Soviet leadership that keeps the Berlin Wall standing, but also the Americans—who have an interest in maintaining European stability and thus the stability of the Soviet Union. Isn't this close to what you are saying?

TREVOR-ROPER   Yes, it is—but in making comparisons we have to look at the objective circumstances. As I've just said, in the earlier parts of the 19th century and, indeed, in some sense right through the 19th century, the British government regarded the maintenance of the Ottoman Empire as being in the general interest of peace and the correct balance of power. By the turn of the century, however, the mood had changed. Nationalism was on the march; it had prevailed in Germany and Italy, and it was undermining the internal cohesion of both Austria-Hungary and the Ottoman Empire. Our policy, therefore, changed too.

If the Soviet Empire can no longer be relied upon to keep the peace but is likely to become the home of uncontrollable national dissensions, then I have no doubt that our governments will no longer consider the Soviets our partners in stability, and will switch from talking to Moscow to supporting the dissenting nations of the Empire. This is already happening in our relations with the East-Central European countries, especially Poland and Hungary, which can quite obviously not be contained within the imperial mould.

Now, you cited Egon Bahr on the Berlin Wall and the alleged American interest in keeping it in place. Let me say this: One reason for the division of Germany in 1945 was because the Russians and the West were afraid that the weight of a united Germany under a revived nazism or militarism could once again become a threat to their security. This, I believe, is no longer so—the objective circumstances have changed.

Let me point again to my slightly metaphysical theory that a nation's drive towards imperial domination happens only twice: the Spaniards tried twice, the French tried twice, and the Germans tried twice—and they are not going to try again. They got such a bloody nose in 1945 that even the generation of grandchildren—and that is the generation now growing up in Germany—knows better than to attempt to start thinking in terms of imperial power. Germany today is a country of highly civilised Europeans who have renounced the historical mission implicit in their national policy from 1870 to 1945. I do not, therefore, regard the unification of Germany as being a potential military threat to the security of the world, and I can see no justification for the Berlin

Wall. A united Germany could, of course, become an economic power which would dominate Europe (even the Federal Republic, on its own, does this to a large extent), but it would not be a great military power. The division of Germany has, therefore, lost a major cause which brought it into being.

The real question raised by the prospect of German reunification is whether unification is possible, in the light of the separate existence of the two Germanies over almost half a century—whether the mechanical separation which has created two different social systems may make the two Germanies difficult or impossible to reunite. My own feeling is that the German people's sense of cultural unity is more important—has deeper historical roots—than their demand for political unity. When Germany was split into nearly 400 principalities, its only unity was cultural unity. It is quite possible that this sense of cultural unity will prove a substitute for a restored political unity, and this might be a good thing for both Germany and Europe.

URBAN   At the risk of digressing for a moment, doesn't this raise a sensitive and (until the problem of modernising the Lance missile gave it fresh relevance) a much-avoided issue: Germany's role in a post-Soviet Europe? British opinion seems to be divided. On one side we have people like Norman Stone (professor of modern history at Oxford University) and Peregrine Worsthorne (of the *Sunday Telegraph*), who argue that reunification would be a great cultural gain and a way of fitting an underdeveloped Russia into a peaceful European framework. On the other we have sceptics such as Roger Scruton (professor of philosophy at London University), who criticises Germany both for her alleged neutralism and for her aggressive idealism. The latter, he thinks, can be switched without difficulty from the adoration of Hitler to the admiration of Gorbachev.

For example, Norman Stone wrote (*Sunday Telegraph*, 23 April 1989) after a recent visit to Germany:

She [the Federal Republic] is, easily, the outstanding European country. She fulfils the role that we used to fulfil of combining economic efficiency, educational excellence and all-round seriousness with political liberalism and respect for people's rights; she is now, in my opinion, the model European country. She is very well placed to offer a bridge by which Communist Russia can cross into the European family.

And Peregrine Worsthorne said, two weeks later (*Sunday Telegraph*, 7 May 1989):

Twice in the past Germany has done incalculable harm. . . . Now its people have a new and incontrovertibly noble dream. Suspicion among the allies there is bound to be; fear, too. . . . Yet they are beginning to ring a little hollow, sound a sour note. For if Europe, the cradle of civilisation, is ever to become whole and healthy again, only Germany, in conjunction with the Russians, can bring this miracle about.

TREVOR-ROPER I broadly agree with Stone and Worsthorne. I have no fears of a revival of aggressive German militarism. In any case, the leading powers, Russia and the U.S.A., are so much more powerful nowadays than they were fifty years ago that they would dwarf the power even of a united Germany. So I do not regard the unification of Germany as *per se* very important. Everything depends on the circumstances.

Facts and Follies in History

URBAN To return to the breakup of empires—aren't our policies towards the Soviet Union most inconsistent? We say, on the one hand, that it is in our interest to support the Soviet Empire so long as it is a guarantor of stability; but we also say in our public diplomacy to the constituent elements of the Soviet Empire—Estonians, Latvians, Uzbeks, Georgians, Armenians—that we want them to be free and sovereign. Talking to the nations of the broader empire—Hungarians, Czechs and Poles—we say this quite openly, while talking to those of the USSR proper we say it by encouraging "national consciousness . . . economic and cultural sovereignty . . ." and the like. But our message is clear. How can we hope to draw stability from the Soviet Empire when we are, in effect, trying to destabilise it?

TREVOR-ROPER Our talk about sovereignty is mere rhetoric. There is no such thing as complete sovereignty for small nations. They can have internal sovereignty, they can have autonomy, but they are not free to conduct independent politics on a world scale. They are parts of imperial systems, although not necessarily politically imperial systems, and they are constrained by economic pressures. It would be wrong if we neglected to mention these simple facts of modern life in addressing the nations of the USSR and Eastern Europe.

URBAN But how would you answer a Pole who said to you: "The world is making a great hue and cry about giving independence to Namibia—but not to Poland. Does an old Christian nation in the middle of Europe deserve fewer rights and less respect than the tribesmen of West Africa?''

TREVOR-ROPER   I believe that the Poles should be independent, but they would have to realise that their independence would not be complete. It would be political independence; but even a most independent Poland would still not be fully in control of its destiny, because it would remain very much a dependent element of the world economy. Just as the economy of the Irish Republic is really dependent on that of Britain, so the economy of the East European states—even if we regarded them as politically independent, as they were before the war—would, in fact, be dependent on either Russia or Germany.

Bulgaria in World War II is a good example. Whatever the Bulgarian people wanted to be, they had to be pro-German because the alternative was being dominated by the Soviet Union. They might not like German control, they might feel that they owed a debt to the Russians who had liberated them from the Turks and created modern Bulgaria; but nevertheless, after the Russian Revolution, if they did not want to be communised, they had to come under German control because they were economically dependent. Even so, they did not declare war on the Soviet Union in 1941 because popular feeling against a move of that kind was well known to the government. But it was the Bulgarians' *de facto* dependence, behind the outward trappings of formal independence, that decided their role in the war, with all its well-known consequences.

An independent Poland might find itself, *mutatis mutandis,* in a similar situation. I would be entirely in favour of the Poles having all the independence they had between the wars. But it would not be full independence; an invisible imperialism would remain. When we talk about spheres of influence that, I assume, is what we mean.

URBAN   Had you been in the position of Wickham Steed or R. W. Seton-Watson, would you have worked for the dissolution of the Habsburg Empire, as they did?

TREVOR-ROPER   Let me try to be precise about this: had I myself been contemplating the advantages and disadvantages of preserving the Habsburg Empire in, shall we say, 1910–1918, I would probably not have wanted its dismemberment. But, of course, if I had been Steed or Seton-Watson—that is to say, a liberal romantic, my mind formed by the liberal nationalism of the late 19th century—then I would no doubt have acted as they did. They were children of their time, and so probably would I have been.

URBAN   Would it have been possible to foresee in 1905 or 1910 that the dissolution of Austria-Hungary would destabilise the peace of Europe?

TREVOR-ROPER   I think it would, but that does not mean that it could have been prevented once the war had started. I believe Austria-Hungary might perhaps have been saved if the empire's nationalities' policy had been less repressive. The Hungarian part of the monarchy was the main culprit. It was ruled by an aristocracy and bureaucracy which treated the South Slavs, Slovaks, and Romanians under their control as subject races. Had the Hungarians agreed to give the Croats autonomy under a trilateral arrangement with Vienna, the monarchy might have been preserved. I say "might" because we cannot be certain; the racial problem of the Habsburg Monarchy was perhaps insoluble. After the loss of the Italian provinces, the great defeat at Königgrätz in 1866, and the introduction of Dualism with Hungary in 1867, the imperial government was too weak and frightened to act in a liberal way and was unable to provide that thin, loose envelope of imperialism that would have retained the loyalty of its subject races.

Whether the Croats gained by being "set free" and then subjected to Belgrade rather than to Vienna and Budapest, is an open question. They had a hearty dislike of the Orthodox Serbs who, they felt, had been barbarised by long Turkish rule, whereas they themselves had profited from the more civilised rule of the catholic Habsburgs. Nevertheless, at the end of World War I, Yugoslav rule meant liberation. But I'm not sure how long this feeling persisted. It was certainly in ruins by the time of the German invasion of Yugoslavia in 1941, and has never fully recovered from the ferocity of the Serbo-Croatian conflict during the war.

The rationale, durability and usefulness of empires has to be judged in the light of all circumstances; that is the only safe rule.

URBAN   Can you envisage Gorbachev saying to some of his more realistic colleagues in the Politburo: "We are over-extended—we cannot indefinitely force restive Poles, Hungarians, and Czechs to stay within the Stalinist frontiers. Doing so has cost us extraordinary economic sacrifices and our reputation in the world. We are going to raid Lenin for suitable quotations to justify what we are doing—'Russia as the prison of nations being turned into free and democratic states,' that sort of thing. We'll do our best to make the transition slow and shock-free, and we'll exact as many concessions from the West as the traffic will bear—in exchange for 'voluntarily' doing what we are being forced to do in any case. So let's look at the books again, and quote chapter and verse for reducing the domains of socialism in the name of Lenin and in the language of Lenin. . . ."

Can you see Gorbachev taking that sort of attitude? Is he already doing it?

TREVOR-ROPER   The great advantage of chapter-and-verse is that you can choose your chapters and verses, and prove almost anything.

I go back to your original analogy with Christianity. The early Christians believed in the Second Coming; they believed it was going to happen quite soon and that the Roman Empire would be utterly destroyed. And they could produce good scriptural texts to support these beliefs. But when the Second Coming did not materialise, and the Roman Empire adopted Christianity as the religion of the state, these doctrines became embarrassing; so they were declared heretical and were suppressed. The Church then reinterpreted the Scriptures and emphasised other texts which would support the new view.

Nevertheless, the early Christian doctrines, together with the dese-lected parts of the Scriptures which had supported them, resurfaced after a time and eventually fuelled the Protestant Reformation of the 16th century. They gave rise to a new messianism and injected into Christianity a new revolutionary content. The Protestantism of Eliza-bethan England, the Lutheran and Calvinist Reformations, the Protes-tant international at the time of the Thirty Years' War, the Huguenots, were all inspired by heresies which had been driven out of the Church more than a millennium before. It is, therefore, perfectly possible that the scriptures of Marx and Lenin, too, will be found to contain heresies which were thrust aside in the Stalinist period and will provide an ideologically acceptable framework for the reduction and reformation of the Soviet Empire.

URBAN   The current reform of the Soviet economy in the name of the NEP period of the 1920s is one sign that Gorbachev and his friends are busy ransacking the books for the right quotations.

TREVOR-ROPER   If continuity in the Soviet domains is to be preserved, the reforms will have to be enacted in the name of the Church—but suitable texts will no doubt be found.

URBAN I often wonder, though, whether Marxism-Leninism isn't so inherently absurd that no reform of it will work at the turn of the second millennium. An heretical expression of something nonsensical remains nonsensical no matter how radical the heresy. After all, Marx's thinking is contemporaneous with the invention of the steam engine and predates the electric light bulb. History has refuted all his main tenets, from the pauperisation of the proletariat to the expectation that nationalism would disappear under the pressures of international class solidarity.

TREVOR-ROPER There is a prohibitive absurdity in almost all ideologies—which does not stop them from being taught and accepted. After all, Christianity contains dogmas which are today impossible for an educated person to believe; but we obediently repeat them.

URBAN But isn't there a difference of appeal between the two? The core of the Christian faith has always been transcendental. Christianity never claimed to be open to rational understanding alone, and Christians have no hesitation in saying *"Credo quia absurdum est."* I can, therefore, see that an heretical interpretation of Christianity will be no more absurd, in Christian terms, than the orthodox interpretation. But this is not so in the case of Marxism.

Marxism claims to be scientific, empirical, and predictive. When *it* goes wrong by the testable evidence of the economy, for example, everything about it goes wrong. It can, therefore, not ask us to extend our confidence to a revised, heretical interpretation. Marxism has, indeed, now shown itself to be wholly absurd in the sense of being inapplicable and unusable on its own terms.

TREVOR-ROPER I have to surrender to that.

URBAN Do you think sophisticated scientists and technologists in the various Soviet academic cities and think tanks would be willing to put up with even a revised Bolshevik ideology?

TREVOR-ROPER Yes, I do. Ideologies can be revamped to an extraordinary extent. They can go into reverse while lip service is still paid to the orthodoxy. Stalinism, too, was a revised ideology, because Marxism denies that "great men" can have a decisive impact on the design of history. Whatever Gorbachev may now be saying about the evils of Stalinism, his own highly concentrated leadership is a backhanded compliment to the Stalinist heresy—it would be hard to imagine a Gorbachev revolution without Gorbachev.

URBAN   Suppose the Soviet system rendered itself meaningless by the force of its own reforms, or were eliminated by the passions of nationalists, economic decentralisers, and the liberal intelligentsia— would a Russia emptied of the international appeal of Marxism-Leninism, but strengthened by Russian nationalism, be an "empire" with which we could more easily live than the present one?

TREVOR-ROPER   I don't think so. Russian nationalism is subterranean but very much alive. It might in certain circumstances, if the Soviet system were to expire, find resonance in some of the other Slav nations and become a menace. Personally, I would prefer to see lip service being paid to communism, because this would be the mere repetition of an empty ritual, far safer for the rest of the world than an exacerbated Russian nationalism. A Russian nationalist government, with all the military and industrial power built up in 72 years of Bolshevism, is not a prospect any European country would be happy to contemplate.

URBAN   Aren't you echoing the voice of 19th-century British imperialism? Support the Ottoman Empire because it keeps the tsar away from the Dardanelles—keep the Soviet Empire going because a Russian nationalist empire is liable to make even more mischief in Central and Eastern Europe than Stalin's Russia has been doing.

TREVOR-ROPER   Yes—in the 19th century it was vital for us in Britain to keep the shipping lanes to India and the Far East open, and the Dardanelles were a key element of our security. In the nuclear age, the prevention of any warlike conflict has become the predominant British and European interest. This is, in my opinion, probably better served by the preservation of an ideologically degutted and economically limping Soviet Empire than by a Russian nationalist successor state.

URBAN   Don't you think, though, that we would be giving hostages to fortune if we helped to uphold the skeletal remains of a system that threatened to bury us only a few years ago? Might the skeleton not be filled out with flesh as rapidly as it lost its vital energy in the 1980s?

TREVOR-ROPER   Of course it might. Anything can happen in history— that is my somewhat unhelpful view. We can only legislate for our own period to the extent that we can foresee events with some hope of accuracy. Before Marxism emerged, the movement which carried a comparable programme of internationalism and rationality was the Enlightenment. The Enlightenment led to the French Revolution. Who predicted the French Revolution? Nobody did. Even in the early 1780s

nobody had the faintest idea that a great revolution would sweep
France, and no one was more shocked by its development than the
writers and philosophers to whose teaching it was afterwards ascribed.

One can make conditional prophecies, saying if this or that were to
happen, then such and such a development is most likely; and one can
buttress that vague forecast with analogies drawn from the past. But
the German idea that history has rules, and that if we learn these rules
we can predict the future (Hegel, Marx, Spengler, and many other
German historians thought in those terms), seems to me to be based
on the wrong premises. I find it no more persuasive than the historical
prophecies deduced from Scripture or from the works of Arnold
Toynbee.

URBAN   My fear is that if today we preserved the Soviet Communist
empire as a stabiliser, it might, in true Hegelian fashion, turn the tables
on us and become a destabiliser again tomorrow. Man's search for
Utopia is always with us, and those conducting the search have seldom
shown any inclination to profit from the disasters of the past.

You may not rate Arnold Toynbee highly as an historian, but perhaps
you will agree with me that he was a man of wide experience. In a
conversation about a similar topic in 1972, Toynbee said to me, "This
nonlearning from patent facts—this obstinate and persistent nonlearning makes me pessimistic. . . . The power of blinding ourselves to
patent facts seems to be almost insuperable."

Are we, do you think, going to be immune from the next outbreak
of Bolshevism if the bacteria of Bolshevism are now preserved for the
sake of world stability?

TREVOR-ROPER   I doubt whether there could be an outbreak again.
Communism has had a good run and has revealed itself to be a failure.
It has now shot its bolt, and I don't believe that anyone except a few
people irrevocably committed to Utopia will try to build a govern-
mental system on it. The ideology will probably survive in heretical
forms and in unlikely places, but if it is world stability that must be our
first concern today, as surely it must, then I am satisfied that an
ideologically defunct, territorially reduced, and internationally assimilated Soviet Empire is more likely to serve our interests than the chaos
that would follow its uncontrolled disintegration.

URBAN   I keep coming back to my tentative parallel with National
Socialism. Would we be taking the same line if a de-Hitlerised, territorially reduced, and internationally cooperative Nazi empire happened

to be our partner in maintaining world stability? And if so, wouldn't we be betraying our trust as a free and democratic civilisation?

TREVOR-ROPER   This seems a simple parallel; but once we analyse it, it becomes less simple, since the implicit circumstances are entirely different. The Russians were our allies in the war. We emerged victorious. We set up the present European system which, with all its defects, has lasted. It is now a question of amending it in one part of Europe.

But you are supposing a totally different situation, in which Hitler has won his war and set up his robber-empire. We are defeated and disarmed. The whole continent is under Nazi domination. Its governments are puppet governments. There is no balance of power. Against this, while it lasts, there can only be resistance movements. This cannot be called stability, or at least it is not a kind of stability that any of us would wish to preserve.

However, moving on to a general plane, I believe that we must always recognise the limits of the possible. In a crisis we accepted the alliance of Stalinist Russia, whose criminal record at that time was worse than that of Nazi Germany. We have had diplomatic relations with Mao's China. One generation is not responsible for the acts of its predecessors. I would have no objection to dealing with a government whose origins were tainted, provided that we did so with our eyes open, for rationally defensible purposes, and from an independent position. But in the scenario which you assume, we would not be independent. So the parallel is not a true parallel.

If Hitler had won the war, I find it impossible to imagine the state of Europe today. We lose ourselves in such speculations.

Spring 1989

Chapter 3

Nationalism and the Balance of Power

A Conversation with Elie Kedourie

Dependence and Independence

URBAN Your best known contribution to the scholarly debate about national identity and nationalism may be summed up in the idea that humanity does not naturally divide into nations and that groups that claim to be "nations" do not have an automatic right to be independent states. It is enough to speak these words to see hackles rising in many quarters of our planet—and not only in places where nationalism rides high. In the Soviet Union, in particular, your claim would have a stormy passage. Your Russian, Ukrainian, Latvian, Lithuanian, Georgian, Armenian, and other critics would at once tell you that the dominant theme of our time is precisely that humanity is naturally divided into nations, and that the Soviet system carried the seeds of its own destruction from its birth in 1917 because Marxism-Leninism had failed to take account of this self-evident truth.

They would quote the fate of the Ottoman Empire, of the Austro-Hungarian monarchy, of the British Empire, Woodrow Wilson's Fourteen Points, Principle VIII of the Helsinki Final Act, and much else to show that nations have both a passive right not to be denied their identity, language, and cultural aspirations, and an active right to

This dialogue appears here with the kind cooperation of the Institute for the Study of Conflict, Ideology, and Policy, Boston University, which published it in *State and Nation in Multi-Ethnic Societies: The Breakup of Multinational States,* eds. Uri Ra'anan, Maria Mesner, Keith Armes, and Kate Martin (Manchester and New York: Manchester University Press, 1991).

101

assert these in the framework of sovereign states, even if their material interests were better served if they remained members of a comprehensive multinational state such as an empire. How would you answer them?

KEDOURIE   The various peoples that make up the Soviet Union were, of course, there under tsarist rule and under conditions of comparable unfreedom. But not many thought of themselves as "nations" and even fewer were seen to be such by the outside world. The idea that nations, however defined, have a right to enjoy independence and a right to a separate state is a *new* idea with complicated roots in Western political thinking. It began with the French Revolution and then spread to the Ottoman and Hapsburg empires, and eventually to all parts of the world.

Of the two great absurdities of our time—Marxism and nationalism— nationalism is, to be sure, the more attractive absurdity: Yet, it is an absurdity and a dangerous one at that. Why do I say that?

There is nothing in human nature or in history to suggest that, because you are a Georgian or an Uzbek, you should risk life and limb, going to the very brink of extinction, in order to enjoy living in an independent state. When you look at the history of some of the new independent states or groups who advocate independence, you will find that in the past these groups were not aware of the need to have political independence, and that those that were independent at one time or another had the kind of independence that did not give them prosperity, or freedom, or anything else that makes life worth living. Today, the Lithuanians, Latvians, Estonians, Moldavians, Georgians, Armenians all want to be "independent states." But if they were to gain independence they would have to take on board the perils of conducting an independent foreign policy, assume the financial burdens of armed forces, and expect to be entangled in quarrels with their neighbors.

Moreover, it is anybody's guess whether these independent countries would survive for any length of time. The dependence of Tadzhiks and Uzbeks and Azeris on the central rule of Moscow is not due to Soviet power as such but to certain historical and geographical conditions, notably to the expansionism of the Grand Duchy of Moscow which swelled into an increasingly powerful Russia under the tsars and swallowed up its weak neighbors. If the Soviet type of justification for Russian rule over these minority republics were to disappear—either because the Soviet system underwent thorough reform or because secessionist movements forced disintegration on the Union—a very powerful Russia would still remain at the heart of the Euro-Asian land mass, and it is more than likely that it would continue to make its power felt among its neighbors. "National independence" for Armenians and Ukrainians would then prove to be an illusion.

URBAN International life, you suspect, is played out in a vast magnetic field, with one or two strong magnets exerting their influence on a large number of weak floaters. The precise quality of these magnets is irrelevant—it is their size that matters. The United States is, on this showing, one big magnet which tolerates no random behavior in Nicaragua or Panama, while the Soviet magnet is equally unforgiving vis-à-vis Lithuania or Azerbaijan. Yet all our declarations from the Atlantic Charter (1944) to the Helsinki Final Act (1975) run counter to these facts of history, if that is what they are. They renounce the notion of "spheres of influence" and underline our support of self-determination and national independence. Are we caught in a dilemma to which there can be no solution?

KEDOURIE Yes, we are. Nothing can erase the fact that Estonia, with a population of about one million, has to go on living side by side with Russia, counting 150 million; or that Eire is a neighbor of a much more powerful Britain. That does not make the dependence of small nations on large ones any more or less moral; but it is a fact of history we cannot ignore.

URBAN But you would surely agree that the current leaders of small nations have more than a little justice on their side when they accuse us of rank cynicism—seeing that we pick up their causes only when it suits our book, and not when justice and equity so demand? For example, the Baltic nations have a well-recognized right to secede from the Soviet Union, both on the strength of the Soviet Constitution and Principle VIII of the Helsinki Agreement. Yet we balance their claims to liberty on the scales of power politics—or "world stability," as we like to call it in our Sunday sermons—ignoring our numerous declarations about self-determination. You will understand that, as one who has spent thirty years of his life talking to Soviet-dominated Eastern Europe about the Western commitment to national liberty, I am sensitive to charges of hypocrisy.

KEDOURIE It would be absurd if I tried to judge which of the groups now constituting the Soviet Union have a claim to consider themselves "nations" and which have not. Let me just say that government by foreigners has been the rule rather than the exception in world history, and the European—in this case the Russian—domination of parts of Asia is far from constituting a novelty. I am ready to concede that in the case of European peoples, such as the Baltic peoples and the Ukrainians, the idea of nationhood and independence has, over the last 200 years, been so powerfully transmitted from Western Europe that it has to be seriously reckoned with as a factor affecting the cohesion of the Soviet Empire and the world balance of power. I am not saying this is a bad thing . . . so long as national liberation is coterminous with the liberation of the individual and constitutional government.

But, as far as the Asian populations of the Soviet Union are concerned, it is far from obvious why they, too, should think that "nationhood" and a national state will best promote their interests. Nation-states are not out of character with European history. They are rather an extension of the condition which, since the disappearance of the Roman Empire in the West, was customarily "Europe," with its feudal divisions, free cities, sovereign republics, and monarchies. But the typical Asian polity is the Chinese Empire, or the Empire of the Moguls, or the Ottoman Empire—large and varied areas administered by a *nomenklatura,* controlled by a single center. Nationalism and the idea of a sovereign nation-state is not something indigenous to Asia, nor is it an irresistible tendency of the human spirit, but rather an importation from Europe which does not fit. Almost any strand of Asian (and African) nationalism, considered as a program of action or a scheme of thought, suffers from artificiality, from being a laborious attempt to introduce outlandish standards and alien categories.

URBAN   On a high level of historical generalization, this may well be the case. But don't the practical requirements of our time call for a different approach? It was "only yesterday" that we saw the tyrannical Soviet Empire as the principal danger to the rest of the world, and we looked upon anything that might weaken that centralized tyranny—especially the spread of nationalism in the non-Russian parts of the empire—as deserving support. It was, we said, in the universal interests of freedom that we should recognize and promote these nationalisms. The risk that they might eventually get out of hand and follow the Mazzini- or Mickiewicz-type of 19th-century European nationalisms struck us as much smaller than the risk of allowing the Soviet system to continue.

Now that the Soviet Empire seems to be in danger of falling apart, we are increasingly confronted with two related and, in my view, surprising, arguments. Firstly, that almost any order is better than no order; and, secondly, that nation-states, especially "new" ones, are not to be encouraged. Those who take these lines of reasoning seem to fear instability much more than they fear the absence of individual and national freedoms. In the nuclear age, I can understand some of our leaders' concern for world stability. But if "natural justice" had any place in international affairs I would argue that those who now advocate the preservation of the Soviet state as a pillar of international stability have very short memories. They seem to forget that, until Gorbachev's arrival, the Soviet leaders never hesitated to subvert the French and British empires, undeterred by any thought that world disorder might follow. Indeed, it was world disorder, and a "socialist" order to be built on its ruins, that they openly and proudly promoted.

KEDOURIE   If you want to stick to practical politics, I would say that encouraging nationalist movements in the Soviet Union is giving hostages to fortune; you may be starting something you cannot control. The rise of national forces and states is not necessarily benign. Take, for example, the fallout after the collapse of the Habsburg Empire. In 1918–19 there was a wave of enthusiasm for doing away with Austria-Hungary on the principle of self-determination as formulated in President Woodrow Wilson's Fourteen Points. The Ottoman Empire too fell apart under comparable circumstances. But what resulted was *not* a group of states free from misrule, living side by side with each other as so many symbols of liberty—but a patchwork quilt of weak states which promoted, with the honorable exception of Czechoslovakia, neither individual freedom at home nor moderation abroad, and which were too feeble to resist either Hitler's or Stalin's aggression. The consequences of the breakup were much worse than the illnesses they were designed to cure.

In any case, we are quite powerless, so far as the Soviet Union is concerned, to prevent or to hasten its breakup. Support for Gorbachev—which seems to be current Western policy—may not ensure his survival; and if he does survive, it does not follow that he would be able or willing to continue the policies which have attracted support from Western governments. Nor is it the case that these policies will infallibly turn to Western advantage.

The Right to Self-Determination?

URBAN   But wouldn't you say that the wrongs committed by the Soviet system and the Soviet Empire are so much greater than anything we can associate with Austria-Hungary, or the Ottoman Empire, that to upset the kind of stability represented by the Soviet system is worth taking a few risks for, even the risk of unleashing a number of unguided nationalisms? None of us can really believe that another Mongol invasion of Europe is imminent and that the massed ranks of the Russian people are our best form of defense . . .

KEDOURIE   Well, what are the great wrongs the Soviet system expresses? They are Moscow's centralized despotism and the Communist ideology—the two being really the same thing. These are, of course, great evils; and it was right that we should have opposed them. But what we can now observe is that these evils have been brought down by the weight of their own absurdity, and they no longer threaten us, for the time being at any rate.

URBAN   Are you certain that they *have* indeed been brought down?

KEDOURIE   I feel that is not an unfair inference seeing the speed with which the system is unravelling. Whatever the results of Moscow's political infighting may be, I take it as read that the Kremlin is now unable to know, much less to control, what goes on in Turkmenistan or Kirghizia. Mackenzie Wallace, that eagle-eyed, late-19th-century observer of Russia, tells us in his book *Russia* (1877) that one day he appeared at a ferry station on the Volga hoping to cross the river as indicated in his timetable. But as no ferry appeared, he asked the local ferry master why the delay. "It says here that the boat should be leaving by now," he told the official, brandishing his timetable. The Russian laughed at this Westerner's pitiful innocence. "The more fool you, if you believe what is printed," he said. I would say this applies to most things Soviet and Russian. *On paper,* Moscow may still be in control of its empire, but in reality it is no longer. Our own policies will, therefore, have to be reordered accordingly.

URBAN   I am not persuaded that national ambitions in East/Central Europe, or in Asia, would respond to this argument. National self-determination (Principle VIII of the Helsinki Final Act) grows naturally out of the principle of individual human rights and fundamental freedoms (Principle VII). We can observe this in the history of the 1848 revolutions, when individual human rights and national rights were two sides of the same coin. 1848 is surely not lost on Asian nationalists; and even East and Central Europeans, who had their fingers severely burnt after the collapse of Austria-Hungary are, again, harking back to an age when it was thought that individual freedom is meaningless unless free men have the right to create free associations—that is to say, sovereign and independent nation-states.

My pessimistic reading of history, however, moves me to go along with your reasoning part of the way and to ask whether the African and Asian peoples aren't destined to go through the same miserable cycle as the Europeans have done, and, indeed, whether some of the East and Central European nations aren't themselves destined to repeat it before merging their identity, under the hammer blows of the next round of troubles, in a broad European framework?

KEDOURIE   The national "renewal" movements of the 19th century, such as Mazzini's Young Italy, did indeed originally equate the idea of individual emancipation with national freedom. It was widely believed in 1848 that the two were indistinguishable, and that free nations composed of free individuals would create a free and equitable international order. But soon it was discovered that this was an illusion. The two were highly distinguishable! First, the states raised on the concept of the nation embraced various forms of national messianism and became internally oppressive and intolerant in their foreign policies. Second, it is impossible to redraw the map of the world in a way that would give us ethnically homogeneous states. This is particularly obvious in Central and Eastern Europe, where large pockets of Serbs live on Croatian territory, Hungarians in Slovakia and Romania, and so on. The tensions between the ideological obsessions of nationalism and what was politically and geographically possible under the Ottoman and Habsburg empires led to the destruction of our civilization in two world wars.

There is now a new factor since the Soviet Union, which is a mere 73 years old, is itself the outcome of an ideological obsession. It tried to impose an ideological vision on the peoples it inherited from the wreckage of the tsarist empire. It instituted a harsh and very oppressive regime; and I can well understand that, reacting to this oppression, the peoples under Soviet rule now tell us that they cannot be sure of their freedom unless they remove themselves from Moscow's central control and become "independent nations." This is a natural reaction, but I don't think it is a wise one. I am reminded of Lord Acton's praise of the Austro-Hungarian Empire. He saw its great virtue in that a large number of nationalities managed to live in it peacefully together. "A state which is incompetent to satisfy different races condemns itself," Lord Acton wrote in his essay, "Nationality." The tolerance of other races and religions, he said, was the absolute criterion of civilized politics; and so it is.

URBAN   But, in the 1990s, how do you explain to a restive Lithuanian or Ukrainian that his now-burgeoning human rights should not include the right to sport his own national flag, the right not to be drafted into a foreign army, the right to control his own economy, the right to have his own national legislation and ultimately the right to full national independence? Isn't it asking too much of human nature to expect these people to heed, in the heady hour of their liberation, "the lessons of history" or any other lessons?

KEDOURIE   Collective human rights do not automatically follow from the human rights of the individual—at least not to the extent that individual rights collectively asserted must lead to demands for national rights and nation-states. For an example: the United States is composed of a great mixture of peoples from all corners of the earth, and so long as one is an American citizen, one has certain constitutional rights and safeguards; but is anybody saying that one has to establish an "independent Republic of Nebraska" in order to safeguard the rights of Nebraskans?

URBAN   Margaret Thatcher, the former British prime minister, gave a similar reply to a Soviet questioner during a BBC phone-in from Moscow. She was asked (by, I recall, a Georgian) whether she supported the rights of minority nations to become independent nations as part of *glasnost* and *perestroika*. She responded cautiously by pointing to the U.S. where people of different backgrounds, language, and culture live together in peace and prosperity. I don't think her questioner was persuaded. To compare the American melting pot with the Soviet Empire or anything occurring in Central and Eastern Europe strikes me as difficult to sustain. In any case, I can, under certain conditions, well imagine a large American state such as California developing a "Californian identity" and a Californian sense of nationhood, based on Ernest Renan's principle that a nation exists when so many people express the view that, by solidarity, sentiment, and "a plebiscite of every day," they are a nation.

KEDOURIE   Renan's analogy is striking. Two points, however, must be made. If a nation rests on a daily plebiscite, so then does the family, and the village community, and friendship, collegiality, social ties in general. So the image, suggestive as it may seem, tells us very little specifically about the nation. In the second place, a nation is not a state, and if we are talking about states, as we surely are here, then a plebiscite cannot possibly be the foundation or the organizing idea of a state. A plebiscite is a vote taken on a particular day. There is no inherent reason why the vote should not be repeated at intervals—but to ground a state on a vote which can change from time to time is manifestly impractical, indeed absurd. A plebiscite, again, can give no guidance about the organization of government, about the constitution, about the judiciary, about the administration. In all of these matters detail is of the essence, the kind of detail with which plebiscites cannot possibly deal.

Of Culture and State Power

URBAN You show in your book *Nationalism* (1960),[1] much more persuasively than I have just done (apropos of the Helsinki Final Act), how the idea of human rights for the individual can turn into demands for national rights—how Kant's idea of individual self-determination became, in the hands of Fichte, a quest for national self-determination and national fanaticism. That you have been criticized for involving Kant in the pedigree of fanatical nationalism does not concern us here; but your emphasis on the great wrong that national self-assertion can inflict on the world (and has, we must concede, frequently inflicted on it) continues to worry me. Need we throw out the baby with the bathwater?

In a similar discussion some years ago, Hugh Seton-Watson made a sharp distinction between national consciousness, which he supported, and nationalism, which he did not:

> If you say that Hitler was derived from the German national idea of the 19th century, Fichte for example, this is true up to a point; what you cannot say is that the national aspirations of Germans for unity, as they were worked out at the beginning of the 19th century under the first impact of Herder's wide influence, could *only* have ended in Hitler. They could have ended in many different ways. National consciousness does not *have* to lead to nationalist movements and conflict. National consciousness *may* lead to nationalism and conflict if it is frustrated. But even nationalist conflicts can end up as a beneficent force, provided that there is statesmanship, wisdom and moderation.

It would, therefore, be very wrong to argue as follows: "Nationalism is a destructive force, therefore let's suppress national consciousness." That is what many governments have tried to do; they justify their repression of the national consciousness of their subjects on the grounds that they themselves stand for a higher civilization. Could there be anything wrong, they argue, in freeing these recalcitrant minorities from the beastly distemper of nationalism? Well, if history teaches us anything it is this, that the attempt to repress national consciousness is almost always self-defeating.[2]

I don't suppose you would disagree with that.

KEDOURIE   No, I would not, but I would qualify it further. The free expression of national consciousness can be most beneficial, and if (speaking in the Soviet context) it means the gradual retreat of Moscow's centralized despotism—who would shed tears for that? But, trying to look into the future, I cannot suppress a certain unease that history might *mutatis mutandis* repeat itself. Just as 1848 resulted, in the long run, in the disasters of unbridled nationalisms and two world wars, so the liberating openings in the present might, unless a great deal of wisdom prevails, lead to highly undesirable consequences. In your conversation with Lord Dacre (Hugh Trevor-Roper)[3] we heard him repeatedly say that he is not afraid of German unification because the Germans have become democrats. He may be right, and I very much hope he is. But extrapolations from present trends are speculative. What we know from the historical evidence is that the kind of nationalist movements we can now see asserting themselves on the ruins of the Soviet Empire did lead, in their earlier incarnation between 1848 and 1945, to extremism, tyranny, and war.

You are familiar with L. B. Namier's work on the subject:

With 1848 starts the German bid for power, for European pre-dominance, for world dominion: the national movement was the common denominator of the German revolution in 1848, and a mighty Germany, fit to give the law to other nations, its foremost aim. *Einheit, Freiheit und Macht* (Unity, Freedom and Power) was the slogan, with the emphasis on the first and third concepts.[4]

Namier called 1848 "the revolution of the intellectuals." An ideological style of politics goes with intellectuals or intellectuals *manqués*. Hitler, I suppose, was one such intellectual *manqué*.

URBAN   Let me try to approach the relationship between culture and national existence from a different angle. You show in your scholarly work that until the French Revolution the idea of nation either did not exist or had wholly different connotations from the ones it has acquired in the last two centuries. At the University of Paris, you remind us, the students were divided into four "nations"—France, Picardy, Normandy, and Germany. The French "nation" included the Italians and Spaniards; the German "nation" were the English as well as the Germans living on the territory of Germany. Religions, empires, and dynasties, you tell us, were the centers of human allegiance and the springs of power.

Would you not agree, though, that so much of European culture—especially in the "young" or reborn nations of Italy, Germany, Poland, Hungary—is centered on the idea of national rejuvenation that we would be losing something essential to our European identity if we disallowed its worth merely because it is "tarred with the brush of nationalism"? Wouldn't we have to exclude, or elaborately "explain," some of the finest poetry and prose of the 19th century, to say nothing about the visual arts and music?

KEDOURIE   Far be it from me to disallow the value of 19th-century culture in any of its significant aspects. But we must distinguish between the cultural and the political, and this is a distinction that runs against the doctrine of nationalism which asserts that the two are inextricably mixed: if you have no political independence, you cannot have a national culture. This is absurd. Groups of people of every kind have and always have had their national culture without being politically sovereign. The idea that a country which rules another, or a group of people who rule another, should impose their language and mores on the ruled is a very recent development. It was certainly not the case in the Ottoman or the Habsburg empires; nor was it true in India under British rule. National culture can certainly exist in the absence of national independence—think of Belgium, or of Switzerland.

URBAN   This may be true if a state grants all its citizens full cultural liberty as do the countries you mention—although Quebec's apparent quest for independence seems to weaken your case. But where this does not exist, it is difficult to see how the aspiration to cultural freedom can stop short of a demand for national liberation and ultimately independence. The cultural and linguistic Russification of the Baltic states is one good example; the fate of the Hungarian minority under Ceausescu's (and now even Iliescu's) Romania is another.

Where a people's right to speak and be educated in its own language is denied, and its history, literature, and traditions are distorted to suit the ruling nation's *amour propre,* doesn't the cry not only for cultural freedom but also for national independence rise spontaneously (if irrationally) from the souls of the underprivileged minority-nations? Can we, in the 1990s, expect Estonians or Georgians to restrict their national aspirations to an Ottoman-style *millet* system? Can we tell them with any hope of success to learn from the dismemberment of the Austro-Hungarian monarchy, when their daily experience tells them that only by blowing the Soviet Empire sky-high can they hope to make a fresh start in their own history?

KEDOURIE   The last thing I want to do is make excuses for Russification or Romanianization. Where the majority-nation indulges in such excesses it can, indeed, expect nothing but robust resistance leading to demands for secession and independence. The Soviet state must reform itself from the ground up, and so must Romania. But arguments for separatism are, I insist, poorly based if they are based on culture. Within the German-speaking world, for example, there are vast differences between the culture of Bavaria, the Rhineland, and Prussia. But should the unification of Germany of 1871 be reversed because these areas might qualify, on cultural grounds, for separate statehood?

Or should the Bretons—or Provençals or Corsicans—qualify for independent statehood because their culture and language are different from French culture and language? Where does this argument end? I remember Sir Isaiah Berlin telling me many years ago that in 1919, at the height of the agitation for "self-determination," residents of a block of flats on Nevsky Prospekt in Petrograd petitioned the authorities for self-determination. And why not? It is absurd, but logical.

URBAN   To deviate somewhat from the line of my own questioning, there appears to be a "law" of history which says: The greater your self-determination the worse your oppressiveness. No sooner did the Lithuanians, in March 1990, declare their independence than they decided to deny self-determination to the Poles in their midst. The Abkhazians fared no better at the hands of the Georgians—to say nothing about the fortunes of the Karabakh Armenian minority in the republic of Azerbaijan. And, before we unduly idealize the permissiveness of the Austro-Hungarian Monarchy, we might also remember that Hungary's emancipation from Austrian tutelage in 1867 did not induce Budapest to pursue a liberal nationalities' policy *vis-à-vis* Slovaks, Romanians, and Croats.

It ill becomes Communist and 'Socialist' critics to castigate the old Hungarian dual-state for its reactionary policies. It was none other than Friedrich Engels who derided, in 1848–49, the claims of the small Slavic races, and of the Romanians (a "decayed nation") to independent statehood. He dismissed the Slovaks as "a 'nation' with absolutely no historical existence," and doubted whether the South Slavs could "botch together a powerful independent and viable nation out of these tattered rags? . . . If the 'eight million Slavs' had to allow the four million Magyars to impose their yoke on them for eight centuries this alone is sufficient proof that the few Magyars had more vitality and energy than the many Slavs."[5]

Aren't you, by the logic of your argument, driven to embrace both the idea of an old-fashioned liberal imperialism as the smaller evil, *and* Marx's and Engels' presumption that "the historic nations" enjoy more extensive rights than the smaller fry? In which case, wouldn't your strictures on nationalism indirectly assist the survival of the tyrannical Soviet Empire?

KEDOURIE   Not at all. What I am saying is that small-nationhood when it becomes *small-statehood* harbors certain great dangers of its own which the world can ill afford. When Woodrow Wilson's Fourteen Points were translated into reality—to the extent that they were—in 1919, European instability ensued because the newly created states were too small to be defensible. It didn't really matter whether they had to face the expansionism of a *Nazi* Germany or a *Bolshevik* Russia—what mattered was that they were small states bordering on a mighty Germany and a mighty Russia. A great power like Russia will always be a source of danger to its small neighbors and so might an enlarged Germany, no matter how liberal and democratic its domestic institutions may be. Occasions will always arise when a big power bordering on an insignificant power will be tempted to dominate the smaller power. Thus, though the centralized Soviet state and its command economy does hide much inefficiency, disorder and corruption, it still wields very great power. It commands a very large and powerful army and a vast security network. We have seen in the Baltic republics with what unscrupulous brutality such power can be used. There have also been recent indications that in spite of the enormous upheavals of 1989 it may not be easy for East European countries to rid themselves of Soviet occupation troops.

URBAN   You say, "no matter how liberal and democratic its domestic institutions may be." Doesn't this rather run counter to what we in the West have been saying since World War II about the foreign policy inclinations of dictatorships and democracies—namely, that governments which are aggressive and coercive *vis-à-vis* their own kinsmen are likely to be even more aggressive *vis-à-vis* foreign nations, and that, conversely, governments based on liberal-democratic principles are much less likely to be internationally aggressive? It was Vaclav Havel, the then newly elected Czechoslovak president, who said in November 1989 that a unified Germany of 80 million people worried him no more than the Federal Republic of 60 million, so long as an enlarged Germany remained free and democratic.

KEDOURIE   First, that a country is liberal and democratic today is no guarantee that it will be so in succeeding generations. In the second place, Germany as a state is a big, productive, and vibrant entity. Because it weighs so much in the world balance of power it is bound to act as a magnet to others and to offer the holders of power in Bonn or Berlin—whoever they may be—the temptation to use that power. We need not assume that they would use it to barbaric ends as the Nazis did. We need not assume anything of the kind, but, speaking from the historical experience, we can assume that at some point Germany might decide that one mishap in a neighboring state might lead to another mishap in another and then to a third, until Germany would feel compelled to make some of these neighboring countries its satellites—if only to put a *cordon sanitaire* between itself and its large rival in the East. This is how great powers behave and how the balance of power is traditionally preserved.

Are Wars Inevitable?

URBAN   But don't our incessant warnings about Germany, forty-five years after the war, boil down to a form of racism—"once-a-German-always-a-German"? Some of our politicians talk as though there were some genetic flaw in the German national character (if, indeed, there is such a thing). I find this ignorant and insulting. Imagine the scandal if they said half as much about Negroes or about Jews.

KEDOURIE   No, I am certainly not implying that the Germans spring from corrupt seed or anything of the sort. What I'm saying is what reason should dictate to those of us who have any acquaintance with history. Here we have a big state and a highly energetic and gifted people placed in the middle of Europe—a state of this kind is in a position to throw its weight about. All I'm assuming is that the

Germans, like the rest of us, are not angels—if they have great power, they will make use of it.

But to return to the balance of power; it seems to me the height of naiveté to assume, as the peacemakers of 1919 assumed, that one can establish an independent Polish state between Germany and Bolshevik Russia and exempt such a Poland from the inevitably conflicting interests of these two big states. It took only twenty years for German and Russian interests to reassert themselves and to destroy the independence of Poland. Without in any way assuming the return of a Stalin in Russia or a Hitler in Germany, I am bound to say that there will always be a Berlin and a Moscow, that these capitals are going to have foreign policy interests which may in some cases make them allies, and antagonists in others. In either case, Poland would be suspended between them, which is an uncomfortable and perilous position for any country to be in. It was, at best, an idealistic aberration, at worst the *hubris* of victory, that induced in 1919 the American, French, and British peacemakers to believe that Poland could survive the clash of great-power interests, or that the dismemberment of Hungary and the establishment of racially heterogeneous successor states could lead to lasting peace.

URBAN   But isn't this rather picking up the language of power politics of an antiquated kind which those born after 1945 in Western Europe, in the U.S., and also the men in Mr. Gorbachev's leadership, have mercifully forgotten or deliberately turned their backs on? I find it most encouraging that so many Frenchmen, Germans, and Italians should think it inconceivable that a fratricidal war could once again erupt in Europe for whatever reason. And they think so, in my reading, not merely because there is a "European Community," nor merely because the nuclear factor would make any such war utterly suicidal, but because the spirit of our time—that indefinable *Zeitgeist* which Mikhail Gorbachev and Eduard Shevardnadze have captured so well— has ruled out war as a continuation of politics "by other means." Then Foreign Minister Shevardnadze's words to the 28th Soviet Party Congress in July 1990 offer good evidence of how far the Gorbachev leadership had ceased to indulge in superpower posturing:

> If we continue as we did before, spending a quarter of our budget on military expenditure, we shall ruin our country. We will then need no defense, just as a ruined country and an impoverished people do not need an army. There is no sense in protecting a system which has led us to economic and social ruin.

That political dinosaurs such as ex-Thatcher minister Nicholas Ridley on the fringes of Europe, and others on the fringes of Soviet political and military life, still cling to the notions and the vocabulary of yesterday's conflicts strikes me as requiring a psychological explanation.

KEDOURIE   These are fine sentiments, and let us hope that they may shape our future. But as an historian who has to consider the past, which is the only evidence he has, I must warn against mistaking the present peaceable pictures for the whole of reality. I am ready to agree that to your young Italian, or young German, it is inconceivable today that he should bear arms against his neighbor; but if you think of the mood of the people when they gather together and are addressed, not as individuals but as members of a crowd, your optimism will need correction. The behavior of a football mob is only the mildest manifestation of the irrationality of mass sentiment, although the mindless behavior of many English soccer supporters can hardly be described as mild.

Mass enthusiasms can grip any population. I can well understand why people demonstrated in East Berlin, in Leipzig, in Prague, and Bucharest against wicked rulers; and it is admirable that, with the exception of Romania, they voiced their anger without bloodshed. But this can change with lightning speed. The Soviet reforms have unleashed passions not only against Moscow and its henchmen—they have also set Azeris against Armenians, Uzbeks against the Kirghiz, Ukrainians against Russians, with all the unabated intensity of earlier feuds. And if you remember the fate of the Armenians at the hands of the Turks in 1915 and a whole series of other genocidal attacks upon one racial group by another (not least in the Muslim parts of the world), then the virtue of national self-determination leading to separate statehood must be seriously questioned.

URBAN   But what do you infer from these deplorable examples—that national aspirations should not be given their head in the age of human rights and self-determination?

KEDOURIE   All I am saying is that if a nation is to become a state, it has to consider the risks of statehood. "Absolute independence" or total subjection to the rule of a centralized despotism are not the sole alternatives, moreover there can and should be a balance of power between states, because that is our only fully tested safeguard against international disorder.

Now, the balance of power is something for *states* to establish, not nations, because states alone have sovereignty. Once a state makes it clear which of its interests are negotiable in the pursuit of international stability and which of its interests are indispensable to its character and survival, a balance of power can be struck with other states making analogous stipulations. This is how international order was tolerably maintained up to 1914.

The small nations which are not states—your Armenians and Moldavians—will have to look very carefully at the perils of independent statehood and find ways and means of living peacefully together in some larger, confederative democratic state, perhaps on the model of the Habsburg Monarchy. This may not fully satisfy nationalist demands; but it might create, in Central Europe for example, a secure haven for several small nations which would, in the absence of such a structure, go on fighting one another, succumbing again and again to the power and influence of their mighty neighbors both in the East and the West. That a grouping of this kind is already under discussion, involving Yugoslavia, Austria, and Italy as well, is a hopeful sign for the future.

URBAN Kuwait—which is neither a separate nation nor of sufficient size to qualify for independent statehood—may have to be satisfied, on your showing, with a subordinate role assigned to it by a powerful Iraq. I am, of course, fairly certain you would not want to subscribe to this proposition, not least because Iraq is a highly undemocratic state which may treat the Kuwaitis no better than it has treated the Kurds. But that is the direction in which I'm led by your reasoning.

Earlier in this conversation (and in several of your books) you pointed out that the nation-state and even the concept of nationhood are alien imports to Asia: "The typical Asian polity is the Chinese Empire, or the Empire of the Moguls, or the Ottoman Empire—large and varied areas administered by a *nomenklatura* controlled by a single center." I would have thought Saddam Hussein's Iraq, modelling itself, as it does, on the Akkadian Empire and Babylonia, would be the sort of state in which smaller peoples such as the Kuwaitis would have to be content to live in a state of dependency—if they accepted your argument.

KEDOURIE Whether one likes Saddam's regime or not, it was in the cards that Kuwait and other sheikhdoms would be at the mercy of Iraq—or of Iran—once British paramountcy disappeared. When it did, in 1971, there was much self-congratulation in Britain that it was to be replaced by a new and promising "regional organization." It was, of course, nothing of the kind—only a house of cards, which has now collapsed. British paramountcy, abandoned for ideological and frivolous reasons, may now be replaced by something altogether unscrupulous and barbaric. In any case, the balance of power abhors a vacuum—paramountcy there has to be . . .

URBAN   You haven't answered Vaclav Havel's point that he is not worried about eighty million Germans forming a single state as long as an enlarged Germany is liberal and democratic. His words encapsulate much that we in the West have been telling the world over the last half-century.

KEDOURIE   The idea that war between democratic countries is unlikely is an illusion. It is, broadly speaking, the same illusion that Immanuel Kant entertained when he committed himself to the thought in his *Perpetual Peace* (1795) that wars would be ruled out if every state were a republic and these republics united in a universal "league of nations." In a world of scarcity there must always arise a conflict of interests between two parties, or two peoples, or two states which will covet the same possessions or advantages for (as they see it) the best possible reasons. You will recall Rousseau's explanation that tyranny came into the world when the first man put a fence around his house. If we accept that, as we should, then it is not far-fetched to say that there is a kind of "original sin" in the very existence of states. Havel is, therefore, in error. Democratic institutions in themselves guarantee no peace. Strong armies and the determination to use them can. The Peloponnesian War was unleashed by a famous democracy . . .

URBAN   But not against another democracy . . .

KEDOURIE   No, but the essential point is that Athens' democratic institutions did not protect the Athenians against the lure of power, loot, and profit. Nor did the democratic institutions of the U.S. prevent civil war between the North and South, nor (to demolish another favorite hypothesis while we are at it) did "highly developed economic relations" and very similar stages of industrial development prevent Germany and Great Britain from going to war in 1914. Nor is it true that "shared civilizations" prevent wars. Germany, France, Italy, and Britain share a civilization and yet they have been at one another's throats twice this century. So I come back to my contention that only a balance of power and one's publicly proclaimed readiness to defend oneself with arms in hand can prevent war.

URBAN   It is a bleak picture which few of my young friends in this country or on the Continent would willingly accept. The call for constant suspicion—for military preparedness, for cultivating an enemy image—strikes them as anachronistic and wicked. Should they go along with your pessimistic reading of history at a time when Europe is being reborn and under luckier stars than marked earlier renewals?

KEDOURIE   None of us can argue with the facts of history. Wars, like human illnesses, happen; often we don't know why a particular war happened; all we know is that it did happen, and we suspect that it is in the human condition that from time to time wars should engulf us. We can deplore them, but we can't ban them.

URBAN   But doesn't your fatalistic analysis almost *invite* war, for might it not induce a peaceloving citizen to say: "If wars are inevitable, I'd better get in my blow first?"

KEDOURIE   It does not, absolutely not, have to lead to such a conclusion.

URBAN   But can we afford to ventilate opinions about the inevitability of war in the presence of nuclear weapons?

KEDOURIE   We have had nuclear arms on our territories since Hiroshima, but that has not prevented destructive conventional wars from being unleashed in Korea, Vietnam, the Lebanon, and between Iraq and Iran. Under the umbrella of the nuclear balance of terror, peoples and governments have found it possible and worthwhile to go to war. I cannot quite understand why a similar thing happening in Europe should be ruled out. A conventional war in the shadow of nuclear weapons could occur in Europe.

URBAN   But don't you think that, even in Europe, nuclear arms would have to be used if one of the belligerents had its back against the wall and had no other means of saving itself? And wouldn't that mean suicide for us all?

KEDOURIE   Once a war has started, no contingency can be wholly excluded, not even the use of nuclear weapons in Europe. My point is that we should not be fooled by our own rhetoric. It is simply not the case that the internal organization of a state is, or ever has been, a guarantee against war. The Soviet Union may be more warlike or less warlike under an eventual multiparty system. So might Germany; so might any state.

URBAN   The young in Europe will, in my experience, just not accept
any idea that a balance of power policy is the ultimate wisdom of
human affairs . . . that, unless you have a gun permanently pointed at
you, there can be no decency and peace among states and nations.
They feel, with Immanuel Kant, that a balance of power policy is "the
immoral sport of sovereigns." Surely, this is a view worthy of
respect . . .

KEDOURIE   Look: Here we are, peaceably talking in my room in All
Souls College in Oxford; but our ability to do so very much depends
on the rule of law in the United Kingdom and a police force which
prevents somebody scaling the garden wall and shooting us down.
There is, in this country, a carefully structured hierarchy of authority,
starting with the monarch and parliament, which everyone accepts;
hence the law prevails.

But in international relations there is no such generally recognized
authority. The international system is essentially still a jungle, and the
law of the jungle can only be tamed if the penalties for disturbing the
peace are loudly proclaimed and imposed. That is what a balance of
power policy is about.

Should One Forget History?

URBAN   Wouldn't you agree that the world around us appears to be
going in opposite directions at one and the same time? There is, first,
a move to larger, supranational formations, of which the European
Community is the most convincing example, fuelled by the idea that
world peace, economic prosperity, and our ecological survival all
militate for supranational cooperation, coordination, and eventually a
single world community. Yet we are also witnessing the rebirth of
fierce nationalisms and separatism both in the Soviet Union and in
Central and Eastern Europe. The Yugoslav state is falling apart along
the old Ottoman-Habsburg demarcation line, with Slovenia and Croatia
opting for independence and a "return" to Europe. Centrifugalism in
the Soviet Union is too well-known to need comment.

Are these two developments indeed going in opposite directions, or
can we assume that the separatism of Estonians, Latvians, Georgians,
Albanians, and all the other small peoples is motivated, not by anti-
Russian or anti-Serb feeling, but by a libertarian determination to be
rid of a centralized ideological tyranny?

If the latter, then your hope that disparate nationalities can peacefully coexist in a federation or confederation would strike me as well-founded. But can we say that the independence movement of the Albanians in Kosovo is rather anti-Communist than anti-Serb; or that the Ukrainians would have nothing against their Russian neighbors if the Soviet Union ceased to be Communist and coercive?

KEDOURIE   These are difficult distinctions to make. Communist domination in the Soviet Union has been represented, for the non-Russian population, by Russians as "elder brothers"; the tyranny of the League of Yugoslav Communists has been of predominantly Serbian coloring (even though Tito himself was half-Croatian). Resistance to one also meant, and still means, hostility to the other. But this coincidence of nationality with oppression should not mean the end of peaceful coexistence between nations of unequal size and different religions and traditions. A confederative structure based on representative government is desirable and perhaps possible once the ideological messianism of communism and fascism is removed from the mixture. Sooner or later the passions of the present nationalistic revivals may become spent, and the desire for civic peace and prosperity may become paramount. And these, in the modern world, cannot be had without wide-ranging cooperation among different national groups and a balance of power among states.

URBAN   Is Margaret Thatcher, then, in error when she says that European unification runs against the temper of our time because events in Eastern Europe and the USSR show the world moving towards national separatism rather than a faceless merger of nations?

KEDOURIE   Generalizations of this kind are, at best, superficial. It is undoubtedly true *at the present time* that most West European countries, with the possible exception of Britain, are prepared to surrender some of their national sovereignty to an elected and accountable European Parliament. To that extent it is legitimate to say that the militant cultivation of national identity has been eroded and the will to further a joint European "good" prospers. Witness, under Article 3 of the July 1990 NATO statement, the appearance of the following words: "The move within the European Community towards political union, including the development of a European identity in the domain of security, will also contribute to Atlantic solidarity and to the establishment of a just and lasting order of peace throughout the whole of Europe."

A "European identity" in the domain of security is a very important addition to earlier language. It has been incorporated at French insistence, and that tells us something about the way things are moving in Paris.

But the parallel in Mrs. Thatcher's argument with Eastern Europe and the nationalities question in the Soviet Union does not hold water. National resentments have come to the surface in these places not because national feeling is a constructive and innately irrepressible force, but because national rights and traditions have been savagely repressed for four and a half decades in Eastern Europe and for seven in the Soviet Union. I doubt whether any of the national groups within the Soviet state would have decided to resort to arms, as the Armenians and Georgians have done, had they enjoyed the sort of freedoms the French- and Italian-speaking population enjoys in Switzerland. The Soviet leaders now openly acknowledge that their troubles in the nationality areas are due to their own follies. For example, at the 28th C.P.S.U. Congress, G. I. Usmanov (secretary of the Central Committee) observed:

> Let's be honest! The so-called resolution of the Nationalities Question that was proclaimed in the past has turned out to be a dangerous illusion. The desire to eradicate ethnic problems based on a distorted and primitive concept of the class approach led to a situation whereby everything that failed to fall within its framework was described as nationalism. There were times when strong-arm methods crudely interfered with the delicate fabric of interethnic relations. There was a deep gulf between the official version and what the peoples saw and knew . . .

I would, therefore, conclude that events in Eastern Europe and the Soviet Union offer no ground for inferences to be drawn either about the desirability or the undesirability, the feasibility or nonfeasibility, of unification in Western Europe.

URBAN   Your insistence on the good that may flow from a renewed balance of power politics sticks a pin into me. I do not dispute its stabilizing effects at various times in the past; but I wonder whether, in the utterly changed nuclear world in which we live, public opinion would stomach any recourse to a balance of power politics and sustain the attitudes that go with it.

As far as the one remaining superpower—the United States—is concerned, we saw, under Nixon and Kissinger in the 1970s, that Dr. Kissinger's Metternichian balance-of-power policies rendered his conception of détente ineffective because the American people either did not understand the complicated game Kissinger was playing, or, to the extent they did understand it, they found it "un-American" and immoral. In Europe, it is true, a new balance-of-power politics would cause fewer eyebrows to be raised, but I think it would tend to resuscitate precisely those now well-forgotten feelings of rabid nationalism which certainly the educated young, and not so young, have spectacularly overcome.

The French and British responses to the fall of the Berlin Wall, and to the first intimations of the unification of the two Germanies, were a sobering reminder that our political masters of the older generation are stuck in the grooves of 1945, if not 1914. No sooner did the Soviet threat appear to be dissolving than conditioned reflexes came into play: language about the need for an Anglo-French nuclear entente began to be heard in the articulations of our politicians and leader-writers. President Mitterrand hoped that Gorbachev would do his job for him by vetoing German unification. Mrs. Thatcher conjured up atavistic images of a German menace on various memorable occasions. Anglo-Polish and Franco-Polish friendships were suddenly revived as a counter to the Polish-German border question; and in the jingoistic wing of our journalistic community dark hints began to be dropped about the impending *Anschluss* of East Germany. In July 1990, the ineffable Nicholas Ridley demonstrated clearly in the pages of the *Spectator* magazine that national and racial prejudice and a balance of power politics are two sides of the same coin.[6]

The European public, and especially postwar generations, had little understanding for any of this. Isn't it worth asking whether it is possible, in the long term, to pursue a balance of power politics and to be constructive, burden-sharing and vision-sharing members of the European Community? In the past, balance of power politics led to war . . .

KEDOURIE   A balance-of-power policy need not go together with nationalistic intolerance. It did not do so in the late 18th century, and even in the 19th it did not become a serious factor until the Franco-Prussian war of 1870–71. A balance of power policy need not be militaristic or pugnacious. All it means is that when one state becomes too powerful for the peace and prosperity of others, the latter try to coordinate their interests so as to balance the might of the former. When Poland was under Soviet control and Communist rule, it would have been laughable to suggest that General de Gaulle should sign a Franco-Polish treaty as reassurance against the German Federal Republic. Germany then had limited power and limited prospects, whereas the Soviet Union, of which Poland was a satellite, was, or so it seemed, all-powerful. But with the Soviet *glacis* in Eastern Europe gone and Germany on the verge of acquiring additional power, it does make sense for Mitterrand, in the 1990s, to think of Franco-Polish friendship as a balance to German hegemony. This sort of thing is as old as history. Human nature being what it is, balance-of-power politics is the best mechanism men have so far invented for keeping a semblance of order in the world.

URBAN Isn't the obverse side of any balance-of-power politics the feeling of encirclement which has cost us so dear? For balance to exist, someone is bound to feel encircled, and that leads to paranoia and worse.

KEDOURIE That is far-fetched. When the French moved to create the "Little Entente" after World War I in order to keep some form of control over Germany (and Hungary), they had a sound idea. Had the Little Entente not been a cardboard contraption, we might have been spared World War II.

URBAN You said a moment ago that a confederative state on the pattern of the Habsburg Empire is one of the most desirable frameworks for the peaceful coexistence of different nations and "nationalities" and the best guarantee against overbearing neighbors. Now you speak in support of the Little Entente which resulted from the demolition of the Habsburg monarchy. Can you have it both ways?

KEDOURIE The kind of incipient multinational federalism we saw in the Habsburg Empire, had it been conducted on truly federal and liberal lines, would have been the right framework for interethnic peace and international balance. But with that gone, the Little Entente was, in intention at least, the right pillar in Central Europe for the containment of a potentially irredentist Germany.

URBAN As the Europeans of the postwar generation see it, there is now a case for saying that Europe cannot be healthy as long as the central and eastern parts of it are mortally injured; and for saying that, because of its geographic position, economic strength and interests, Germany is perhaps the only, and certainly the main, European country able and willing to sanitize these cancer-ridden organs of our continent for the benefit of the whole of Europe as well as, of course, Germany's own. Does it make sense to revive the ancient suspicions, the dated vocabulary, and old power-political machinations of our grandfathers in the wholly changed circumstances of the turn of the millennium? Isn't it as important to forget some of the experiences of history when the times call for amnesia as it is to remember them?

Some of the current (1990) pronouncements of our British and French political leaders about the future of post-Soviet Europe remind me only too well of Clemenceau's backward-looking policies at the 1919 Paris peace conference. This is how John Maynard Keynes, who was present as a member of the British delegation, described them:

> Clemenceau took the view that European civil war is to be regarded as a normal, or at least a recurrent, state of affairs for the future . . . European history is to be a perpetual prize-fight, of which France has won this round, but of which this round is certainly not the last . . . This is the policy of an old man, whose most vivid impressions and most lively imagination are of the past and not of the future. He sees the issue in terms of France and Germany, not of humanity and European civilisation struggling forwards to a new order.[7]

KEDOURIE I can see that there is a good argument to be made for suspending the suspicions of history, erasing the past and starting again with a clean slate. I can see that this has an appeal to the young and the idealistic. I am not saying such an approach is wrong or unduly naïve. All I'm insisting on is that states do have natural interests and that these interests do increase as the power of the state increases. It is perfectly true that the West German Federal Republic is almost a model democratic state with a faultless record in its international relations. But it is precisely Central and Eastern Europe that has always been Germany's main target for expansion, and it is precisely that area which will now come under German economic hegemony.

We do not have to suppose that a united Germany would once again become an ideological, or even a conventional, expansionist power, on the pattern of Kaiser Wilhelm's Germany, to fear a certain economic imbalance developing in the affairs of Europe in the wake of the retreat of Soviet power. A prudent man will ask himself: How would Germany use its fresh economic hegemony in the long term? . . . because there are all sorts of ways in which a strong state can overawe weaker neighbors. What would happen if Germany did do another Rapallo? What if it said to its NATO allies: We will no longer agree to the presence of your forces on German soil unless the nuclear discrimination against Germany ends and we acquire nuclear forces similar to those which the French and the British have . . . Who could say *no* to such an approach?

URBAN   Aren't we jumping a little too far ahead of history? Our current problem, which will tax our purses and our imagination for a long time to come, is how to manage the retreat of communism and rehabilitate 100 million Central and East Europeans, as well as some 280 million "Soviet" people, from the ravages of the Communist system. Should we, in the hour of this greater challenge to our ingenuity, worry about the end effects of European recovery when the recovery itself is entirely open to question? To express in 1990 fears of "German domination" strikes me as rather like saying: "This surgeon will, if I'm lucky, remove my cancer—but won't that make him too powerful over my life when I've recovered?"

KEDOURIE   Rehabilitation is, as we know from the Third World, something for the East and Central Europeans themselves to undertake. Our assistance can be only marginal. And we have to ask whether they have the material, historical, and spiritual resources to do it. The history of the Balkan nations after their emancipation from Ottoman imperial rule is not encouraging. Nor is that of the successor states of the Austro-Hungarian monarchy, or Hungary itself. With the exception of Czechoslovakia, they managed their affairs disastrously. What parliamentary democratic traditions existed in Poland and Hungary at various times in their history cannot be said to be alive after half a century of lawlessness under communism. They will have to write an entirely new chapter in their history—what they have in front of them at the moment are just so many blank pages. It is, therefore, by no means certain that the successor states to Soviet hegemony will manage their affairs, either among themselves or in their domestic politics, any better than they did after the retreat of Habsburg and Ottoman power.

URBAN   My own analysis tells me that the Polish, Hungarian, Czech, and Slovak reserves of democracy are a bit more substantial than you have indicated. But assuming that they are as thin as they would appear to you, I am cheered by a remarkable and paradoxical phenomenon. Marxism-Leninism preached a libertarian creed and prosperity—but practised oppression and scarcity. The oppression has been overthrown but the libertarian creed has made its mark. It is now fuelling Central Europe's quest for democracy and social welfare. Communist rule has turned out to be in some ways the people's "university." During my recent visits to Central Europe I saw a great deal of very intelligent understanding of what democracy is about and the clear will to make it work. Constitutions are being made or amended, and institutions put on the statute books.

KEDOURIE   Ah, but there lies the whole problem. Democracy cannot be made to order. I don't think you can create institutions by legislation. Look at the constitutions of the U.K., Canada, or the U.S. and ask yourself: How do they work? Are they guaranteed by the deliberations of some college of lawyers or other formal arrangements? You will find that they rest on a balanced society in which substantial interests check and control one another. It is, more particularly, economic interests, over which no one can ride roughshod, that guarantee the equilibrium and make it impossible for either a dictator or single-party rule to arise.

Most Central and East European countries have an historical deficit in these characteristics; although they might acquire them, it would be taking hope too far to say that they are likely to become democracies simply because Soviet power is on the retreat and their national independence has been restored. Your point that the spirit of democracy in Central Europe appears to be asserting itself by inspiration drawn from the "good Marx"—

URBAN   A phrase I didn't use . . .

KEDOURIE   . . . and the egalitarian undercurrents of Sovietism is an interesting one. But let me say that the "good Marx," what is called the early Marx, was laughably Utopian. He provides no basis for any practical politics. In brief, the only certainty we have at present is great uncertainty.

URBAN   May I refer you to Aristotle's words about the effectiveness and ineffectiveness of constitutions: Namely, that constitutions are worthless unless they are grounded in the customs and conventions of the people. It may well be true at the moment that Central Europe is without a web of countervailing economic interests, but it is certainly not the case that either the Poles, the Czechs, or the Hungarians lack the traditions that make for a *Rechtsstaat* and political pluralism. Hungary's *Golden Bull* (1222), to take one example, is almost as old as the *Magna Carta* (1215) and makes comparable stipulations limiting royal privileges and prerogatives.

But, coming closer to our time, we have the example of postwar Germany to consider. There was nothing in German history up to 1945 that would have induced a reasonable man to believe that from the heritage of Nazism—from the ruins of the German cities, from the human débris of the lost war, from the influx of millions of destitute expellees, the rampant hunger and homelessness—a liberal, democratic, prosperous, and generous German state would arise and flourish so quickly. But it did. The most successful society in German history sprang from such inauspicious beginnings.

Central Europe today is, it seems to me, in an incomparably more fortunate situation than Germany was in 1945. The Czechs, Poles and Hungarians have housing, food, a functioning railway and a postal system. Their cities, though badly polluted, have not been laid waste, their menfolk are not in prisoner of war camps. They are all in the process of creating a free and democratic order to the applause of the rest of the world. They are ethnically entirely homogeneous (if we discount the Czech/Slovak dichotomy as a seedbed of conflict) and will soon be rid of all foreign troops. If a defeated and war-torn Germany could surmount its *Nullpunkt* in 1945–47, albeit with Anglo-American assistance, I cannot quite see why an undefeated and war-spared Central Europe should not be able to do the same—to be sure, with Western assistance, which is now forthcoming, reinforced by the prospect of eventual admission to the European Community.

KEDOURIE   Your comparison is unpersuasive. In 1945 the Western powers had a keen and wholesome memory of how their victory in 1918 had been mismanaged. They were determined not to repeat the mistakes of Versailles. They were even more keenly aware that the real victor of World War II was the Soviet Union, with Stalin (and Stalinism) at the helm. A hungry and clueless Germany was waiting to fall into the hands of Stalin, from which the fall of a hungry, clueless and increasingly Communist-subverted Western Europe would have followed. Western fears increased when totalitarian Communist rule was extended to the whole of Central and Eastern Europe. The Marshall Plan, the creation of the West German Federal Republic, and NATO followed. The German media were reorganized on American models; German trade unionism and codetermination in industry were introduced under British auspices. These were the keys to the birth and success of German democracy. Why was all this done? Because we had a vital interest in having a free, prosperous, and strong Germany on our side in our contest with the Soviet Union.

Central Europe can count on no really comparable Western assistance. I am ready to concede that we do have an interest in seeing the Central European countries prosper under liberal-democratic dispensations—for we do not want them to sink into chaos. Much less do we want them to seek salvation in dictatorial rule whether of the left or the right. But the threat from the Soviet superpower is assumed to be no longer there, and our assistance is bound to be less committed than our assistance was to Germany. Central Europe will essentially have to fend for itself under difficult conditions. The West is going to help, but the analogy with postwar Germany does not strike me as convincing.

Other considerations also weigh against the analogy. Forty years and more of bureaucratic Stalinism have created layer upon layer of people with a vested interest in perpetuating the inefficiencies and corruptions of the command economy. The socialist tyranny has also utterly destroyed the legal order necessary to a free society. It will take a very long time to re-establish—and to accustom people once more to the institution of private property, and the opportunities it can open up.

You quoted Aristotle about the effectiveness and ineffectiveness of constitutions. Well, one of Aristotle's main concerns was how to forestall revolution and disorder. He was, of course, talking about very small societies and assuming that political action was organically connected with the personal virtue or lack of virtue of every citizen: "A state is good only when those citizens who have a share in the government are themselves good" (*Politics,* Book VII, 3).

We no longer live in small societies, and we no longer link our political analysis to the virtue of the citizen—

URBAN   More's the pity . . .

KEDOURIE   That may well be, but we don't. Aristotle's purpose was to identify and then to remove the distemper of social extremism; and he offered certain wholesome remedies. When there is a revolution by the rich, he said, and aristocracy degenerates into oligarchy, everyone who does not belong to the victorious rich is not only dispossessed but also disenfranchised.

How, he asked, is this to be prevented? What you have to do, he answered, if you are an oligarch, is to recommend to your fellow oligarchs that your oligarchy should, first and foremost, look after the interests of the *demos,* the people, the poor. And he goes on to say that, by the same token, if the people come out on top and there is "democracy," it should be the first business of the people's representatives, i.e., the democrats, to take care of the interests of the rich. Now this is the kind of spirit the builders of the new democracies in Central Europe might profit from; but I doubt whether, in the wake of the passions aroused by communism, they are likely to do this in the short run.

URBAN   I would say that their search for social equity is already in the making. The new democracies seem to be looking for a "social market economy," based more on the Swedish, Austrian, or German models than the one advanced by Thatcherism. They want to combine the productivity and abundance of the free market with a number of cushions and safety nets provided, out of general taxation, by the state. Doesn't this strike you as a modern equivalent of the Aristotelian principle?

KEDOURIE   In intention—perhaps. But I cannot see how it can be put into practice since these post-Communist societies have as yet no private wealth from which competing political interests might issue. And if private wealth creation is to be restricted, democracy in Central Europe will have a hard row to hoe. There is and can be no shortcut to constitutional and representative government. After the war, earnest civil servants in the British Colonial Office were busy writing scrupulously fair constitutions for the British colonies in Africa. Look now at their handiwork.

URBAN   But you are surely not suggesting that the inability or unreadiness of African tribesmen to create democratic societies is a clue to how the Czechs, the nation of Jan Hus, or the Hungarians, with their ancient tradition of constitutional government, will behave in the next several decades?

KEDOURIE   The analogy may strike you as far-fetched, but it is not wholly irrelevant. It is certainly relevant to the future of the Turkmens, Kirghiz, Uzbeks, Armenians, and Azeris, should they ever attain independence.

URBAN   A last word about power politics: I suppose the revulsion the postwar generation feels against any balance of power politics is due (as they see it) to its transparent immorality. Fighting an ideological war—hot or cold—is morally simple to justify. When a nation is asked to put down an ideological empire—whether nazism or Stalinism—it is asked to fight not only for the national interest, but for a conception of the world it regards as just, and against one it regards as unjust and tyrannical. But when ideological antagonists disappear and the balance of power means balancing power among states with similar institutions and a shared social order, the popular psyche is confronted with a very different problem. Democratic Frenchmen, democratic Germans, democratic Britons, and democratic Italians are then told to prepare themselves for arm-twisting and worse against one another—because this or that state is "getting above itself," has a better economy, or is simply overshadowing the pride, status or "station" of others.

Those born after 1945 throughout Europe find this 19th-century manner of looking at our world intolerable; they want to see no further installments of the story "The European Civil War, 1914–89."

KEDOURIE   What is moral in public affairs is never easy to determine. Moral judgement is likewise never an open-and-shut affair. To quote Grotius, in politics and war a way has to be found between those who say that in these matters nothing is lawful and those who say that everything is lawful. In 1941 Britain and the U.S. allied themselves with Stalin's Russia, knowing full well that Stalin and his system were loathsome and alien to everything Britain and America stood for. But they felt even more strongly that the primary threat to their freedom and perhaps to their survival came from Hitler's Germany. An alliance even with Stalin was necessary in order to defeat nazism. This was balance of power politics at its cruellest.

In the mid-1970s, former president Richard Nixon, to take another example, played the "China card." He made his peace with and even befriended Mao Zedong because he was anxious to isolate the Soviet Union. But did Nixon think that Mao and his "Red Guards" were one whit better than the thugs the Soviet leaders let loose on the people on countless occasions? Not at all. Nixon acted on cool calculation, but in the service of a higher good which was attained.

URBAN   Wouldn't you agree that in both these cases the Western powers' balance of power politics were motivated by moral and philosophical considerations? Nazism had to be defeated because it was a totalitarian despotism and a menace to the world, and the Soviet system had to be isolated and overcome for the same reason. However, in the post-Nazi and post-Communist world, any balance-of-power policy would involve like-minded people and identical social systems holding one another in check by a combination of economic pressures, military threats, and government-inspired nationalisms. Forgive me for saying it again: The young in Europe, the new generations, will have no truck with that. They will feel, with St. Augustine, that any peace attained by such methods is a "peace of the unjust"—that any future conception of "collective security" must not rest on insecurity. That is why, it seems to me, they support in their great majority the unification of Europe. Can we fault their thinking? Aren't they, in fact, advocating a higher conception of balance among nations—one that would put cooperation and integration in the place of ransom and blackmail?

KEDOURIE   If we are quoting St. Augustine we have to remember that, for him, justice is attainable only in the Heavenly City. You have, in this conversation, repeatedly quoted the young and their views. Youth in itself does not guarantee virtue or wisdom. On the contrary, to the extent that these goods are attainable, they are more easily attained by the old. It is not for nothing that the hymn of a demagogic movement like fascism was *Giovinezza, giovinezza!* But this was no rejuvenation . . .

Your mention of youth reminds me of a passage by Aldous Huxley which it is ironical to recall in the present context. It occurs in that marvellous anthology of his, *Texts and Pretexts,* published in 1932. It was the first book I bought for myself as a schoolboy, and it gave me an incomparable insight into Western poetry. Huxley has a chapter about old age in which he quotes a couplet from the Elizabethan poet Thomas Bastard:

> Age is deformed, youth unkind,
> We scorn their bodies, they our mind.

Huxley goes on to say:

Things have changed since Queen Elizabeth's days. "We," that is to say, the young, scorn not only their bodies, but also (and above all) their minds. In the two politically most "advanced" states of Europe this scorn is so effective that age has become a definite bar to the holding of political power. Communism and fascism appeal for the support of youth, and of youth alone. At Rome and Moscow, age has been disfranchised . . .

Later on in the same passage Huxley says: "To a white traveller who visited him, 'Give me hair-dye,' was the agonized cry of the greatest of African chiefs. 'Hair-dye.' He was going grey. Not long afterwards his warriors speared him to death."

In its self-certainty, youth is (as the poet says) indeed unkind.

1990

Chapter 4

A Tale of Two Empires

A Conversation with Otto von Habsburg

URBAN Lord Dacre (Hugh Trevor-Roper) holds the view that in a world in which national passions run high, empires are stabilising forces which we dismantle at our peril. For a long time, he says, both the Ottoman and the Habsburg Empires were forces of that kind. Given the world's many sources of political and ecological instability, even the Soviet Empire, especially the Soviet Empire in its present state of enfeeblement, is (he observed) preferable to the disorder that would follow its dismemberment.

How do you, as head of the House of Habsburg and legatee to the traditions of the Austro-Hungarian monarchy, see this comparison? Can we legitimately set side by side the Habsburg Empire, as an erstwhile guarantor of European stability, with the Soviet Empire as a present or future guarantor of world order?

V. HABSBURG The differences between the Habsburg and Ottoman Empires on the one hand, and the Soviet Empire on the other, are much greater than the similarities. The Habsburg Empire was characterised, certainly in the last phase of its existence, by compromise, stability, and quiet cooperation. The Latin tag, *et tu felix Austria nube,* was not a far-fetched *aperçu*. Most of the nations that made up the Empire had joined or remained part of it because it was within the Empire that they saw their interests best defended. The same goes, although to a smaller degree, for the Ottoman Empire. I deplore the consequences of Ottoman militancy on European soil, but I cannot close my eyes to the fact that Islam was a force of spiritual cohesion, some of which is still effective or has recently been reborn on the

133

former territories of the Empire. What is more, and what is often forgotten, is the tolerance which Islam under the Ottomans extended to minority nations and religions. The Jews, for example, enjoyed a longer and more profound period of relative freedom under the Ottoman *millet* system than they had done before or were to enjoy right up to their emancipation under the Enlightenment.

The Soviet Union offers a radically different picture. Whereas the Habsburg Empire was a multinational community, the Soviet Union is a colonial empire. Some of it goes back to the Tsarist conquests of the last three centuries, other parts have been acquired by the Bolsheviks since 1917.

The Soviet leaders are not unintelligent. Under Gorbachev they have come to realise the importance of words and symbols in international communication. They are now making strenuous efforts, through their fifth columns in Western Europe and the United States, to induce our public opinion to believe that the Soviet Union is a multinational state like, shall we say, Switzerland, and not a colonial empire ruled in all essentials by a single nation. The truth is that the Soviet Union is an empire under Russian tutelage. The Russian nation is the ruling nation (albeit itself unfree), and all the other nations and ethnic entities, whether large or small, are subject nations. You can best observe this in the Baltic states where the influx of Russians and the use of the Russian language have played havoc with the national identity of Lithuanians, Latvians, and Estonians, so much so that, as a reaction to fifty years of Russification, all three Baltic states are now in the process of redefining themselves as national, and eventually independent, republics. We can see the same process in action in Moldavia, where the local and essentially Romanian population wants to return to the use of the Latin alphabet and to Romanian as the official language of the republic.

Now there was, admittedly, a certain Magyarisation in the Hungarian half of the Austro-Hungarian monarchy, but it would have been unthinkable for the leaders of Austria or Hungary to abolish the writing or language of a minority nation. Yet this is what has happened in Moldavia. Bulgaria, with its persecution and expulsion of the Turkish population, was another terrible symbol of Communist imperial intolerance, and so, of course, was Ceausescu's intolerance of the Hungarian and German languages and cultures. There may be other examples.

URBAN   To be fair to the Gorbachev reformers, let me say that your analysis of the nationality question is shared by many of them. For example, on 1 September 1988, Yuri Afanasyev, the Russian historian, said in an interview: "The model of national relations that existed before *perestroika* must be discarded." What we have today, he observed, is "a strongly centralised state on Stalinist lines. We do not have autonomous republics, but rather provinces subject to the centre."

V. HABSBURG   Yes, and for all these reasons I feel that the Soviet Empire cannot escape the law of colonial disintegration and cannot be looked upon as a guarantee of international security. Decolonisation has run its course in all the other colonial empires—the Soviet Union is bound to go the same way. In 1962 I talked to General de Gaulle about the future of the Soviet Union. "I have great pity for the Russians," he said, "because they have Algeria within their own walls." This was a wise observation. Exactly how wise is even clearer to us today in the light of the creeping pulverisation of the Soviet Union.

URBAN   I wonder, though, whether in a generally volatile world it might not be in our interest—as Lord Dacre suggested—to keep the Soviet Empire stable. When you think of that nightmare of unruliness that holds much of the Near East and Middle East in its grip, do you not feel that we need a relaxed Soviet Union as a partner in world stability?

V. HABSBURG   Whether we need it or not—we cannot get it. I am deeply sceptical about the whole idea of conceiving the Soviet Union as a source of stability. One lesson we ought to have drawn from Mikhail Gorbachev's years in power is the system's patent fragility. There is unrest in Uzbekistan, Tajikistan, Kirghizia; there is interethnic strife between Georgians and Abkhazians, between Armenians and Azerbaijanis, and between Russians and virtually all non-Russian nations and nationalities. The Baltic states now look upon themselves as being under military occupation on the argument that the Nazi-Soviet pact of 1939 was invalid *ab initio,* so that the incorporation of the Baltic states was invalid, too. Leading members of the Soviet establishment—Valentin Falin, for example, on 23 July 1989, on German television—have now acknowledged that there were secret protocols attached to the 1939 pact, and at least one authentic copy has been identified. Roy Medvedev, in his revised version of *Let History Judge,* makes the same point and, significantly, on 24 December 1989, the Congress of People's Deputies of the Soviet Union finally added

Moscow's official acknowledgment. Meanwhile, on 22 August 1989, a commission of the Supreme Soviet of Lithuania had declared the Nazi-Soviet pact to be illegal and the subsequent incorporation of Lithuania into the Soviet Union to be without legal force. Four days later, the Central Committee of the Soviet Communist Party came out with a threatening statement. On 11 March 1990, Lithuania declared its independence and the Soviet state—under its newly elected, all-powerful president—is doing its best to thwart the Lithuanian people's constitutionally guaranteed right of self-determination.

None of this makes for stability. In fact, it has all the makings of international disorder. Peaceful order in the Soviet Union can only be obtained if self-determination is restored to every nation that has been forcibly deprived of it. So, personally, I cannot conceive the Soviet Empire as a partner for world stability but, rather, as a source, and probably the main source, of instability. Add to the ethnic factor all the other, and increasingly visible, factors of social unrest—the evaporation of the authority of the Communist Party, strikes generated by shortages of food and consumer goods of all kinds—and you have the prescription for trouble in virtually every area in which earlier empires encountered trouble as a prelude to their disintegration.

URBAN   There was a widespread belief (conceit might be a better word for it) in the nineteenth century that nations, and especially empires, had to have a "mission." The French thought their civilisation equalled human civilisation par excellence, which it was their duty to propagate; the British saw themselves as harbingers of the rule of law and parliamentary government; the Russians believed that their mission was to defend Christianity against the Turks and to save a cynical and effete Western Europe from itself. Only the Austrian Empire did not have a mission. Or did it? If we were to append a single tag to the Habsburg Empire and leave it there for our successors for easy identification, would you say that tag would be the coexistence of cultures under one European Culture, with a capital C?

V. HABSBURG   Indeed, I would. You see, the very existence of Austria-Hungary was a cultural statement. There appeared in Vienna some years ago an excellent book under the title, *Das blieb vom Doppeladler, Auf den Spuren der versunkenen Donaumonarchie,* by Ernst Trost, one of Austria's best historical writers.[1] Trost went in search of the cultural heritage of Austria-Hungary from Chernovitz to Cattaro, and he was right in first assuming, and then finding, a profound cultural link binding all the Empire's constituent elements into a somewhat undefinable but very real whole. That link, that Habsburg-inspired life style, still exists. But when I say that the Habsburg Empire was first and foremost a cultural community, I have to add in the same breath that it was a cultural community with a mission, and the name of that mission was the defence of Europe. Had we not defended Europe against the Turks in the Danube valley, we would not be here today; we would be praying in some mosque on the Rhine or the Seine. The danger of that happening was very real.

None of this is to say that I deny the mission of other empires, or the mission today of the United States with its roots in the Old Testament and the faith of the Pilgrim Fathers. (That faith has by now disappeared in its narrow sense, but its penumbral effects still dominate American thinking.) The Habsburg Empire, and Austria-Hungary in particular, are best understood as a tree of many branches that grew from a single root but has shed its seed in many directions, fructifying its neighbours and being enriched by them in turn. The defence of European culture and civilisation was the great idea the Habsburg Empire stood for.

URBAN How would you answer historians who contend that the smaller and mainly Slavic nations of the Austro-Hungarian monarchy did not enjoy the same cultural and civic freedoms as the two ruling races of Austrian Germans and Hungarians? Before and during the First World War, R. W. Seton-Watson and Wickham Steed, for example, fought a long and successful campaign in support of Czech, Slovak, and South Slav separatism on the argument that these small nations were ripe for independence and the Empire stood in the way. Even sympathetic observers of the Monarchy such as Leo Valiani and Edward Crankshaw ascribe its fall to the unwise nationalities policy of Vienna and, especially, Budapest. They seem to go along with the view that the accession of Archduke Franz Ferdinand would have put an end to the inequitable rule of the Hungarian magnates by revoking the 1867 Austro-Hungarian Dualism, setting in train the reorganisation of the Empire on federal lines and giving equal rights to the small nations.

V. HABSBURG Minority rights must be understood in their historical context. Some of the national cultures you have mentioned are of very recent vintage. The whole idea that national consciousness and national culture have a specific political meaning which governments and the members of other cultures ought to respect did not begin stirring until after the French Revolution. Even Magyar culture, although of long and respectable history, did not assert itself in the form in which we know it until 1848. Up to 1848, Latin was the official language of Hungary, and Latin, not Hungarian, was the language spoken in the Hungarian assembly. Much the same goes for the Czechs. For centuries, Prague was a completely German-speaking city of German culture. Think of Charles University which was and is an ancient seat of German learning, or, in our time, of Rilke and Kafka who lived in Prague but wrote in German.

Governments do not normally jump ahead of public consciousness—they usually lag behind it. New perceptions are always the work of creative minorities. The majority are stuck in the grooves of conventional wisdoms and time-sanctioned responses. They are reactionary in the literal sense of the word. It is, therefore, not quite fair to criticise the Habsburg Empire for not having taken hasty steps to satisfy the demands of what were initially small groups of national minority leaders and, in some cases, a few individuals. Until about the outbreak of the war the demand for secession was just not there. Indeed, even during the first two years of the war, most of the Czech and Croatian nationalists, while asking for extensive rights, protested their loyalty to the House of Habsburg. It was not until 1914 that Thomas Masaryk himself reluctantly embraced the idea of secession, realising that he was assisting in the destruction of what was irreplaceable.

The same slow development from a small nucleus of committed individuals to public awareness may be observed in the history of social consciousness. It was only in the nineteenth century that certain social thinkers began to feel that society had a collective responsibility for its weaker members. Communal solidarity with the poor and disadvantaged would have struck our ancestors in the eighteenth or seventeenth century as preposterous. And look at the depressingly slow pace at which the ecological bundle of problems has been able to penetrate the skulls of our contemporaries. The threat to our environment has been there for a hundred years. Books have been written about it and speeches made in all languages, but it was only about twenty years ago that an unwilling public began to take the facts on board and governments began to feel obliged to respond to public anxiety. The British, always the slowest in the Western convoy, held back until a couple of years ago on the contention (a) that ecological problems did not exist and (b) that they were the expression of the hidden agenda of the Far Left.

In brief: The Habsburgs did not act because the idea that a profound minority problem existed did not become publicly assimilated until the turn of the century. Please remember that the first constructive solution of the ethnic question was the Moravian Agreement in the early years of our century (1905). Historians who apply today's standards to yesterday's problems write poor history.

URBAN   Professor István Deák of Columbia University observed on Hungarian television in June 1989 that, in the course of his researches in the Vienna State Archives, he had occasion to examine confidential files of officers of the Austro-Hungarian Empire. He was interested in their social background and the ratio of the various nations and nationalities in the officer corps as a whole. He found to his surprise that, while the files went into great detail about the officers' suitability for promotion on grounds of intellect, responsibility, leadership qualities and the like, nothing at all was said about their nationality or mother tongue. Deák felt this was testimony that at a certain level the monarchy was astonishingly egalitarian and free from national bias.

V. HABSBURG   I do not find that at all astonishing as far as the nationality factor is concerned. That the officers' mother tongue was not noted either is more surprising because the language of command was German and, later, Hungarian on the Hungarian side of the armed forces; but officers serving with units other than German-speaking were required to be well enough versed in the language of the troops under their command to be able to communicate with them on service matters (*'zum Dienstgebrauch genügend'*).

But, as I say, I am not surprised that the files were silent about nationality. It did not matter what nationality an officer belonged to, and many of them did not even realise that they belonged to a nationality. They all carried the emperor's or king's commission, and that made them equal in the eyes of all. If you study the names of senior officers during, shall we say, the last 100 years of the Empire, you will find a very liberal representation of Czechs, Croats, Poles, Slovenians, and other minority nations, in addition to Austrian Germans and Hungarians.

URBAN   I suppose the Emperor Franz Joseph and then your father, the Emperor Charles, looked upon himself as head of a multinational and multicultural family. The legal bond holding the Empire together was not Austria but allegiance to the House of Habsburg by treaty or marriage.

V. HABSBURG   Absolutely. Both Franz Joseph and my father felt that they were citizens of the whole; and we can see in retrospect that they were perhaps the last citizens of the whole. Yugoslavia in our own day offers a telling parallel. Tito was probably the last Yugoslav. He believed in the federation and held it together. With his death, Serbs, Croats, Albanians, and Slovenes began to reassert their tribal loyalties and Yugoslavia is now in the process of disintegration. There are no more Yugoslavs.

URBAN   But that, I suppose, is where the parallel ends—for in no other respect would I, for one, care to compare Tito's short-lived rule with the history of the Habsburg Empire.

V. HABSBURG   I would agree with that.

URBAN   Without wishing to pry into your private life unduly, may I ask you whether the state's unconcern with race and nationality was also reflected in the personal behaviour of the Emperor Charles and the Empress Zita? What sort of a personal tradition was handed down to them, and then to yourself, from Franz Joseph?

V. HABSBURG   Race and nationality never played any role in the thinking of our family. Even religion did not. My father was a modest and very mild person. It was difficult to rouse him to a state of anger, but I remember a scene at our dinner table—it must have been in 1918—that made a deep impression on me. Somebody at table made an anti-Jewish remark. My father flew into a rage and told this person very bluntly what he thought of him and where he should go. You see, for us it was an unquestioned and unquestionable fact that the Empire was multinational. It would have struck us as monstrous (and, of course, highly impolitic) to discriminate on grounds of race, nationality, or religion. We just did not think in those terms.

URBAN   In a conversation at the end of 1987, Sidney Hook, the distinguished American philosopher (now alas dead), told me that young American Socialists during the First World War looked with much greater favour upon the Kaiser's Germany and the Austro-Hungarian Monarchy than they did on the Allied powers. One of the reasons for doing so, he said, was the Emperor Franz Joseph's even-handed policy vis-à-vis the Jews: "Most of the community in which I lived . . . were much more sympathetic to Germany and Austria than to Tsarist Russia. Britain and France were unfamiliar countries to them . . . I still recall their boasting of the number of famous German Jews who were accepted at the court of the Kaiser and their sympathetic words about the Emperor Francis Joseph of Austria whom the Jews praised as someone who had protected them from anti-Semitic ethnic groups during the Austro-Hungarian Monarchy." Hook's view is very much in line with what you have just told me. Was this even-handedness in the Habsburg family a matter of conscious policy or did it come without effort?

V. HABSBURG   We never talked about it; it came without effort. Take, for example, the aristocracy in Hungary: The fact that Manfred Weiss had been elevated to the baronetcy was considered to be entirely just and natural because he had great industrial achievements to his name. That he was a Jew did not count as a plus or a minus. The fact that he belonged to one denomination rather than another just did not enter our family's thinking. One could cite other examples.

URBAN   A comparison, then, with the practices of the multinational Soviet Empire would not redound to the credit of the Soviet Union?

V. HABSBURG   Indeed, it would not. In the Soviet Union racism— racism, that is, at both the popular and the poorly disguised official level—plays a major role. Look at the *Pamyat* organisation with its rampant racism and open anti-Semitism. Boris Yeltsin was a candidate of *Pamyat* at the last elections and obtained a very impressive majority. I find this alarming. True, he was not a candidate of *Pamyat* alone, but he came out on top with the support of a movement that has the makings of nazism. At the meetings of *Pamyat* some of the old Nazi language has shamelessly surfaced. Russia's misfortunes under communism are ascribed to a world Jewish conspiracy. The so-called Protocols of the Elders of Zion are bandied about. Who prints these and how are they distributed? I find it distressing that many Western commentators celebrate Yeltsin as a great dissident democrat and do not detect the voice of a Nazi-type extremism among the people who support him.

I am following these trends in the Soviet Union rather carefully, and I would not exclude the possibility of the Communist system transforming itself, via national bolshevism, into a kind of Russian national socialism—

URBAN   Not into a corporatist system of the somewhat milder, fascist kind, as some Sovietologists suggest?

V. HABSBURG   No, into a National Socialist system proper; current developments in the Soviet Union point to outright nazism. A few years ago, Assen Ignatov, a former Bulgarian Communist, pointed out in a book[2] that, after the collapse of communism, national socialism would be the wave of the future. Collectivism, in order to survive, would have to take on many of the features of nazism. We are, I believe, already witnessing the Soviet Union going down that road.

URBAN   Taking the idea of culture a step further: would you say that the kind of Europe we are in the process of hammering out needs a "dominant theme" even if it does not need a "mission"? That dominant theme, it seems to me, could not be any of the leitmotifs of the earlier incarnations of Europe: It could not be a Europe that defines itself against the "barbarians" (as the Greeks did), nor could it be a Europe that is coterminous with Christendom. Would not a United Europe at the turn of the millennium naturally define itself as a Europe of European Culture—much as you have said the Habsburg Empire did on a much smaller scale?

But if the new Europe were to draw its inspiration from European Culture, would culture prove strong enough to secure the allegiance of Germans, Frenchmen, Italians and Britons? De Gaulle once observed that Frenchmen would fight and die for France, but no one would die for a customs union. Would Europeans die for European Culture, or the "common house of Europe," if we could agree on the meaning of that nebulous term?

V. HABSBURG   I strongly believe that a United Europe is going to define itself around the idea of European Culture, but not, as you imply, because the older definitions have become anachronistic, but because European Culture is a living thing which will, as time goes on and we acquire a more profound consciousness of belonging together, gain in strength and depth.

There is, apart from culture, also another feature that distinguishes us from other nations and continents: we are more freedom-loving and more liberal than they are. Even in the United States we can observe how the drive for equality sometimes threatens to strangle freedom, while we in Europe are prepared to accept a certain amount of inequality because we put a high price on individualism. European society is the most individualistic society yet created. Erik von Kühnelt-Leddihn makes the observation that if we polled 100 Frenchmen as they were coming out of a Paris metro station we would find that there were almost as many views as there were interviewees: some would say they were monarchists, others would be anarchists, flat-earthers, Trotskyists, Catholics who believed in the retention of the Latin rite, philo-Semites and anti-Semites, Arab-haters and romantic admirers of Arab culture. You would get the whole spectrum. But if you ran a similar exit-poll at one of the New York underground stations you would probably find that out of 100 people, 99 would be conformist. There lies the difference. Great diversity within a fundamental unity is the hallmark of European culture.

URBAN   How does so much emphasis on the rather decentralising factor of individualism tie in with your views as a leading Federalist?

V. HABSBURG   There is no contradiction. Federalism is going to preserve the differences; it is for us to see that it does. This goes *a fortiori* for the smaller languages. These are extremely significant for the profile of European Culture as a whole. Our technocrats are, from time to time, inclined to belittle and resent manifestations of "smallness," but they must not be allowed to get away with it. I strongly believe that even the smallest languages are integral parts of our heritage, and if they die, something in our common culture dies with them. Take Hungary for an—admittedly somewhat untypical—example: Its language is outside the Indo-European mainstream and inaccessible to most Europeans. It is spoken by about 13 million people but has a literature that is second to none. I speak Hungarian and I am familiar with Hungarian life and sensibility. I would feel impoverished if Hungarian culture were somehow to be given less prominence in the concert of European cultures than the culture of the more numerous nations.

URBAN   You clearly do not feel that Margaret Thatcher, the British prime minister, is justified in fearing that European unification might lead to an *identikit Europe*.
    Let me look at the Soviet Union for a parallel. Whatever we may think about the Russification of the national republics of the Soviet Union, it is nevertheless true that the small languages and cultures have survived (under the protective shield of ethnography, folkloristic research, and the preservation of national "monuments"), and will perhaps survive even better if Gorbachev's policies are put into effect. In Yakutia, for example, there is a tiny nation called the Yukagirs who live in Nizhny Kolm and number only 850 people. A local ethnographer maintains a record on each and every member of the Yukagir nation. He has compiled a Russian-Yukagir dictionary and designed a Yukagir written language. Would not this attention to the ethnic factor, if it occurred in our own environment, be overwhelmed by the homogenising momentum of European unification?

V. HABSBURG   I do not know much about the Yukagirs, but I do happen to remember that the Yakuts have become a minority in their own land owing to Russian immigration, and the percentage of Yakuts in the general population of Yakutia has been halved in the last fifteen years. There is a form of apartheid in Yakutia, the Yakuts being dismissively referred to as "tight lids" by the Russians because of the Asiatic cut of their eyes. The very name of Yakut (meaning "I drink") is a Russian invention which the Yakuts, who call themselves *sakha,* deeply resent.

Nothing of the sort could happen in a United Europe. The tendency in Europe is for more national self-determination and a much expanded use of minority languages such as Flemish, Gaelic, and Romantsch, rather than the extinction of small cultures under the impact of uncontrollable impersonal forces.

Coming back to Mrs. Thatcher's observations in her speech at Bruges in Belgium, an *identikit Europe* is an Aunt Sally no one should take seriously: She put up an enemy in order to shoot it down, but in reality there is no such enemy. Naturally, there are, as I have said, technocrats in the European bureaucracy who do tend to work not only for European unity but also uniformity. This is a *déformation professionelle* and has to be opposed. Dealing with it will be one important element in our work in the newly (1989) elected European Parliament as part of the general debate on federalism.

Let me go back a couple of steps in the history of the European Community to explain what I mean. The Treaty of Rome incorporated an absolutely decisive idea—the idea of the free-market economy as a commitment enforceable in law, that is to say, in the European courts. This saved France from the excesses of socialism in 1981. Today, my French Socialist colleagues tell me privately (they will not do so in public) that this stipulation of the Treaty of Rome was the greatest blessing the European Community could have bestowed on them, because it prevented them from carrying out the follies of their original programme.

By a similar token, the follies of uniformity and central control can and should be prevented either by a new statutory interpretation of the existing treaty, or perhaps by a new treaty which would enshrine the idea of "subsidiarity." Subsidiarity means that no problem arising in Community affairs is to be referred to a higher level for resolution until all means of dealing with it at a lower level of competence have been exhausted. My impression is that we do need a new treaty to make the principle of subsidiarity crystal clear and enforceable in the European courts. It would ensure that we have adequate defences against excessive uniformity and centralisation in the economy, in culture and administration—in other words, it would see to it that Mrs. Thatcher's fears remain fears—and nothing more.

URBAN   May I take you back to de Gaulle's view that Frenchmen would be prepared to die for Marianne but not for a customs union. Would not European Culture, even a Federal Europe, be too weak an inspiration to generate European loyalties of the visceral kind we would need in critical situations?

V. HABSBURG   I do not think so. Marianne is an idea and Europe is an idea so long as we do not identify Europe with the statistics of the European Community. De Gaulle was right: no one would die for the standard of living—which would be a contradiction in terms, anyway. But I am convinced that people would die for our freedom, our cultural values, and our way of life. People fight and are prepared to die for symbols, but these are a long time in coming. You do not start with the symbols. Europe is now in the process of establishing itself as a new reality. It will have its own frontiers, its economic and "federal" interests, its distinct way of life and culture. The symbols will grow out of these organically as they always have done in history.

URBAN   Would it be a mistaken reading of your career to say that your leadership as a European Federalist and member of the European Parliament is an indirect attempt to create, on the ruins of the Habsburg Empire and the Second World War, a revamped version of the Habsburg Empire?

I suspect your name will be remembered in the history books as that of a man whom destiny deprived of the opportunity to be emperor and king but who, after the shocks of two world wars, extracted the good that he found in the Habsburg idea and applied it on a much larger scale to the whole of Europe. Can you see yourself in that light? Will historians write that Crown Prince Otto had lost an empire in the centre of Europe but helped to create one embracing the whole of Europe?

V. HABSBURG   I would not disagree with that reading of my role if future historians did me the honour of writing about me. Notwithstanding the protestations of many modern historians, there are lessons to be learnt from history. Certain ideas stood the test of time, while others were aborted before they could have flowered into practical policies but are nevertheless relevant to our time. The ideas incorporated in the Holy Roman Empire, which was a federal state, are one seminal guide to my thinking; but I would go back further in history and say that I regard Burgundy as the earliest source of my inspiration, because Burgundy, with its moving frontiers and multinational composition, was a great example of civic freedom, cultural accomplishment, and diversity within an overall unity. Burgundy began as a kingdom in the South of France, then moved into the northern areas and expanded into Germany around the time of Charlemagne. From the Holy Roman Empire there is, via the Habsburgs, a straight line leading to Austria-Hungary which was, in effect, a belated and residual but none the less very real legatee of the Holy Roman Empire. I ought to qualify this to the extent that Hungary had, of course, been a kingdom in its own right since the first millennium and cannot, therefore, be so clearly subsumed under the Holy Roman heritage as Austria. But it is certainly true that the Austrian Empire would not have arisen had it not been for the disappearance of the Holy Roman Empire and the consequences of the Napoleonic wars.

The man who first offered us an intellectual bridge, as a matter of conscious policy, between the Holy Roman Empire and the European present was Count Richard Coudenhove-Kalergy. In 1923, at the age of 29, he was the first to realise that after the fratricidal mess of the First World War, Europe had to be rebuilt as a single civilisation on pan-European lines. I merely follow in his footsteps.

URBAN   I appreciate your modesty, but would you not say that your leadership of the Pan-European Movement and your advocacy of federalism are more than a coincidence—that they flow directly from the Habsburg view of Europe and, indirectly but through your person as head of the House of Habsburg, from the idea of the Holy Roman Empire?

V. HABSBURG   Well, let somebody else answer that question for me. The day I obtained my German naturalisation—which was a precondition for standing for election to the European Parliament—Franz Josef Strauss, the then-Bavarian minister-president, said to me: "Thank God—the Holy Roman Empire is back with us."

URBAN   Let me now look at the present state of the Soviet Empire and ask whether analogies drawn from other empires, notably the Ottoman and the Habsburg, might be reasonably applied to it.

Two points seem worth making. First, the *raison d'être* of the House of Osman was unchangeable by definition: The Ottoman Empire existed for the sole purpose of fulfilling God's will on earth by spreading Islam. When that missionary consciousness declined and sheer military strength held together the various parts of the empire, the end was in sight. It was, it is true, an end very long in coming, and it would be disastrous for individual liberty world-wide if the demise of the Soviet Empire were to be as protracted. Do you, nevertheless, see an analogy?

V. HABSBURG   Bolshevism as a missionary idea is completely exhausted. As a Polish joke has it, communism is the longest and most painful road from capitalism to capitalism. Between the two world wars and for some years after the Second World War, many people in both Eastern and Western Europe (as well as some in the United States) believed that communism as practised in the Soviet Union was the wave of the future. They did so despite Stalin or, as some historians maintain, because of Stalin. By now any sympathy with the theory of communism is confined to a small and dwindling nucleus of Western intellectuals. In Russia and Eastern Europe, communism is an acknowledged failure and dead.

Not so Russian imperialism. This exists, built as it is on Russian nationalisms of various strengths and colourings. But while the Bolshevik type of missionary ideology had an international audience, Russian imperialism does not and cannot have one. It appeals to Russians only, and, we should add, not to all Russians, much less to all Slavs. I cannot believe that, for example the Croats, Slovenes, Czechs, or Poles, having burned their fingers with the Bolshevik variety, would embrace a new pan-Slavism under Russian auspices.

Just how utterly exhausted the communist belief system is can be gauged from the behaviour of members of the Communist parties of the Baltic states. On paper, they are still Communists if party membership means communism, but their entire behaviour, including their voting record, has now put them on the side of the nation to which they belong. Estonian "Communists" have shown themselves to be much more Estonian than Communist. Having rejected Sovietism, they are most unlikely to embrace Russian imperialism.

There is also the demographic factor which will soon put a natural ceiling on the appeal of Russian imperialism. Population growth in the Asian parts of the Soviet Union is much higher than in the Russian and Slavic area as a whole. The birthrate of the Soviet Muslim population is similar to that in underdeveloped countries, whereas the birthrate of the Russians is comparable to the low rates we have in Western

Europe. The catchment area of Russian imperialism is getting smaller in relative terms.

URBAN   Granted all that, I still wonder whether a determined regime at the head of the Soviet state could not hold down almost indefinitely restive Ukrainians, Georgians, Uzbeks, Latvians, or Moldavians with the sheer force of arms. That is how the Ottoman Turks stayed on top of their empire for centuries, and that is how, it is now feared by Soviet liberals, a disintegrating Soviet establishment might react to the turmoil under *glasnost* and *perestroika*. An article in *Komsomolskaya Pravda* on 5 August 1989 put it with great candour: "The country is being shaken with ethnic clashes like bouts of a disease . . . Clashes and conflicts follow one another, and the reports from various regions of the country are reminiscent of dispatches from a theatre of war . . . Where are the law and order and state security bodies which only recently showed such might in uprooting every shoot of dissidence and which saw a threat to our foundations in a slim volume by an emigré writer? Today, it is not literature that people collect under cover of night but dumps of weapons and explosives . . . The state is incapable of ensuring the security of all its citizens." And on 9 September 1989, Gorbachev himself warned against "scare stories of imminent chaos and arguments about the danger of a coup or even of civil war."

V. HABSBURG   I do not believe that force, at the turn of the millennium, can achieve what it could in earlier centuries. The world has shrunk; information has become ubiquitous. Shortwave radio and television see to that, so that even illiteracy is no longer a barrier. In the nineteenth century the Bulgars in their mountains and the Kirghiz and Uzbeks on their steppes could be sealed off from the rest of the world. They were outside the political processes of our civilisation. Not so today. Events in our world are global in their impact and it is, therefore, much harder to keep fissiparous states together by old-fashioned military means.

URBAN   But frightened imperial establishments do not take a long-term view of things. They want law and order here and now. Could they not enforce it in the Soviet Union for a substantial period of time?

V. HABSBURG   I doubt it. The tempo of devolution is fast, and if you read some of Gorbachev's speeches between the lines, Gorbachev himself appears to be aware that time is running out on his system. There may, of course, be a temporary tactical reaction to the Soviet Union's present troubles: a change of leadership, martial law, military government, preventive internment, a diminution of republican rights and freedoms. These may turn the clock back by three or five or ten years, but what is a decade in history? National consciousness and the will to independence are unconquerable. You can (as Horace said of nature) "cast them out with a fork, but they will still return."

URBAN   Now, to the parallel with the Habsburg Empire. The domestic upheavals that followed the collapse of the Austro-Hungarian Monarchy are one of our best examples of "Imperial Hangover." After defeat and dismemberment in 1918, Hungary fell into the hands of a Communist regime, followed by Romanian occupation and the Regency under Admiral [Miklós] Horthy. It came under Nazi and then Soviet control. Austria was gripped by an identity crisis and ideological fanaticism which culminated in civil war in 1934. It was "cured of imperial hangover only by seven years of Hitler" (in the words of Hugh Seton-Watson).[3]

If the Soviet Empire is now heading for slow disintegration, is it your judgement that the metropolitan nation—Russia, and especially the Russian political class—will be gripped by analogous crises when the scale of the disaster is finally realised? Is the Soviet Empire heading for colonial wars as the French were in the 1950s in Indochina and Algeria?

V. HABSBURG   The fear of colonial wars and signs of an Imperial Hangover are already discernible in the behaviour and utterances of the Soviet establishment. The words you have just quoted are not a bad example. I remember talking about the end of empire to an East European Communist leader who shall remain nameless. He was extremely frank in telling me that his greatest fear was that his children might be killed in the last colonial war in history. He envisaged cataclysmic events to follow seventy years of monolithic rule, and he could not see how disaster could be averted. So I think your parallel with Indochina and Algeria is probably right, with this important difference that the French metropolitan state was protected against the direct impact of colonial wars by the oceans, whereas the Russian would not be.

Speaking as a European, I would say that once the Soviet Empire has gone the way of all empires, we would then have to try to integrate the Russians into Europe, but only as Russians. Whether this could be done soon after the demise of their empire is anybody's guess. I expect Russian Imperial Hangover to take a course very similar to that we have witnessed in our time in other countries. As you well stated in your question, whenever an empire collapses, a suicidal mood spreads over the metropolitan elite and frequently way beyond the elite. Deprived of a grand theme, they tend to question national identity and the worth of their society. That was the case with the suicide of Austria in 1938 and the dramatic events that had led up to it. There were similar convulsions in metropolitan France after the collapse of the French Empire and, although on a smaller scale, similar tremors have shaken Portugal since 1974. I should put it like this, at the risk of mixing my metaphors: You suffer a mighty fall from a window on the tenth floor of a high-rise building, but somehow you survive. The trauma is immense; it will take you a long time to start living a normal life again, if indeed you ever will. That, I think, is the sort of danger threatening to engulf the Soviet imperial civil service and the establishment as a whole.

URBAN   You said that some form of nazism would be the first Russian reaction to the loss of Soviet superpower status—

V. HABSBURG   Yes, I foresee a National Socialist phase—or a violent reaction along Chinese lines. I do not exclude the possibility that *Pamyat,* ultraconservatives in the Party and the military might join forces to accomplish it (the military, mind you, have lost so much self-confidence since the debâcle in Afghanistan that their role in any state leadership must be treated with scepticism). Then, to repeat, I foresee a great colonial war, or several wars, within a time frame of two or three decades. It is not only that the deprived nations will rise against Russian colonialism and against one another, but they will be egged on and supported by their coreligionists and racial brothers across the Soviet frontiers in Iran, Pakistan, and China.

In sum, I foresee cataclysmic developments which may not remain isolated. That is why I feel that European unification must be pursued with speed and determination so that by the time all these things come to pass we in Europe have a modicum of security. Politically and psychologically, the collapse of a great empire produces a chain reaction just as terrible in its effects as a nuclear meltdown. A political Chernobyl is what we have to brace ourselves for.

URBAN   You hinted a minute ago that the Red Army, too, might be facing a crisis—

V. HABSBURG   Yes, the Red Army's administrative structure is antiquated and rigid. The social differences between officers and men are great and the abuse of authority on the part of virtually everyone of superior rank or influence towards those of inferior rank or influence is widespread. For the first time, these problems are now being openly discussed in the Soviet press—which does not mean that they are also being resolved. Bullying unfortunately exists in almost every army, but in the Red Army (where it is euphemistically described as "nonregulation relations") it has reached unheard of proportions and ferocity. None of this helps military morale.

I had the occasion recently to consult officers from the Central European armies of the Warsaw Pact who had been seconded for one reason or another to the Soviet forces. They brought back reports of great tensions subverting discipline throughout the Soviet armed forces, especially on ethnic lines. As long as the Red Army seemed invincible, these tensions could be held in check or papered over. But, since the defeat in Afghanistan, the notion of invincibility has been much weakened. For let us make no mistake about it, when General Gromov crossed the River Termez on the Soviet-Afghanistan frontier, with tears running down his cheeks, he was bringing up the rear of a defeated army. At the time, we in the West did not fully realise just how bitter this defeat had been for the Red Army and public opinion, but we can now tell from the evidence that it was great and its repercussions are widespread.

URBAN   There is, then, in your reading hardly any aspect of the Soviet system or any corner of the Soviet Empire that is not in profound crisis in the wake of Mr. Gorbachev's reforms?

V. HABSBURG   That is indeed so—but "my reading" is not mine alone; it seems to coincide with the reading of many people who think about these matters.

URBAN   Let me ask you a highly hypothetical question which you may or may not want to answer: If you were head of the Soviet Empire anxious to avoid its disintegration (a big if), what would you, speaking from the Habsburg experience, advise your colleagues in the Party and government to do and not to do?

V. HABSBURG   I am not sure whether any advice could be successful at this stage, but I would advise them to restore, and restore at top speed, the political, cultural, economic, and religious rights of all nations and nationalities within the Empire including the Russians, because we must remember that the Russian people are fellow-sufferers, even though Soviet imperialism was, in effect if not in name, carried out under their leadership.

URBAN   Would you go so far as to advocate the right of secession which is, in any case, guaranteed in the Constitution but has never been honoured in practice? Surprisingly, and to prove your point, Valentin Rasputin, the popular Russian writer, suggested recently that, to save its soul, Russia might do well to secede from the Union.

V. HABSBURG   Yes, I would. Sooner or later, independence has to be granted—so why not do it under peaceful conditions and obtain whatever good will can still be obtained from the aggrieved minorities? If anything is likely to slow down disintegration, speed in extending rights to the national minorities is the thing that might do it.

Another piece of advice I might offer my colleagues in the Soviet Party and government would be to look at analogous events in other parts of the world and read their implications. The death of the dictatorship in Spain should be of especial interest to them—as, indeed, it is already widely acknowledged to be to many of the East and Central European Communist leaders. I happen to know many Spaniards; I witnessed the expiry of the Falange, Spain's monolithic party under Franco. I saw their self-confidence in decline and their will power deserting them. On my recent visits to Central and Eastern Europe I had strikingly similar experiences. Leading members of the various Communist parties and "patriotic fronts" displayed the same attitudes, frequently even using the same words, as I had heard from Falangist dignitaries during the last years of Franco's rule. I could sense the same, desperate, last-minute efforts by the beneficiaries of a dying system to save their privileges. I remember one leading Communist telling me quite openly that he hoped to find ways and means of giving his particular organisation a new title which would keep his staff in their jobs and himself in possession of his privileges—though he dressed up the last point in the appropriate weasel words.

Members of the former establishments were fascinated by the history of the Falange. They could see that the Spanish ideological dictatorship was the first in history to be liquidated without revolution and bloodshed, and they wondered how the Falange had done it and whether they could escape as lightly. Not for nothing was the Spanish ambassador one of the most sought-after personalities in the Communist-run states in Central and Eastern Europe! His advice was thought to be crucial to their survival.

The curious thing was that the former East European Communist establishments were just as shaky in countries where there were no pressures from below as in those in which such pressures existed. Well before the November/December 1989 collapse, I found the *apparat* in Bulgaria, for example, surprisingly destabilised. A senior Bulgarian Communist (I will, again, mention no names) said to me in conversation: "As a Communist I should tell you . . ." But then he stopped short of actually telling me and added: "Ah, but I will not say it as I know it's so very unpopular." I was astounded. Did a leading Bulgarian power holder not have the courage of speaking his mind in a private conversation? My explanation of all these phenomena is the total loss of legitimacy and self-confidence. Communism is so dead that it cannot be buried.

URBAN   You stress the possible relevance of the Spanish model . . .

V. HABSBURG   Gorbachev's renunciation of the Brezhnev Doctrine, in his speech to the Council of Europe, for example, on 6 July 1989, will now be tested in Poland and Hungary. That the new Polish prime minister is a leader of Solidarity does not, yet, mean that power has slipped out of Communist hands, although the "leading role of the Communist Party" has certainly been badly battered. But Poland has a long way to go before we can say that it has become a free and independent state in the sense in which Spain has.

URBAN   A Spanish government in which the minister of the interior and the minister of defence had to be certified friends of the United States would not go down well in Spain or in the rest of Europe—

V. HABSBURG   No, it would not, and that is why, despite the quantum leap in Polish affairs, it is too early to celebrate. Whatever one may think of the incompetence of Communists in the economy, they have inherited from Lenin a shrewd tradition of power management.

URBAN   How would you describe the secret of Spain's peaceful transition?

V. HABSBURG   Franco had the foresight to create a substantial middle class; middle class people are unlikely sponsors of revolutionary experiments. Then, by an extraordinary stroke of luck and perhaps wisdom, three very different actors played into each other's hands: There was the king waiting in the wings and there were, eventually, Felipe Gonzàlez and Manuel Fraga Iribarne—that is to say, one man representing, by birth, the traditional order of Spain, another the Socialist opposition and a third the outgoing system but carrying a revised message. All were agreed to promote a free and democratic system, and they did.

In some ways Hungary and Czechoslovakia at the turn of the decade may be close to a Spanish kind of solution.

URBAN   What are your feelings as head of the House of Habsburg when you visit a country like Hungary—a country that makes you feel welcome, a country that could have been your realm if history had taken a different course, a country which is now trying to claw its way out from under the rubble after forty-odd years of misrule?

V. HABSBURG   Firstly, I am pleasantly surprised to see the Hungarians unbent and doing so well. Secondly, I see it as my task to help them in clearing away the rubble and, more specifically, to assist Hungary in its effort to rejoin the European family of nations. A United Europe plays a significant part in the Hungarians' imagination. We must not fail them.

URBAN   Do you harbour any personal bitterness because you are not the king of Hungary and cannot provide the kind of stability that King Juan Carlos brought to Spain?

V. HABSBURG   No, I do not. When I consider what a terrible job it is to be king, I thank God that I am a member of the European Parliament.

URBAN   Are you impressed by Benedetto Croce's observation that "all history is contemporary history"—what with your background as crown prince to the throne of Habsburg fading naturally into the post-Communist revival of Central and Eastern Europe?

V. HABSBURG   I would agree with Croce to the extent that contemporary events are, inevitably, a replay of earlier instances in the successive activities of men, although they are unpredictable in detail. Envelope forecasts are in order—anything more precise is not. It is in this sense that I feel that my heritage and experience have given me much to be grateful for in my attempt to serve as midwife to the birth of a new Europe.

1990

Chapter 5

What Is "Soviet"—What Is "Russian"?

A Conversation with Adam B. Ulam

The Key to Tyranny

URBAN   Much confusion and considerable resentment have been caused in Sovietological discussion by the cavalier use of the words "Soviet" and "Russian" as interchangeable adjectives. Those who believe with Alexander Solzhenitsyn that the Communist system is of Western provenance and has been imposed on the Russian people are profoundly offended. Others say that Russian traditions and political culture are so strongly woven into the fabric of Soviet Communism that it is nonsensical to search for a clear distinction. Far from being a matter of mere semantics, the quarrel touches upon the very nature— the durability and changeability—of the Soviet system.

If "Soviet" did correctly apply to all things Russian, then we in the West would be inclined to take a harsher view of Russian society than we would if we were persuaded that "Soviet" and "Russian" were not only *not* coterminous, but were clearly antithetical. In other words, we could either say that the Soviet system was as alien to the Russian nation as it has shown itself to be to Poles, Czechs and Hungarians, and shape our policies accordingly. Or we could say that the Soviet system was what the Russian people have sustained and defended for seven decades, and shape our policies to fit *that* view.

Where do you stand in this conflict?

ULAM   In everyday parlance the two are used interchangeably. This may be wrong but it is done, and I feel that not to do so would be pedantic. I prefer to make a distinction whenever clarity demands that we should; but it would be pretentious not to say "Soviet" for "Russian" and vice versa, occasionally. In most cases it is perfectly clear what we are talking about—whether we say "Russian" or "Soviet."

URBAN   I would have thought communism would have resulted in a very different system if Marx's ideas had been put into effect in Italy or Holland rather than Russia—

ULAM   Yes, it would. . .

URBAN   And it is, therefore, difficult to deny that the Soviet system carries the birthmarks of Russian traditions and culture. Wouldn't this argue for a very thin distinction between "Soviet" and "Russian"?

ULAM   It's difficult to deny the strength of the Russian component. Let us, however, also remember that the Russian origins of the Soviet system have been used—by sympathisers and apologists on the Left— to underline the grave imperfections of the Russian realisation of Marxism, and to argue that, but for those origins, Marxism would have had a better chance to produce an acceptable model with appeal throughout the world. In either case, the conjunction between the corruptions of the Soviet system and the backwardness of Tsarist Russia from which it arose is broadly recognised—whether to condemn the system because it is "Russian," or to rescue Marxism from "the Russian connection."

On balance, however, I am not inclined to stress the link between Sovietism and the Russian heritage. It is striking that in several countries communism has assumed almost the same characteristics as define the Soviet system. The French Communists, for example, were for a long time just as obedient to Moscow as any oblast chief under Stalin in the USSR. They followed Soviet propaganda in every detail. No feat of mismanagement was too outrageous for the French party not to present it as "an economic victory," and no lie too transparent not to embrace it as a triumph of the truth. If *national* environment is the decisive influence on political behaviour, why did the French Party behave as it did?

No, communism has the notions of autocracy and imperialism deeply embedded in its dogmatic scheme, and wherever communism triumphs it tends to produce a tyrannical system. The Russian background certainly added to the depredations of Soviet Communism, but it is insufficient to explain it. It is *communism* that accounts for Soviet despotism, not the history of the Russian people.

URBAN   Wouldn't you say that the French Communists obeyed Moscow because it was the world's anti-capitalist power centre, and thus the ultimate guarantor and paymaster of their existence—and not because they were propelled into submissive behaviour by Communist doctrine? "Polycentrism" notwithstanding, we have little experience of Communist parties that are not, in one way or another, beholden to Moscow.

ULAM   Moscow as the ultimate anchor did, of course, have a powerful impact on the French Party's behaviour. But the source of French dogmatism was not just the power of Moscow, but the whole body of Communist thought.

The Chinese Party offers another good example. Quite early in their political life, the Chinese Communists diverged from Moscow. Yet, in their model of communism today, autocratic "Stalinist" features are as firmly established as before they came to power, and later under Mao's stewardship as leader of the ruling Party. I am also convinced that in Germany, had the local Communist rebellions turned into a nationwide revolution in the early 1920s, as Lenin hoped, that nation would have ended up as a dictatorship very similar to the one Lenin founded and Stalin perfected in Russia. The key to the tyranny of communism is communism, not the country in which it is enacted.

URBAN   Richard Pipes thinks otherwise. He seems to believe that the Soviet system is a product of Russian history and political culture at least as much as of Bolshevism.[1]

ULAM   Pipes thinks the system is a logical continuation of tsarist autocracy. This is unjust to prerevolutionary Russia, which was opening up in different directions, including liberal and Westernising ones. I would not deny the impact of the Russian milieu—how could one? But it is greatly exaggerated to say that Bolshevism is specifically and exclusively *Russian,* and to single out Russian political culture for special condemnation.

URBAN   But wasn't there fertile ground for collectivism and egalitarianism in the Russian *artel* and *mir*—as many late 19th-century Social Democrats argued? These men and women were in a hurry. They were worried that if they went by the book of Marxist theory, Russian society could not undergo a final Communist revolution before it had gone through "capitalism" and "a bourgeois revolution"—and that would take time. . . . Hence, they said, the existing collectivist *mir* system in the Russian villages should be used as a shortcut to Communism—there was no need to wait for a bourgeois revolution.

Wouldn't you say that the spirit of egalitarianism in the Russian countryside predisposed Russia to accepting first Leninism and then the full egalitarian rigours of Stalinism? Even under Gorbachev, seven decades on, egalitarianism is a massive stumbling block to economic reform and private enterprise. The peasants are reluctant to accept the land they are offered under Gorbachev's leasehold arrangements, and many of the newly formed cooperatives have had to be closed down in response to public anger. Don't these signs rather confirm the view that in some respects "the spirit of Bolshevism" isn't fundamentally at odds with "the spirit of Russia"?

ULAM   No, I don't think they do. It's true that Marx himself, in an incautious moment a few years before his death, said that Russia might (as an exception to the rule) "skip" the stage of bourgeois revolution and capitalism, and advance, through the *mir* system, straight to a Communist revolution. But most historians would disagree with the view that the *mir* background automatically predisposed the Russian Muzhiks to embracing collectivisation.

The best proof that this was not so was the bloody resistance they offered to Stalin's collectivisation campaigns in the 1929–32 period and the passive resistance they have offered ever since—ultimately compelling the régime to start re-examining, under Gorbachev, the whole concept of collectivisation. That the Russian farmer is now hesitating to accept land is not due to his innate reluctance to take charge of his destiny, but to the haunting memory of what happened to his father and grandfather under Stalin's terror—and how "the *NEP*-men" were treated when Stalin decreed that the New Economic Policy had come to an end.

URBAN   You have said that wherever communism takes hold, a tyrannical system is bound to emerge because of the inherently totalitarian character of Bolshevism. Aren't there other explanations? I would have thought reasons could be found in the history and traditions of any nation to explain why its particular form of communism (or fascism, or whatever) is the most wicked.

For example, arguing from certain strands in French history, one could say that the French habit of driving logical argument to its extremes and the glorification of *la Révolution* and "the people" make

French Communism a most likely candidate for tyranny. In Germany, the combination of the spirit of Hegel, militarism, and the cult of efficiency would argue for an equally nasty form of German Communist despotism. In Romania, we need hardly look beyond the heritage of Vlad the Impaler, the spirit of the Ottoman janissaries, and the Iron Guard to explain why Ceausescu's now-toppled dictatorship was the worst of them all.

So, while I am not disputing your point that the trigger to the rise of all these unpleasant forms of government was, or could be, the totalitarian doctrine of communism, I do believe that every nation has in it the capacity to turn any political idea into a particularly nasty—or an acceptable and civilised—dispensation. There are, it seems to me, strands in every nation's history that can be summoned to support this-or-that form of development—good or bad. But our problem with Bolshevism is that it chose, or perhaps saw itself forced to build on, the most retrograde elements in the Russian heritage.

ULAM   I think we are really both saying the same thing. There *is*, as I've said, a Russian element in the Soviet form of communism. It stems from a particularly authoritarian conception of socialism in the nineteenth century, to which were added a very Russian form of xenophobia and Russian nationalism. Leninism inherited all these, and although Lenin thought of himself as a sworn enemy of great-Russian chauvinism, Russian nationalism nevertheless became a determining element of the Soviet system. Under Stalin it came out into the open as a strong Russian chauvinism.

But, with all that, I believe that the totalitarian character of Communist régimes stems from the basic tenets of communism itself. I do not disagree with you that suitable elements from the national past can be summoned to give it colour and legitimacy, but the basic impulse is the letter and spirit of Communist thought. Communism has to be tyrannical and imperialistic *because* it is communism.

Blaming the Intellectuals

URBAN   I am pressing you on this point because it has been accepted wisdom in most of our foreign ministries (until the arrival of Mikhail Gorbachev) that Soviet expansionism and Soviet foreign policy are best understood as Russian expansionism and Russian foreign policy in a new guise. Nikolai Berdyaev observed in the 1940s: "In 1917 we believed that Communism had swallowed up Russia; today we see that Russia has swallowed up Communism. . . .'' It is a view widely held.

ULAM   But it is mistaken. Foreign ministry officials are, of course, trained to recognise and deal with political power of the traditional sort. Few of them take the trouble to acquire more than a nodding acquaintance with ideology, which they find alien and impenetrable. Hence their failure to grasp the ideological driving force behind Communist imperialism.

URBAN   One reason why our foreign ministry officials tend to have an imperfect understanding may have to do with the schizophrenia in Russia itself. The dominant mood in the Soviet state today is nationalistic, whereas Western observers tend to equate the progress of enlightenment in Soviet society with the progress of "Westernisation." Both exist, and if we restrict our view to the rhetoric of *glasnost* and *perestroika,* Westernisation in the shape of the Gorbachev reforms appears to be in the ascendant. But underneath that thin guise, Russian culture and the popular ethos still revolve, symbolically speaking, around the traditional triad of Tsarism, Orthodoxy, and Peasantry. It is this reality that Western observers have some difficulty in grasping, and when they think they have understood it, they simplify it down to "Fascism . . . pogroms . . . the Black Hundreds."

This is unhelpful enough, but it is even more unhelpful (and much more important) that so many Russian intellectuals seem to be ashamed of their native culture, and share the Western presumption that the worth of Russian civilisation should be judged by its ability to meet certain standards which emerged in France and Britain in the eighteenth and nineteenth centuries under entirely different conditions. Isn't this Russian proclivity for self-punishment puzzling and dangerous?

ULAM   It's true enough that the Slavophile and neo-Slavophile elements in Russian behaviour are largely inaccessible to the Western observer. But this is also true of the particular type of nationalism in Poland and Hungary; and because our knowledge is so limited, we may be in for surprises both in the Soviet Union and in Eastern and Central Europe. Slavophilism was, as I have said, accompanied in the nineteenth century by a strong streak of liberalism. "We are essentially a European nation," the liberals said. "Certainly we have a specifically Russian contribution to make to European civilisation, but our basic European credentials are unassailable. In the past, we were ruined by autocracy and backwardness—but we shall no longer tolerate either the first or the second."

It was this nineteenth-century liberal tradition that went into socialism and communism, and resulted, under Stalin, in its grotesque perversion. Westernising thought ended up in Stalin's boastful chauvinism, expressed at its most extravagant in his famous toast, at the end of the war: "To the Russian nation." It was the Russian nation, he said, that had stood by the country at the time of its worst trials—meaning that it had stood by Stalin; which is, in my view, not a compliment to the Russian nation. It is for all these reasons that enlightened Russians are now thoroughly alienated from the Communist Party. They see in it a force that combines the tyranny of Leninism with the obscurantism of the Slavophiles.

URBAN   Enlightened Russians may do, but haven't the unenlightened masses a different view? I tend to believe that Nina Andreyeva, the Leningrad "re-Staliniser," represents more than a fleeting nostalgia for orderly and more "Russian" times. In an interview with the Hungarian newspaper *Magyar Hirlap* (8 December 1989), she said:

> I reject every form of private property. . . . In order to force a road open to private property, the "leading advocates of *perestroika*" demand the creation of a special class of politician in the shape of "a highly educated parliament." This, they say, would assemble "the best brains of the nation"; that is, academicians, economists, lawyers, and other representatives of the intellectual élite. If we consider that there are only 77 such persons among 1,000 Russians but among Jews the ratio is 474, then it is not difficult to figure out whom exactly these people want to foist on us as our leaders. Behind the slogans of "a highly educated parliament" and "the best brains of the nation," we can detect a malicious and power-seeking Zionism.

ULAM   You are saying that this kind of reactionary outlook is more popular than the views of the enlightened intelligentsia who support Gorbachev. Perhaps so. Equating the Jews with ill-gotten wealth and wrongful influence has a long history in Russia, and beyond Russia. No time is better suited for the revival of such anti-Semitic aspersions than a time of acute shortages of food and other consumer goods.

Yet the faceless masses have seldom, perhaps never, played a decisive role in Soviet or Russian affairs. Reform and revolution came almost always from the top. (Gorbachev's spiritual forebears are Peter the Great and Alexander II.) I am persuaded that the Nina Andreyeva type of "fascistoid Stalinism" is weakly supported by the opinion-making top segments of Soviet society, if indeed it is supported at all. This does not, alas, make it unimportant; but it does limit its operational influence under existing conditions.

The overriding sentiment in the Soviet political class today is a sense of shame: "We are a nation of slaves ruled by scoundrels—we have spent much of our history trying to do something about our backwardness, but with little success." It is this sentiment that has induced Solzhenitsyn to say that Marxism-Leninism is an international creed imposed on the Russian nation by a minority, under conditions of a lost war. There is some truth in that; but its acceptance as a fact of history does not mean approval of the Nina Andreyeva type of neo-Stalinism. And Solzhenitsyn would, of course, be the first to stress that.

URBAN   Apropos Solzhenitsyn, isn't there a lack of clarity in the current Soviet intellectual landscape? After the February Revolution of 1905 (and let me just say that in Vladimir Bukovsky's reading there is an analogy between that and the current "pre-revolutionary" upheavals under Gorbachev), the Soviet intelligentsia imposed upon itself a thorough self-examination in order to pinpoint the causes of the Revolution's failure.

In the celebrated volume *Landmarks* (*Vekhi*, 1909)[2], a conclusion emerged which deserves a brief mention. Some of the contributors to that symposium—Bulgakov, Berdyaev, Struve, and Frank—expressed the view that the débâcle of 1905 had been due to the Russian intelligentsia's immaturity and its inability to free itself from the bondage of Orthodoxy and Utopian conceptions of socialism. Even the most left-wing and outwardly atheistic Russian *intelligent,* it was said, was a Christian and a puritan by temperament. His idealism was so concentrated on the universal realisation of the people's happiness that he had neither the time nor the will to concern himself with promoting the good of his neighbour.

> For all its striving for democracy [Sergei Bulgakov observed], the intelligentsia is merely a special kind of aristocratic class arrogantly distinguishing itself from the philistine crowd. Whoever has lived in intelligentsia circles knows well their haughtiness and conceit, their sense of their own infallibility, their scorn for those of other opinions, and the abstract dogmatism into which all learning here is cast.[3]

And this is how Peter Struve described the character of the Russian intelligentsia at the turn of the century:

Credulity without a creed, struggle without creativity, fanaticism without enthusiasm, intolerance without humility—in short, here was and is at hand the complete form of religiosity without its content.[4]

Assuming, with Vladimir Bukovsky, that Russia under Gorbachev is undergoing a kind of dress rehearsal for a much more radical upheaval, does the role of the Soviet intelligentsia today remind you of its forefathers' lacklustre performance around 1905?

ULAM   It's easy enough to blame the Russian intelligentsia for the failure of Russian reformism. A similar charge was made against the intelligentsia of the 1870s, before the wave of reaction set in that followed the assassination of Alexander II in 1881, and, most notably, after the 1905 revolution.

Bulgakov's remarks do contain some truth, and not merely about the Russian intelligentsia. We recall the infatuation with Marxism which characterised many West European and American intellectuals in the 1930s, and which continued to be a strong force in French intellectual life until the mid-1970s. But it is an oversimplification to blame the failure of the reforms after 1905–1906 on the Russian intelligentsia alone. The tsarist system was simply not strong enough to withstand the forces unleashed by the October Manifesto, *perestroika*'s predecessor; and consequently, confronted with the pressures brought about by World War I, it collapsed—and would still have collapsed even if the intellectuals had acted more responsibly.

It is true that the Soviet scene in 1990 might, in some interpretations, suggest a perversity inherent in the Soviet intelligentsia. Having first greeted Gorbachev's reforms with great warmth, the intellectuals now cry: "Not enough! Not enough!" But, again, the major threat to the reforms comes *not* from the intelligentsia, but from the inherent weaknesses of the system once it has stripped itself of its authoritarian integument.

It is questionable whether anything approaching a democratic system is compatible with the preservation of Soviet federalism. It is even more questionable whether the present conditions of political unrest and disintegration would allow for those sweeping economic reforms which the country needs if it is to be rescued from its deepening crisis.

In brief, I am all for taking a critical view of the shortcomings of the intelligentsia, whether in the Soviet Union or elsewhere. But we should have a sense of proportion, and *not* blame everything on "the damned intellectuals"—which in a way is as unfair as blaming the afflictions of the human condition on an ethnic group or an economic class.

Stability and Suffering

URBAN   We started by questioning the use of "Soviet" and "Russian" as interchangeable epithets in Sovietological discussion. Another temptation—though of an entirely different kind—is to think of Communist ideology as a religion, and to compare its history with the history of other religions, especially Christianity. Richard Lowenthal, one of the most distinguished elder statesmen in Soviet studies, wrote a book about communism as a "secular faith," and Sovietological literature abounds in examples which compare the Sino-Soviet split to the dual Papacy, Stalin's show trials to the work of Torquemada during the Spanish Inquisition, and Marxism itself to "Christianity gone awry" (to use the words of Arnold Toynbee). Indeed, Father Oswald von Nell-Breuning of the Society of Jesus, one of the architects of the German policy of industrial codetermination, attempted to find answers to the question whether Marx's idea of public ownership could actually be justified in terms of "primitive Communism" as indicated by certain verses in the Acts of the Apostles.

Is it your view that analogies of this kind might be offensive to Christians or to Communists? Are the psychological and morphological similarities between the two strong enough to justify comparisons, even at the risk of causing offence to one side or the other?

ULAM   Religion and ideology, in their pure state, are not at all similar. But, in practice, in our own century, the similarities are strong enough to justify, indeed to demand, comparison. "Socialism," as interpreted by Stalin, Mao, Kim Il Sung, and Ceausescu was a kind of religion in that it exacted from the faithful (and not only from them) absolute belief and unquestioning obedience. Marxism itself, of course, demanded no such thing, but "existing socialism" did; and it is, as far as the Soviet Union is concerned, only during the last few years that an attempt is being made to remove its totalitarian-religious incrustations.

I believe, therefore, that general comparisons are not unfair, even though they may hurt the feelings of genuine believers—on both sides. The damage they may do on the Communist side is probably small, as there are only a handful of idealistic Communists left. But I can see that the many people who believe in religion as a great and beneficial spiritual force may find it disturbing to be told that a nominally aetheistic, secular creed, which has become best known to us as a means of acquiring power and practising repression, is a "religion" comparable to, say, Christianity or Judaism.

If you asked a Stalin or a Mao whether he thought the analogy false, I'm sure he would say yes—but he would (if he were sincere) probably add in the same breath that the religious incrustations of communism were his own doing, for there were only so many ways in which a political programme could be inscribed in the minds of primitive peasants—all of them irrational, and with a symbolism resembling the symbols of religion.

This makes it more difficult for historians not to make the comparison with genuine religions. But even if the religious symbolism of Stalinism and Maoism is discounted and the Utopian doctrine of communism is examined in its naked state, scholarly comparisons with faiths of an eschatological character are still in order; and have, indeed, been so often made that they fill shelves in our libraries. Whether they please or displease the reader is not central to the concerns of scholarship.

URBAN   There is yet another sensitive issue in Sovietological analysis which is associated with the "What is Soviet?—What is Russian?" controversy, but is not identical with it. It has to do with the suspicion—or prejudice—that, left to their natural inclinations, the "dark masses" of Russia would give rise to a state of anarchy alternating with national extremism, if not outright fascism. Some Russian émigré historians (Alexander Yanov, for example) have pointed to the allegedly deep historical roots of this inclination, and called it "the Russian idea." They fear that, with the expiry of communism, the Communist Party of the Soviet Union would transform itself into the Russian Orthodox Party; and that the resulting messianic Slavophile state would pose as great a threat to the West as the Soviet system did at its most powerful.

I do not share these fears, but could their discussion be offensive to intelligent Russians and—more important—do you as a student of Russian history find that prediction persuasive?

ULAM   I cannot conceive how discussion of the problem could offend. Democracy in Russia is unlikely to make headway unless the Russian people are confronted with the whole panorama of views that exists in the world, including the views historians take of the Russian past and present. This is what, among other things, Gorbachev and his supporters are doing, and I don't think Western historians should do any less. It is condescending to believe that we should give the Russian nation an expurgated or softer view of what we think of them than we give the French or the Germans. It is *that,* in my opinion, that would offend. . . .

I do not share the historical analysis of Yanov and his associates. My own reading of the Russian psyche and of recent Russian and Soviet history persuades me that the emergence of a nationalist/fascist state after the demise of the Soviet system is most unlikely. Why do I take that view? Because Russia has already had a recent experience of fascism and totalitarianism under Stalin, and is most unlikely to want to undergo another. Stalinism was decked out with internationalist slogans, but it was in all essentials the kind of system whose rise from the ashes Yanov and his friends predict and fear.

However, nations do not make the same mistake twice. If the Russian people were bent on a nationalistic imperial Russian policy, they would be eager to go into Azerbaijan and put down the rebellion. They are not—as we can tell from the Russian mothers' protest in Krasnodar and Stavropol against the call-up of their sons, and the young reservists' own reluctance to fight. Nations bent on empire do not behave like that. Afghanistan has taught the Russian people (and the Red Army) a lasting lesson. They have no stomach for wars which have no conceivable relevance to their own welfare and which point to a further deterioration of Russian living standards—quite apart from the human losses that would inevitably result.

But let us assume that right-wing nationalism of an extremist kind won out, and Russia came to be ruled, under the official cover of a revived Leninism/Stalinism, by a *Pamyat*-inspired system. What would, in fact, happen? Well, it's difficult to imagine nations such as Lithuania, Estonia, Georgia, or Moldavia, which are already on the verge of breaking away from a (nominally) "internationalist" Soviet Union, agreeing to stay within a radically nationalist Russian empire. Least of all could the Ukraine be expected to do so. And if we follow that logic far enough, we are left with a purely Slavic or even a purely Russian rump state—which would represent so startling a turn in history that we must suspend all speculation.

For all these reasons, I don't believe a radically nationalist, neo-Stalinist, Russian restoration is on the cards. I can imagine a democratic but spiritually inspired, perhaps even mildly authoritarian system replacing Marxism-Leninism on the lines Solzhenitsyn may have in mind, but an unholy alliance between *Pamyat* and neo-Stalinism is, in my view, most unlikely to prevail. The Soviet hard-liners would, of course, like nothing better than a return to the old certainties and privileges—but all the evidence I have seen of the state of public opinion points the other way. Central Europe and the Baltic republics are the formative influences in Russia today, not the grotesque ideology of a racially pure, orthodox (or, as some would have it, "de-Christianised") Russia pursuing its statehood under the unforgiving discipline of Leninism.

URBAN   Looking at the decline of the Soviet Empire from the Western point of view, there is an opinion abroad, shared by many of our leaders, that a rapid and uncontrolled disintegration might pose so great a threat to world stability that our dislike of the Soviet system should now be tempered by our even greater dislike of chaos. The consequences of the colonial wars that would follow the collapse of Soviet power can (it is said) already be felt in the wake of Azerbaijan. Lord Dacre (Hugh Trevor-Roper), for example, takes the view that empires mean a certain world security and that we ought to support them, as long as they are supportable, for want of a better alternative.[5] Margaret Thatcher, the British prime minister, has expressed the opinion (sharing a platform with Gorbachev and Shevardnadze) that both NATO and the Warsaw Pact should stay in place. These are indirect ways of saying that we ought not to hasten the demise of Soviet power, for the Warsaw Pact has never been a pact in the accepted sense of the term, but a naked expression of Soviet hegemony.

Do you support the "rather-the-Soviet-system-than-anarchy" school of thinking?

ULAM   No, I don't; and I don't believe these are the alternatives. I don't take the opposite view either. I do not hold to *fiat justitia, pereat mundus* (let there be justice, though the world perish), which tends to be the view taken by libertarian American idealists. My hope is that change in the Soviet Union will be gradual and nonviolent. But this caution does not lessen my enthusiasm for radical change.

I'm not one of those who believed in the 1960s and '70s that the USSR was a great military threat to Western Europe. In retrospect it is even clearer now than it was twenty years ago that the Soviets had no intention of invading us, and very probably didn't have the staying power to do so. Yet I would insist that the USSR before Gorbachev's accession was a source of permanent world instability because of the oppressive and expansionist nature of the system. The excommunication of Tito, the suppression of the 1953 Berlin uprising, the troubles in Poznan and Warsaw in 1956, the Hungarian Revolution, the occupation of Czechoslovakia in 1968 were tremendous threats to the stability of Europe. Also, the Soviet régime was repeatedly finding itself under domestic pressures. There was a great temptation to defuse these by the traditional method of canalising the people's pent-up emotions into external adventures. In 1973 (to take one example), escalation of the crisis in the Middle East was avoided by the thinnest of margins.

In sum: There are dangers attending the fall of any great empire, but on balance I incline to think that disintegration of the iniquitous Soviet system is infinitely less destabilising than its continuing existence would be.

URBAN   For seventy-odd years we have been working and praying for the cloud of Soviet Communism to lift from our affairs without cataclysmic upheavals. Now that it is happening, isn't it a little disingenuous of our leaders suddenly to discover the dangers of the fall of the Soviet Empire and of German unification? I would have thought this might be a time for some quiet rejoicing.

ULAM   I agree. Liberal democracies have got so used to looking for the down side of things that they can't recognise a victory when they see one. One has to be a Russian or a Czech to appreciate the full significance of what is happening.

URBAN   In the West, we have been spared the imposition of a totalitarian Utopia which has haunted the world for the best part of two centuries; but we have managed to keep our heads above water only because we were standing on the shoulders of submerged Russians, Poles, Czechs, and Hungarians. If human affairs were governed by a sense of justice and men's eyes could be lifted above interest rates and the monthly mortgage repayment, wouldn't we owe these guinea-pigs of history some restitution, in the spiritual sense of the word, if in no other?

ULAM   In principle—yes. And that is what many Russians, including Solzhenitsyn, feel very strongly. There is an old Russian idea (shared in the nineteenth century by many Poles) that Slavic suffering does penance for the whole of Christendom. But history has no "law of communicating vessels"; the water levels do not adjust, and are probably not adjustable. The inequity of history is a hard and tragic truth for ordinary mortals to assimilate.

Two Cheers

URBAN   Let's assume for a moment that the growing instability of the Soviet Empire *is* a danger to world stability. Was there some point in postwar history when the Soviets could have stabilised their holdings and we might have accepted that stabilisation as being of mutual advantage?

ULAM There were several such points. A decade or two ago, when internal pressures within the USSR were still dormant, the Soviet leadership could have designed a long-range plan for the "Finlandisation" of most of East and Central Europe, on the argument that the cyclical outbreaks of unrest and rebellion would sooner or later become an uncontainable disease. It should have done so at the time of the Polish upheavals, in 1980–81, at the latest, but it missed that opportunity. Now it is too late. Governing élites seldom have the foresight to anticipate the sort of troubles that do not immediately impinge upon their calculations and interests.

URBAN But doesn't the evaporation of the Communist parties, and the introduction of the multiparty system and the market economy, in fact mean a belated "Finlandisation"? Moscow's former satellites seem to remain tied to the USSR in defence terms, as Finland is, but they are heading for full domestic sovereignty.

ULAM Czechoslovakia and Hungary have asked for the withdrawal of Soviet troops, and Moscow has agreed. This does not formally, or automatically, mean their, or Poland's, departure from the Warsaw Pact; but the decision to ask for a Soviet evacuation does in practical terms come pretty close to it. In any case, with the defection of the whole of Central and Eastern Europe from the political *glacis* of the USSR, the Warsaw Pact has in effect fallen apart.

Some of our political leaders who speak about the need to keep NATO and the Warsaw Pact in balance produce two arguments. First, that it is important to keep NATO in good working order in preparation for a rainy day, because you can never tell how the turmoil in the USSR might end. We can all agree that this is rational. The second argument, however, is not rational. It says that the Warsaw Pact has to stay in place in order to reassure Gorbachev's critics that the crumbling of the outer Empire will not jeopardise the inner Empire's long-term security interests. This is supposed to be part of the help we are giving Gorbachev.

But there is a fly in the ointment. If the nations of Central and Eastern Europe do not want to be members of the Warsaw Pact—and it is clear that they do not—on what moral or pragmatic grounds can we in the West tell them that they should remain members, seeing that we have been busy telling them for the last thirty-five years that the Warsaw Pact was merely an expression of naked Soviet hegemony and that their enforced membership was an insult to their dignity and national self-determination?

Principle VIII of the Helsinki Final Act is about self-determination. We cannot possibly want to keep the Warsaw Pact alive *and* use the Helsinki Agreement as the spine of a new European settlement.

In many ways, therefore, we are past the stage of "Finlandisation" in East and Central Europe. Also, any "Finlandisation" Moscow may have been planning did not, in my opinion, foresee the defection of East Germany. Yet that too is happening. What is more, Moscow is accepting all these developments.

URBAN   Aren't our critics in the East, then, justified in saying that no sooner had Moscow renounced the Brezhnev Doctrine than the West decided to sustain it?

ULAM   That charge could legitimately be made—but nothing we do will sustain the Warsaw Pact. It is in a state of collapse, and so is the Soviet will to keep it going. The whole postwar European settlement will have to be rethought.

URBAN   "Helping Gorbachev" puts me on my guard for yet another reason. Suppose we managed to pull the Soviet economy out of the ditch and upgraded the existing model of socialism into one efficient enough to sustain a humane welfare-socialism with a low military budget and an inward-looking foreign policy. Wouldn't that encourage the derailed train of socialism to be shunted back on to the main lines again, on the argument that socialism has, after all, had the strength and courage to overcome its afflictions and return to its pristine inspiration? Achille Occhetto (leader of the Italian Communist Party), Tony Benn (of the British Labour Party) and others have already argued in favour of this, and have been applauded by *Pravda* (25 January 1990) for having done so.

Is it in our interest—is it in the human interest?—that so flawed a conception of man and society should have another lease of life?

ULAM   I am a liberal with conservative leanings. I do not believe with Hayek and Friedman that a *laissez-faire* capitalist market economy is the only road to the creation of wealth, and through that to a more prosperous and caring society. Nor do I believe that there are *no* circumstances under which a socialist economy could work. Yet I am persuaded that the Soviet type of socialism as an idea and an economic blueprint is now totally discredited; internationally speaking, it has lost the game. I do not believe that the stain of the Soviet experiment, and of Stalinism in particular, can be removed from the fabric of socialism.

There may be regions in the world—Latin America, for example—where for one reason or another the appeal of some variants of Marxism will survive for a while. But socialism as the great Utopian adventure of our time is stone dead; and it died from the Soviet-Russian connection.

URBAN You and I have spent a large part of our lives studying and criticising the Soviet system. Now the system is facing an appalling crisis, and for the very reasons we always said that it would. We don't expect a pat on the back; has history ever been kind to men who were right before their time? Yet I am a little astonished by the almost deafening silence of our political establishments and our colleagues in scholarship. Apart from lone voices in the *Washington Times* and the *Wall Street Journal,* few have publicly acknowledged that Robert Conquest, Leonard Schapiro, Hugh Seton-Watson, Adam Ulam, Melvin J. Lasky, and Alain Besançon (for example) have been right all the way, or that Radio Free Europe and Radio Liberty have just won a thirty-five-year war against great odds, both in the U.S. and in their target area.

ULAM When you think of all our statesmen and stateswomen who fraternised with and fawned upon people like Ceausescu, Kadar, Gomulka, Gierek, Honecker, Brezhnev, and Andropov—perhaps we should not be too surprised. In scholarship, too, there is so much egg on so many faces that one had better not go into the details.

URBAN I should imagine that your biography of Stalin, which you wrote almost twenty years ago, must give you a good deal of satisfaction. It has been confirmed in almost every detail by the revelations that come our way day after day from the Soviet Union. Modesty probably prevents you from celebrating (though in the "hard" sciences less accurate analyses and smaller discoveries have earned their makers many a Nobel Prize). But do you feel the kind of joy that made Leonard Bernstein mount two great performances of Beethoven's Ninth Symphony on each side of the fallen Wall of Berlin (and change the choral section's opening word from *Freude* to *Freiheit*)?

ULAM Of course, I am gratified that I have not committed too many gross errors; but my joy is restrained—and for two reasons. One is the natural anticlimax that follows every victory: The truth has ultimately triumphed, but at what price? Who can bring back the men and women who were sacrificed by the millions to a savage Utopia? Who can heal the wounds, or cut across the tragic spiral of revenge and counter-revenge?

The second reason for my restraint is our apparent inability to learn from what has happened. The demise of Soviet Communism has been the defeat of a great evil. It should have given rise in our own society to a form of thanksgiving, to a great spiritual renewal, seeing how narrowly we escaped. But that is patently not happening.

In the U.S.A. we have a society that is much less desirable to live in than American society was twenty-five years ago during what we should perhaps label "the pre-Beatles phase of Western civilisation." We have drug-taking and crime on a vast scale; moral licence; contempt for learning and for ideals of excellence; a loss of respect for anything of permanent beauty and good report; a levelling down of manners and standards of decency in daily commerce with fellow men and women. I give two cheers for the disintegration of communism—but withhold the third.

End of the Lesson?

URBAN   Isn't it interesting, though—and rather depressing—that some of those very unpleasant features of Western society which you have listed are being greeted in the Soviet domains and in Eastern and Central Europe as symbols of moral renewal, emancipation, and liberation? In Mongolia, for example, a rock 'n' roll song (by the Honk Band) which criticises bureaucracy in Mongolian life is becoming the unofficial anthem of the protest movement. In Russia, "the Age of Rock" is said to have begun with student opposition to the 1968 invasion of Czechoslovakia. Throughout the Communist and formerly Communist territories such phenomena—rock music, drugs, lack of work discipline, sexual promiscuity—are celebrated as consecrated methods of defeating the homogenising Soviet system, in much the same way as our own student rebels of the 1968 generation felt that they were rising against a depersonalising, materialistic, uninspired, capitalist society.

ULAM   The Soviet dissidents' embrace of our junk culture is sad but understandable. In Soviet and East European eyes, any relief from a drab, uniform reality is pregnant with revolutionary meaning—especially if it can be said to come from Paris or New York. Whether it is based on nonsense and can lead to (as it has already led to) the most personally and socially undesirable consequences is a realisation that comes much later, if it comes at all. It is repellent enough to listen to the deafening music-making of a drug-addicted American "under-class"; but I find it almost unbearable to watch their Russian and Czech imitators. We can only pray and hope that when liberation is accomplished, these countries may be liberated from junk culture too.

URBAN   What about the satisfaction you must feel on account of your scholarly books and the applause you have won in what used to be hostile territory?

ULAM   I do have a sense of satisfaction, but it is incomplete. We have had confirmed what we already knew from our laborious researches; some details have been added but these do not change our picture. However, my primary interest in Stalin was not just to find out what he did, but to discover what assumptions prompted him to do those ghastly things. "What explains Stalin?" was the question that exercised me; and I still haven't got reliable answers.

Take one of the basic problems of Stalin research. Here is a man who slaughtered millions. Did he really believe that, in one way or another, they were guilty of something which he genuinely thought was criminal? (After all, we know that 99.9% of those executed were completely innocent of harbouring even vaguely anti-régime senti-ments.) Or did Stalin think of the killing of millions simply as an efficient method of ruling the country—a way in which a man running Russia *has* to exercise power?

These are fundamental questions; but nothing written or done in the Soviet Union in recent years has really helped to clarify them. Person-ally, I lean to the second supposition, but I have no solid evidence to prove it.

URBAN   Aren't we, despite the enormous literature on the subject, still groping for an explanation of the psychological roots of the whole period of Stalinist terror? I notice that Alexander Yakovlev, speaking as head of the Politburo Commission charged with the "rehabilitation" of the victims of the Stalin era, said in *Moscow News* (7 January 1990) that his researches into the period left him baffled. He was appalled, he said, not only by the thoroughness of the Terror, but by the eager cooperation of so many people. Stalin's most recent biographer, Gen-eral Dmitri Volkogonov, on the other hand, holds that, in the same

way as some people are born without sight or hearing, Stalin simply
lacked a moral faculty.

ULAM I'm quite willing to grant that Stalin was amoral, but even
monsters like Hitler and Stalin have elements in their mental make-up
which can help us to understand the way they saw things. As historians, we are interested not just in condemning Stalin—which is easy;
everybody's doing it now—but in identifying the intellectual and psychological roots of Stalin's thinking. That is a challenging task in its
own right, but it is even more important as a guide to future policy and
an early warning to public opinion—"This is what you ought to watch
out for . . ."
    Morality apart, if Stalin's guide to action was simply the practicality
of terror—i.e., "This is the best and only possible way to govern
unruly Russians"—we are still left with a question. At what point did
Stalin realise that terror was becoming counterproductive? At what
point did he say to himself: "If I have another 50,000 miners shot,
there won't be any coal production. . . . If I have another 200 military
officers executed, the Red Army will cease to be an instrument of
Soviet power . . ." And so on. Was he rational in the use of terror?
And if he was, what were his parameters?

URBAN Have any of the revelations under *glasnost* weakened or
qualified your work on Stalin?

ULAM Details have emerged that appear to contest some of my
inferences, but they don't affect my conclusions. The mystery about
the Kirov affair continues.[6] My friend Robert Conquest has been after
me for saying that we still have no "smoking gun" evidence, even
though Soviet statements now clearly imply that Stalin was the insti-
gator of Kirov's assassination. In 1956, Khrushchev had hinted as
much. However, hard evidence has yet to be brought to light.
    Trotsky's violent death in Mexico, on the other hand, is no longer
shrouded in mystery. Soviet sources have joined the rest of us in
ascribing Trotsky's murder to Stalin. My own work on the subject has
also been quoted . . .

URBAN Isn't this yet another piece of evidence to show that Alexander Zinoviev is misguided in saying that no Western observer can
understand the workings of the Soviet system?

ULAM That's nonsense, of course. Soviet historians and publicists
daily acknowledge their debt to Western scholarship, on the subject of

Stalinism and on many other topics which were undiscussible in the USSR for the greater part of Soviet history. When "de-Leninisation" comes into full swing, the work Western scholars have done on Lenin should have an equally profound impact.

URBAN   If and when the myth of Lenin is also destroyed, will that not remove what remains of the glue holding the Party and the Union together? I notice, however, that one of the new "parties" within the CPSU—the Democratic Platform—assumes the opposite. It claims that Leninism is so discredited that the CPSU will disintegrate if it *does* hold on to Leninism. Its best known leader, Yuri Afanasyev, has stated, "The existing party has no future because it is a Leninist Party . . . . We must reject all features of a party which traces its origins back to Lenin."

ULAM   "De-Leninisation" would face the leadership with a tremendous psychological problem. If you give up the creed and symbolism of Lenin, what remains? Nothing. This was fully recognised by M. F. Nenashev, chairman of Soviet Radio and Television, when he said at the Central Committee's ideological discussion on 26 January 1990: "We are at the crucial point where Vladimir Ilych Lenin is the last frontier."

If Lenin is dropped too, the Empire will either fall apart or will have to be held together by brute force. Coercion could happen under some form of neo-Stalinism or under a militant Russian nationalism. Whichever it was, it would not be a pretty or peaceful affair. Gorbachev and his friends have every incentive not to allow the so far largely academic criticisms of Lenin to engulf the country. But whether they can completely stop this from happening is another matter. In a country in which Soviet artillery fire had to be used to sink the Soviet tankers which were blockading the Soviet port of Baku, anything can happen.

URBAN   With the expiry of Marxism-Leninism as an ideological blueprint, a great void has been created. What sort of cause will all those people now embrace who feel almost genetically deprived without an overall ideological commitment but can no longer find satisfaction in communism? Doesn't the spectacle of so many fanatical minds seeking a new outlet rather frighten you?

ULAM   The loosening of spiritual and intellectual loyalties, whether they take the form of decline of religions or of ideologies, is always followed by a time of acute danger. The old compasses have lost their magnetic north, and there is nothing yet to take its place. A completely mature man might argue that the mark of ripeness is precisely the ability to do without such compasses. But we must be realistic, and acknowledge that the majority of human beings require a commitment to church, nation, or ideology, or some combination of these.

Predictions are difficult. In Western Europe and the U.S.A. the decline of Christianity as a universally accepted spiritual undercurrent of our life has been accompanied first by worship of the demigods Stalin and Hitler, and then by sectarian cults borrowed from the Orient and from psychology. In 1968, it was clear enough that the loose energies of the young were seeking an outlet which they could not identify. They were long on frustration but short on any constructive purpose. In France, "imagination" was said to be enough to qualify as "power," and in Germany some of the young rebels thought it was "better to burn a store than to run one." I remember a French journalist exclaiming when he saw the students march on the Champs Elysée: "They haven't had a war for twenty-five years." And that was probably a good part of the explanation.

More recently we have had the women's movement, the sexual revolution, and the drastic reform of the Catholic Church; but these moves towards emancipation are unlikely to be proper substitutes for the radical aspirations which an all-embracing communism satisfied but can satisfy no longer. I have no patent remedy. I fear what you fear.

URBAN   In Poland, some hopeful bishops talk about the birth of a Roman Catholic belt stretching from Lithuania in the Baltic to Croatia on the Adriatic—it would, they think, constitute a wholesome spiritual influence between an apostate West and an unpredictable post-Communist East.

ULAM   I really cannot see Catholicism assuming a wide political role. In Poland it acquired great power and influence under communism, but it is already slowly retreating under the impact of the practical requirements of a secular democratic society. The same is bound to happen elsewhere in Eastern Europe. The Church thrives under oppression more than it does in a free and permissive society. The rapid de-Christianisation of Britain is one good example, even though Britain has an established church, and the monarch is officially "Defender of the Faith."

URBAN   That leaves us with the unsavoury possibility of nationalism coming back to occupy the vacant pedestals.

ULAM   That is a possibility. Nothing is *impossible* in history. Who would have thought, more than 300 years after the Ottoman Turks had been chased back from the outskirts of Vienna, that there would be an Islamic revival, and that Muslim fanaticism would grip Iran, much of North Africa, and now the Turkic world?

But apocalyptic parallels have to be treated with caution. The disintegration of the Soviet Empire will not, in my opinion, take us back to 1910. A reunited Germany will not be anything like the Kaiser's Germany, much less the Third Reich. The U.S.A. will not withdraw from the affairs of Europe as it did in 1919. And European unification will not be sunk by a new Rapallo. I am optimistic enough to believe that Hegel was wrong when he concluded that we learn from history that we do not learn from history.

URBAN   But wouldn't you agree that (as a Hungarian quip has it) "a pessimist is simply an informed optimist"? And aren't you an eminently informed person?

ULAM   I'm afraid the Hungarian joke is slightly off target for once. We do learn from history, though we do not always learn enough or in time. I am optimistic enough to believe that the fratricidal "Thirty Years' War" that wrecked our civilisation between 1914 and 1945 has been no end of a lesson—of which the unification of Europe is our best evidence. The past has to be both respected and, often, rejected.

1990

Chapter 6

End of the Bolshevik Utopia

A Conversation with Milovan Djilas

A Revival of Bolshevism?

URBAN Our first colloquium[1] was committed to print in those now distant days, in 1977, when the Soviet Union under Leonid Brezhnev seemed to be one of the world's two superpowers and Western governments thought they could, at best, slow down but not reverse the creeping growth of Soviet hegemony and Soviet-style socialism. I had to come to Belgrade to see you because Tito's regime prevented you from going abroad, and even our correspondence and telephone conversations were monitored by the Yugoslav security services.

Our second long conversation[2] was conducted in 1988 in an altogether different climate. You came to see me in England because Tito had died and you were free to travel. The Soviet system was disintegrating but the Empire was intact, although its *glacis* in East and Central Europe was crumbling. So was the cohesion of Yugoslavia.

Speaking as we are today in a Serbia that has seen free elections but decided to support a Communist-inspired government under Slobodan Milosevic, a question comes to mind that should exercise us more than any other: have we seen the end of Soviet-style socialism, or is it, as a leading Croatian politician recently told me, a time bomb that may yet unexpectedly explode?

What I am asking is not whether the Soviet Union might, with or without Gorbachev, revert to oppressive policies at home and revanchist ones in Eastern Europe, but whether Marxism-Leninism has finally

179

exhausted its appeal and is now so discredited that we need no longer fear it as a domestic threat to free societies.

Of all contemporary witnesses of communism I believe no one can answer that question with greater authority than Milovan Djilas. You played a critical part, first in the establishment of Soviet-style communism, and then in its demythologisation and destruction. Has the nightmare finally lifted, or are our celebrations premature?

DJILAS   In the Soviet Union and Eastern Europe, Bolshevism is dead as an organised system of beliefs and practices but remnants of it are alive and kicking. These are difficult to eradicate. Even in Hungary, where liberal parliamentary reform has gone far, the country's economic structure suffers from the legacy of communism. Property relations have been fundamentally changed, the enterprise culture is as good as dead, and the central control of the economy has not been as thoroughly repudiated as its ghastly record would have justified.

Even in Yugoslavia, the economic heritage of Bolshevism goes on debilitating us. Take Croatia, where Franjo Tudjman's government has come to power as a result of free elections with a liberal-conservative national mandate. Yet, despite this libertarian programme, Croatia has, so far at least, not been able to shed the economic straitjacket of the old Communist system. The same goes for Serbia, with this important difference: whereas in Croatia serious efforts are being made to reduce the share of "socialist" ownership, the current Serbian leaders are (half-heartedly, I must add) trying to protect it, even though they are eager to attract Western investment and open the economy to the free market. But then, Serbia voted Slobodan Milosevic and his Communists into power, whereas the Croats did the opposite.

Our experiences since the autumn of 1989 may be summed up in a sentence: Even though the Communist parties have lost power throughout Eastern and Central Europe, the damage they have done to the economic welfare of these countries is much more profound than any of us first suspected. When you abolish private property, eliminate the private entrepreneur, diabolise the profit motive, and persist in doing these things over a period of two or three generations, you are doing something very fundamental to the entire social structure and culture of your society. Even in East Germany, where the Communist economy was claimed to be functioning with (relative) efficiency, the present state of the economy is utterly dismal when measured by West German standards. All this breeds serious unemployment, social dislocation, radicalism and a (one hopes temporary) loss of faith in freedom and democracy.

URBAN   Your position has always been that under Soviet-style "socialism" the control of power is the powerholders' overriding consideration. The economy comes, in highly un-Marxist fashion, a poor second—

DJILAS   I still hold to that view: The economy is subordinated to the political ambitions of the Party and to its ideology, but that does not mean that the economic earthquake of communism has not produced absolutely tectonic shifts in the whole of society, which normal governments find very hard to correct.

URBAN   Marxism coming into its own by the back door?

DJILAS   No. The Bolsheviks realised that they could not come to power in classical Marxist fashion—by manipulating the economic base of society and doing little else. But having grabbed power, they reorganised the economic structure of society so thoroughly that they have made it very difficult for their successors to re-create a market-based system.

URBAN   So when the Soviet side insisted in 1989 that German unification must not involve the reversal of the postwar expropriations of land in East Germany, it tried to make sure that the "achievements" of Sovietism would leave a lasting mark on a united Germany?

DJILAS   That must have been the Soviet aim. Whether the Soviets will succeed in doing so is quite another matter.

URBAN   However this might be, my curiosity concerns not so much the economic consequences of Marxism-Leninism as the durability—or otherwise—of the belief in Utopia and the cry for revolution. We live in a period (who would have believed it was possible?) in which the revolutions we are experiencing in Europe are all directed *against* Bolshevism and the various governments it has spawned or imposed.

   Can you see Marxism-Leninism trying to reassert itself in our time with any chance of success? Are there people in Russia, Poland, or Bulgaria who might still believe that Marxism-Leninism provides a coherent body of answers to the social, economic and cultural problems of industrial and postindustrial societies at the turn of the millennium?

DJILAS   No, I cannot. There are definitely no Leninists to be seen in the former Communist domains, and virtually no Marxists. All remaining Marxist strongholds are in America and the West European universities, and they are more in the nature of intellectual chic than serious thought. There are and always will be people who believe that Marx was an important social thinker, but the sharp end of Marxism is discredited because it has failed.

In Yugoslavia we had a number of people who thought that Tito's break with the Soviet Union had been a grave error and worked for its reversal. There were the so-called Cominformists whom Tito had locked up, under cruel conditions, on the island of Goli Otok, and it may be that some of these old-timers genuinely believed in the tenets of Bolshevism.

We also have a new Communist Party of Marxist-Leninist inspiration, but this is a small group which has no impact on Yugoslav life. There is, furthermore, the moribund League of Communists, composed of old Party members, of partisans from the Second World War and of army officers. This, too, is a weak affair and getting weaker by the day. Any role it has so far managed to retain for itself has been due to the army connection but this, too, is a diminishing asset because the army connection has in reality been a Serbian nexus which has no future in a revamped Yugoslavia.

I am saying this while conscious of the fact that the army is trying to play umpire in the conflict between Serbs and Croats but is frequently accused of being an instrument of Slobodan Milosevic. This is not quite the case. To the extent that both want to prevent the disintegration of Yugoslavia, they have something in common. But the army leadership has its own philosophy, and I would find it difficult to believe that it would lend itself to an attack on Tudjman's Croatia. If it did, that would be the end of Yugoslavia, for one of the first consequences of such an intervention would be the disintegration of the army itself. The troops would get out of their uniforms and walk home because no Croat, Albanian, or Macedonian would fight in what would, in effect, be a Serbian army.

URBAN   Didn't we have a foretaste of this in the wake of the Croatian anti-army demonstration in Split in April 1991? A Macedonian soldier had lost his life, whereupon Macedonians demanded that their sons should be withdrawn from service in the federal army—

DJILAS   Yes, that was an ominous sign for the army. Yet I do not believe that Yugoslavia will fall apart. My tentative forecast is that it will survive as a loosely knit commonwealth of sovereign republics which will agree to pool some of their powers for the common good. There might develop a common market, a joint army side by side with national militias, and a common foreign and defence policy. The European Community is the model Yugoslavia might follow—a community set to achieve all three phases of the unification foreseen by the Delors blueprint. But Yugoslavia as we have known it since the end of the First World War no longer exists. We are in a period of transition.

URBAN   But no West European model would permit the kind of unilateral declaration of independence which the predominantly Serb-populated Krajina district of Croatia has declared on behalf of the local Serbian population, and especially the violence that accompanied it.

DJILAS   The independence of Krajina and the demand for its incorporation in Serbia (which is not a neighbour) cannot survive. The local Serbs have suffered some discrimination, and the Croatian government would do well to confer more ethnic rights on Serbs in the Krajina; but the armed rebellion that has taken place there cannot be allowed to succeed. No Croatian government could survive if Krajina's self-declared independence were tolerated.

The Croats under Tudjman have made some mistakes. Croatia's postwar constitution stated that Croatia was the home of both Croats and Serbs; recently, however, it was declared to be the land of Croats only. This made many Serbs feel that they were unequal members of the community and bred great resentment. The extreme nationalists sponsored by Milosevic and Draskovic exploited and further inflamed this feeling, and that is how the local rebellions in Croatia came about. Also, they were compounded by the heritage of the war: Many of the Croatian police were Serbs. The wartime partisans who had fought the Croatian Ustashas were predominantly Serbs, and a tradition of selecting Serbs for both police and army service had established itself throughout Yugoslavia. Tudjman, understandably, did not like this and purged the Croatian police of its Serbian component. This caused further resentment.

URBAN   Vuk Draskovic told me that he and his party would not allow Serbs to be left under Croatian rule. The memory of the wartime genocide of Serbs by the Ustashas was so strong, he said, that no Serb would be left under Croatian control "for a single hour." How is Yugoslavia going to form a commonwealth as long as sentiments and language of this sort prevail?

DJILAS   I have no sympathy with Draskovic's statement. The Serbs have lived with that memory for forty-five years. Why the sudden discovery? Of course, the Serbian people are exceptionally sensitive and easily provoked. They have certainly been provoked by a deliberate campaign of "revelations" showing, or purporting to show, for example, how, during the war, Serbs had been thrown into caves by Croats and buried alive. Some of the Serbian press drew the absurd conclusion that this kind of thing could happen again, that the Croats were fascists and Tudjman's government was an Ustasha government. This was pure incitement and a grave travesty of the truth.

I know Tudjman. He is an ex-Communist who ceased to be one many years ago. He is in charge of a democratically elected conservative government. So, why the campaign against him? Draskovic is weak in Croatia and Bosnia and has an interest in radicalising the Serbs and lowering their threshold of tolerance. Milosevic, for his part, could not afford not to support, openly or otherwise, the hotheads in the Krajina because, since the last elections, his popularity in the urban communities of Serbia has been sharply on the decline. The fanatics of Krajina are much to the right of Milosevic who is, after all, at heart a Communist. But he is sensitive to the charge that he is insufficiently loyal to the Serbian nationalist cause. Hence his support for the Krajina separatists for fear of being branded a traitor—an accusation which falls easily from the lips of the Krajina Serbs.

URBAN   The democratic elements in Serbian politics are hard to identify, although there are some. It is the old Communist authoritarianism and the new nationalism that seem to dominate the scene. A man of reason would find it hard to make a sensible choice—

DJILAS   That is putting it charitably. You may be surprised to hear that at the general elections I supported Milosevic against Draskovic. It was, alas, a choice between two evils, but Milosevic seemed to me to be the lesser evil. This is no great consolation; throughout my life I have tried to avoid such choices (even though I may not always have succeeded). Draskovic would generate even more intolerance than Milosevic is doing. The army, the Serbian civil service and the remains of the old partisan organisations would not support a Draskovic-led administration—much less the Croats, Albanians, and Muslims. Draskovic stands for the Chetnik tradition, which is discredited.

URBAN   But Draskovic assures everyone willing to listen that he is guided by democratic principles—

DJILAS   Lately his slogans have become democratic, but these tell us very little about his intentions. He believes that the Muslims in Bosnia are in fact Serbs, and the Macedonians South-Serbs. He believes in transforming Yugoslavia into a Greater Serbia. The "independence" of Krajina would not be the last frontier adjustment he would demand from the Croatians. He would have similar designs on Dalmatia and other parts of the Union. Draskovic's election would ensure the immediate and probably bloody disintegration of Yugoslavia. That is why I judged Milosevic to be the relatively lesser evil of the two.

URBAN But isn't Milosevic pursuing a similar policy? He, too, appears to be a pan-Serbian nationalist who is trying to make his intentions look slightly more respectable by wrapping them in the flag of Yugoslavia. In a speech on 30 May 1991, he seemed to be backing the campaign of violence by Serbian gunmen in Krajina, describing it as legitimate self-defence against a "fascist" Croatian government.

DJILAS Milosevic's intentions are probably the same as Draskovic's. Milosevic has declared for Yugoslavia, but a Yugoslavia defined by himself, and this is why he is, in effect, anti-Yugoslav in my judgement. He has tried to impose a blockade on Slovenia and tariffs on Croatian exports to Serbia. A man who intends to keep the Union intact does not undermine it with mindless actions of that kind. In any case, both measures have failed, and Milosevic's policies are by now in some ways similar to those of Draskovic, whatever the differences in their rhetoric. Milosevic, too, is aiming for a Greater Serbia which would unite all Serbs inside and outside Serbia. But this is, of course, a fantasy. It could not be achieved without civil war.

It is as absurd an ambition as Hungary's would be if the Hungarians now tried to bring the whole of their diaspora under the roof of the Magyar state. Wisely, the Hungarians have given up trying to do so. Twice in our century they were let down by their nationalistic leaders and catapulted, first in 1914 and then in the Second World War, into war on the losing side. This was, for Hungary, a national tragedy. I earnestly hope that the Serbs will be better advised.

Democracy in the Balkans

URBAN We have been sidetracked. Is communism likely to rise from the ashes? Has it, indeed, been reduced to ashes? These were the questions we set out to answer. Let me try to make them relevant to the present state of Yugoslavia and ask you a question which is on the lips of a great many Westerners, puzzled as they are by the extraordinary ethnic diversity of Yugoslavia. Are we witnessing a struggle between, on the one hand, liberal democracy as represented by freely elected governments in Slovenia and Croatia, and a freely elected communism in Serbia, on the other? Or are we simply seeing a revival of old ethnic feuds between expansionist Serbs and separatist non-Serbs? In other words: Is the conflict one between freedom and authoritarianism, or between chauvinism and chauvinism?

DJILAS   I'm afraid it is predominantly the latter. What we are seeing is a revival of those deplorable nineteenth-century conceits and grand delusions which led to extreme nationalism and two world wars in our century. The struggle between Serbia and Croatia is between two ambitious nation-states: Serbia wants a Greater Serbia, and Croatia wants an enlarged Croatia. The two are on a collision course.

That said, it is true that communism has left a wider and deeper legacy in Serbia than in other parts of Yugoslavia, but as time passes even this is becoming less obvious. For example, the Serbian media, especially television, reformed themselves out of all recognition after the March 1991 demonstrations in Belgrade, and they can now be said to be every bit as free as the media in Croatia and Slovenia. When certain leading people in Croatia claim that the present conflict is between Western democracy and a Balkan brand of Bolshevism, they are talking nonsense.

URBAN   What about the Bosnian Muslims? I was told by Slobodan Milosevic's mentor, the writer Dobrica Cosic, that certain Muslim leaders now claim their numbers run to almost five million and that some have even begun to voice demands for an autonomous Muslim republic. I should imagine their national ambitions have as little to do with the heritage of communism as those of the Slovenes and Croats?

DJILAS   They have to do with communism only in the negative sense that the Muslims, like the Slovenes and Croats, are hostile to it and thus also to Serbian rule, which they see as a vehicle for prolonging the Communist tradition. The Muslims' great problem is that the Croats tend to see them as Croat Slavs who happen to be Muslims. Croatia is very conscious of the 750,000-strong Croatian minority in Bosnia and is eager to boost their numbers. If the Croat thesis that all Bosnian Muslims are Croats could be made to stick, then Croatia's territorial claims on Bosnia might attain a measure of plausibility—or so the Croats like to think. This is, of course, a tall order as Muslims make up about 40 per cent of the Bosnian population and are the largest ethnic group there. I believe the Croatian demands have no chance of finding acceptance even though, in their opposition to Orthodoxy and the Serbs, the Muslims in Bosnia tend to ally themselves with the Croatian Catholics. It is conceivable that they will throw in their lot with the Croats if Serbia attempts to question the autonomy of the Bosnian republic.

The Muslims do, in fact, recognise their Slavic identity but maintain, at the same time, their religious loyalty to Islam. Before the Second World War, the Bosnian Muslims were not too much of a problem. They lived in a state of almost medieval backwardness and were smaller in number than they are today; but in the last half-century they have developed into a more numerous and modern nation and will have no truck with the Croat claim that they are Croats with a difference. They are now hatching plans for Muslim sovereignty.

URBAN Do they identify with the Turks? Do they hope to be supported by the international Muslim community?

DJILAS No. The Serbs have a habit of calling these Muslims "Turks" because of their religious links with the Ottoman Empire—

URBAN In the same way, I suppose, as the Bulgars tend to call some of their own Muslims "Pomaks"—

DJILAS Yes, and these Bosnian Muslims have been despised and discriminated against by the Serbian population in much the same way as the Pomaks have by the Bulgarian population.

Just how strong this opposition to all things Serbian is among the Muslims was vividly shown by their wartime willingness to side with the Nazis and fight the Partisans. Imam Hussein, the grand mufti of Jerusalem, came to Bosnia to help the Germans to organise a Muslim force, the SS Handzar (sword) division. It consisted of some 12,000 men, and I can tell you from experience that they were excellent fighters. The Germans committed the mistake of not thinking of this expedient earlier in the war. The Muslim SS were not thrown in against us until 1944, by which time the Germans' chances of defeating us were small. But the Muslims, under German command, were formidable opponents.

URBAN What happened to them at the end of the war?

DJILAS We shot those we could lay our hands on, but the majority dispersed and disappeared.

URBAN   If these Muslims were considered to be Croats by the Croats, how did Pavelic's government in Zagreb look upon the formation of an independent Muslim SS division?

DJILAS   They did not, of course, like it. Pavelic had proclaimed these Muslims to be the flower of the Croatian nation, and he even found a corrupt Muslim leader to represent the Muslims in his government. It did not take the Muslims long to conclude that the embrace of Pavelic meant the embrace of Catholicism, and they decided to seek independence by allying themselves with Nazi Germany. It didn't quite work out the way they had hoped.

URBAN   Isn't it remarkable, though, that forty-five years of Communist rule had so little success in making the multinational Yugoslav state conflict-free and homogeneous? To the extent that the Communists were at all willing to recognise the significance of the national factor, they told us that national animosities would wither under the impact of a classless Socialist society.
    Well, they could not have wished for a finer testing ground than Yugoslavia—which gave the lie to their theory. I suppose Tito's heavy-handed rule was a response to his awareness that the theory was bogus—

DJILAS   Tito's trouble was that early in the game the Communist movement in Yugoslavia split into national submovements. To have the universalistic programme of communism entrusted to nationalistic Communist parties and nationalistic Communists made nonsense of the claim that communism was the friend and saviour of the working man everywhere.
    But Tito's troubles did not end there. Once nationalism was allowed to creep into the practice of communism, it was soon realised by the nationalists that they could do a lot better outside the constraints of the Communist framework. National communism, though fine as a transition, always struck them as lacking authenticity. Hence the rise, in Tito's last years, of the authentic call of nationalism in all the republics. Tito, I must add, considered himself to be above nationalistic struggles. He was a Communist first and then a Yugoslav—perhaps, it is said, the only Yugoslav. He was deeply afraid of Serbian nationalism because he believed the Serbs were an expansionistic race with hegemonistic ambitions, way beyond their numbers and power.

URBAN   Do you, incidentally, consider yourself to be a Yugoslav?

DJILAS   I am strongly for Yugoslavia, and even if the union fell apart, I would still support the idea of Yugoslavia. But I do not consider myself to be nationally a Yugoslav. I am a Serb from Montenegro—a Serb with certain Montenegrin peculiarities of his own. How do Montenegrins differ? The way Bavarians differ from the rest of Germany: very little to the eye of an outsider, but in subtle ways quite a bit to those who know.

URBAN   Does it not strike you as significant that those Central European countries which had been part of the Habsburg Empire (or, if you like, Austria-Hungary) are finding their way to parliamentary democracy with relative ease, while those which were under Ottoman Turkish occupation have, so far at least, failed to respond to the collapse of Soviet hegemony with fully libertarian reforms and a free market economy? The transformation of Poland, Hungary, and Czechoslovakia is not matched by the halting democratisation of Romania and Bulgaria. Serbia elected a semireformed government, and Albania first walked down a similar road.

Do you share my assumption that it is the Ottoman heritage, reinforced perhaps by the traditions of Orthodoxy, that accounts for this surprising dichotomy? Or is it some latent Bogomilism in the souls of Bulgars, Bosnians, and Serbs that has subliminally motivated these nations to opt, in tolerably free elections, for the egalitarian rhetoric of a native "socialism," despite their bitter experiences of it for so many years? Our best example of the dichotomy is Yugoslavia itself, with the Croats and Slovenes clearly opting for free parliamentary institutions, human rights and a free market, and the Serbs, under Communist leadership, wiping out the self-determination and human rights of their Albanian minority whilst, at the same time, demanding self-determination for their own kinsmen in Croatia.

DJILAS   All these factors are playing a part. The Balkan countries were reared in the cradle of strong royal bureaucracies which were hierarchical and intolerant. No Balkan country developed a "normal" liberal society in which cultures, traditions, religions and languages could peacefully communicate and enrich each other. Serbia began to Europeanise itself in the middle of the nineteenth century. The peasants were released from serfdom, but the number of educated young sent for further study to Italy, Budapest, and especially Vienna was small and their influence negligible. Even at the outbreak of the First World War, for all the outward display of European life styles, all

Balkan countries were peasant lands with centuries of backwardness to make their advance slow and painful.

URBAN   Isn't it also surprising that the Socialist-Communist vote in the Balkans was strongest not, as we in the West expected, in the towns and industrial centres, but in the countryside? This was uniformly so in Romania, Serbia, and Albania.

DJILAS   Yes, Belgrade, for example, voted against Milosevic but the rural population supported him. How do we account for this? You are not right in saying this was a vote for communism, certainly not in Serbia. It was a vote, on the part of a great many frightened and ignorant people, for economic and social security. It was a vote for order. The choice in Serbia was between Milosevic and Draskovic. Many thought Draskovic's election would usher in an era of grave instability, and Milosevic's propaganda went to great lengths to confirm the peasants in their fear that a radical change would mean instability and poverty. The spectre of unemployment and inflation was conjured up as the price of privatisation; retired people were told they would stop getting their pensions; and nationalistic slogans were paraded to give the socialist appeal a strong native flavour.

URBAN   National socialism?

DJILAS   I would say: socialist nationalism, a mixture really—an authoritarian message suffused with elements of genuine democracy which (as I said before) we undoubtedly have now in Serbia, even under Milosevic. All political parties can freely organise, and so can the media.

URBAN   Would the Kosovo Albanians not have a different view?

DJILAS   Yes, they would. Their rights have been seriously restricted, and the suspension of American economic support for Yugoslavia as a single state is clearly part of the West's answer to that violation of human rights.

URBAN   Similar reasons to the ones you have just mentioned would seem to account for the Socialist-Communist vote in Romania, Bulgaria, and Albania. Doesn't the syndrome you describe—the fear of disorder, of diminishing pensions, of the return of the landlords, of inflation, joblessness, social insecurity, and so on—amount in fact to saying that socialism-communism has, after all, not lost its appeal even though Sovietism may have expired?

DJILAS   There will always be people who fear the economic and political power of others, and there will always be powerholders who abuse their privileged positions. But the existence of the fear of inequality should not be equated with a vote for communism, much less with a vote for the Soviet type of communism. Communism cannot be communism without a seamless ideology. I have often said it but will say it again: Ideology for a true Communist is not a goal in its own right but a means to an end, and that end is power. Nevertheless, ideology provides the all-important intellectual cement and the vocabulary of Communist rule. Without it communism cannot aspire to power or stay in power.

Now, the Socialist-Communist vote in the rural areas of the Balkans is in reality not a vote for communism because it is wholly without ideological content. Much less is it a vote for Bolshevism. Both are dead—stone dead. I have here a Serbian Communist magazine called *The Socialist,* which is subsidised by the Yugoslav state. Recently I gave it a long interview. This is its last number. The state can no longer afford to subsidise it—it has no readers left. That, in a nutshell, is the true story of communism and ideology in the Balkans in 1991.

URBAN   But you wouldn't say the same goes for the Soviet Union, would you?

DJILAS   Some basic "Communist" attitudes are undoubtedly still with us—even in Yugoslavia. The intolerant bureaucratic behaviour of the Milosevic party is a warning that democratic elections and free media do not in themselves make a democracy. The methods used by Milosevic's adherents are in reality the methods of communism with the signs slightly altered. At one stage the Party even tabled a motion in Parliament which would have banned all opposition. It did not, of course, succeed, but that the attempt should have been made at all does not bode well for the future.

URBAN   My impression is that the same, highly incomplete repudiation of communism goes *a fortiori* for the Soviet Union. And my fear is that as long as the basic institutions of Sovietism survive, in no matter how attenuated a form, the danger of a revival of Bolshevism and of Soviet power cannot be dismissed from our minds as wholly imaginary.

DJILAS   I don't think you are right there. The future of Bolshevism is organically bound up with Soviet imperialism. The Soviet Empire is in a state of rapid unravelling. Imperialism now exists only within the

Soviet Union, and even there it is weaker by the day. In his contest with the Western world, Gorbachev has had to give up position after position. Military overextension; the ill will which Soviet expansionism of the 1970s had created in the Western chancelleries; the burden (economic as well as psychological) of keeping large forces in Central and Eastern Europe, of pouring countless billions into bottomless pits such as Afghanistan, Cuba, Yemen, and Ethiopia—all these have made it absolutely inevitable that the Soviet Union should give up ideological militancy, surrender its forward positions, and repudiate its role as a superpower on the march. The Soviet system cannot, in my view, survive the collapse of Soviet imperialism because the world mission of the Soviet Union was an essential element of the *raison d'être* of Bolshevism—and that mission has fallen by the wayside.

URBAN   But could it not survive internally—on the now admittedly unfashionable "communism-in-one-country" principle—so that it might fight another day? Even shorn of some of its peripheral republics, the Soviet Union would remain a huge, potentially rich, and militarily significant power.

DJILAS   This might be so if Gorbachev succeeded in turning the Soviet system into a fully democratic system. But he is patently not doing so, and he is not even attempting to do so. Gorbachev's objective is to reform the Soviet system. But the Soviet system is unreformable. One can destroy it and perhaps start again, but no one can reform it. It is my considered opinion that Sovietism is in a state of rapid disintegration, and so is the Soviet Union. I do not, therefore, share your fear that Bolshevism might survive in a rump Soviet Union.

None of this is to deny Gorbachev's historic achievements. He put an end to Stalinism, opened the windows on the Soviet past, and allowed fresh and enquiring minds to question the taboos of an oppressive ideology. But apart from his splendid rhetoric (and I do not underestimate its importance), Gorbachev has not, in actual fact, achieved much. He ushered in a form of parliamentarianism which is a half measure; his marketisation of the economy and his attempts to privatise are half measures too. So is his plan for revamping agriculture, restructuring the Union and so on. He has failed in all these things because he has not had the courage to follow through—because he has been trying to mend what is unmendable. Therein lies his personal tragedy and that of the Russian nation. As in some ancient Greek drama, the protagonists are led to their doom by the iron law of their own character, even though they are fully aware of what they are doing.

Farewell to Utopia?

URBAN   One chapter of modern history is behind us—the egalitarian Utopia of Marxism-Leninism has collapsed, but I find it difficult to believe that the vacuum it is leaving behind will remain unfilled for long. If you were a young man of eighteen and were carried by the same kind of idealism as made you embrace revolutionary communism in the 1930s, what cause would attract you?

DJILAS   I would want to be what I am now—in the first place, a writer. My personality has not changed, nor have my basic ideas. In Yugoslavia I would support, if we had one, a social democratic party, or any liberal democratic party seriously engaged in the business of creating social justice.

URBAN   Suppose you were a young Italian or Frenchman—

DJILAS   In Italy, I would support the Communists under their new management because their programme strikes me as just and realistic; but I might also support a Craxi type of socialism—on balance, the Communists rather than the Socialists, because the Italian Communists have a weightier programme for ending social inequality than the Socialists.

If I were a young man in Germany, France, or England, I would find it difficult to attach myself to any existing movement because all the causes I can see in these countries are narrow or ephemeral, and usually both.

The ecological movement would certainly attract my idealism, but only in a half-hearted manner because it lacks fire. I would give a wide berth to the women's movement because the feminism that is now fashionable is narrow-minded and aggressive in its attitude to men. I am, and always have been, for the equal rights and opportunities of both sexes, but I am an anti-feminist because politicised viragos are a hindrance to the attainment of sexual equality. Anti-racism? Yes, I would, of course, oppose racism in all its forms, and I would also be strongly opposed to every form of nationalism even though I have, as a writer, a profound stake in language and the national tradition. But this would not lead me to embrace nationalism because I find it dangerously incompatible with the principle of interdependence which characterises the modern world and will do so even more emphatically in the future.

URBAN   We seem to be running out of worthwhile causes of the single-issue kind. Communism and fascism/nazism had, like religion, a more universal appeal. Can you see a successor to them arising?

DJILAS   I cannot predict the future. A body of new and attractive ideas may arise—perhaps some call for a new Utopia, who knows?

URBAN   But you are one of the famous scourges of Utopia-mongering, especially of social Utopias—have you changed your mind since we last spoke in 1988?

DJILAS   No, I have not. I have of course often condemned the Utopia of communism, but I do recognise that Utopian thinking is an elemental urge that at one time or other grips most people.

URBAN   What hope is to Christianity, Utopia is to the secular mind?

DJILAS   Yes, that sort of thing.

URBAN   Can you see some variant of Christianity filling the vacuum?

DJILAS   Not in the long run, and not in Western Europe. There is a Christian revival in Eastern Europe, feeding especially on the Catholic church's record of resistance to communism. There is a revival of Orthodoxy in Serbia and an advance of Catholicism in Croatia, but I consider these to be temporary. Under pluralism and Western-style secularisation they are bound to wither. In Poland, the Church's influence has already begun to wane. When I speak of Utopia as an ineradicable component of human thinking, I do not equate it with religion, although some Utopias move in the borderlands of faith.

URBAN   When the former American president, Jimmy Carter, and Zbigniew Brzezinski launched their campaign for human rights, many felt that this was a cause every civilised human being could and should embrace as our answer to inequitable governments of every kind, whether of the Left or the Right. Do human rights satisfy your longing for some vision that would go beyond mere pragmatism?

DJILAS   There is no better idea around at the present time. Its roots are Judeo-Christian: All men are children of the same God and must consequently enjoy equal rights. Well and good in countries where such rights do not exist or are flagrantly abused. But do human rights have a dynamic message in England, or France or Holland, or Switzerland? I doubt it, because human rights in these countries are on the whole amply guaranteed and respected. In the United States they have a limited appeal to the extent that there is a clientele for them in the black and Hispanic population, but beyond these they can hardly engage the imagination of men and move mountains. They are short of a fighting element—

URBAN   You were clearly right in saying that the basic inclinations of Milovan Djilas have not changed over the years: a "fighting element"?

DJILAS   Any commanding idea of the sort we are looking for must open up some new perspective. What perspective? you may ask. I can imagine some vision comprising elements of both science and religion but modern and rational in its appeal and thus fully accessible to everyone.

URBAN   Doesn't that sound a bit like "scientific communism"?

DJILAS   No, that is, of course, not what I have in mind—but what precisely it might turn out to be is something for the future.

From Faith to Heresy

URBAN   You and I, Milovan Djilas, have spent many a revealing (and very pleasant) hour together over the past decades, discussing the story of your life and the rise and demise of communism with which it is inseparably connected. History, we are nowadays told, offers no lessons—but perhaps historians do. If you were to write an epitaph for yourself, how would you like to be remembered?

DJILAS   I have no lapidary message to impart, but to the extent that I have been able to distil a modicum of clarity from the troubled waters that surrounded me all my life, it is this: "Fight and be fully stretched in the service of some great idea, but be aware that you can never attain it."

URBAN   It may not be very sensitive of me to ask you to explain an epitaph, but having done worse things to you in the course of our conversations, could you develop that idea?

DJILAS   Fight sincerely, fight to the best of your ability, try to make certain that your idealism is trained in the right direction—but be always mindful of the imperfections of this world, the fallibility of man and the random events that may ruin the best of your intentions.

URBAN   Like Sidney Hook in an earlier colloquium (see p. 17), you seem to be sharing Immanuel Kant's idealism—and caution: "Out of the crooked timber of humanity no straight thing can ever be made." In your youth, you seemed to have your eyes fixed on the "straight thing"—since the 1950s were you increasingly conscious of the "crooked timber" . . .

DJILAS   Yes, but despite the disappointments and abuses, we should never renege on our idealism. Even so terrible a man as Adolf Hitler had some. Asked on one occasion (I quote from memory), "What is your socialism trying to achieve?," Hitler answered, "When my belly is full but millions of German workers go hungry, action has to be taken to put things right."

Far be it from me to compare my idealism to Hitler's, or my idea of socialism to his, but I do believe that as long as hungry people, maltreated people, people manipulated by this or that authority exist, we must do what we can to help them, and we must do so using all our idealism and enthusiasm, because short of these our help is going to be wholly ineffective. It is, alas, going to be partly ineffective anyway because oppression, exploitation, manipulation, prejudice, the uneven-handed dispensation of justice are innate in the human condition and can never be completely overcome.

Communism made an attempt to eradicate these evils—but at an insupportable price. It claimed that human nature could be changed by social engineering: by the abolition of private property, the state control of education, censorship, and the manipulation of the media, and by a general levelling down to egalitarian poverty and ignorance. It was trying to create a society of robots, and robots would perhaps have fallen in line with the demands of Communist ideology. But real human beings, ordinary men and women, did not; and we must take it on board that they never will. In my old age, I'm not even sure whether it would be a good thing if the crooked timber of humanity (to use your quotation) could be straightened out completely. Would you or I like to live in a state of unadulterated goodwill—in a society of automatons?

URBAN   Now you sound like an advocate of Original Sin. Are you saying there are sins that are good for us—*felix culpa*?

DJILAS   I am not conscious of that implication, but recently my wife Stephanie and I paid a visit to a monk in his monastery, and I tried to convey to him a bit of my life experience. I said by way of (as I thought) challenging him: "Man cannot live without sin." The monk went one better. "Anyone alive for half an hour must be a sinner," he wryly observed.

I think we need a certain amount of wickedness in the world to sharpen our minds and hone our swords against. Look at the dialectic of good and evil in the recent Gulf crisis. The West did a good thing by putting an end to Saddam Hussein's aggression against Kuwait, but gave rise to an arguably much greater evil by inciting the Kurds and then betraying them. What accounted for this? An ahistorical view of history and the nonexistence of political foresight on the part of the Americans; an unwillingness to credit the survival of evil in a defeated tyrant; and a rush to "get the boys home." None of this takes anything away from my appreciation of the splendid military conduct of that short war, but it does illustrate my point that the Manichean contest between Good and Evil is part of our lives at the level of states as much as between individuals.

URBAN   What you are saying is that our problems at the end of the millennium still resemble nothing so much as the labours of Sisyphus. The stone seems forever to be rolling backwards—

DJILAS   Not quite. If you look at the history of the last hundred or so years, it is not unreasonable to claim that the stone has, in absolute terms, moved slowly uphill, despite terrible relapses. Our task is to maintain the pressure, knowing full well that the top of the hill will forever remain beyond our reach. But Europe in 1991 is a better place than it was in 1939 or 1945, and the West of Europe is an incomparably better place. The worst tyrannies have been defeated, there are no concentration camps on European soil and all state ideologies have gone up in smoke. Sisyphus has made some headway.

URBAN   But isn't it one of the remarkable facts of our age that some of the great initiators of rolling the stone uphill have come from the ranks of the erstwhile true believers in Utopia—prodigal sons whose "repentance" is more instructive for us than the behaviour of "ninety-nine righteous people who do not need to repent" (Luke 15: 7)?

Your own career provides one of our best examples of the merits of "heresy," and in one of our earlier conversations you acknowledged as much when you said: "Those who are seen by the world, and the church to which they once belonged, as heretics usually get better billing in history than those who are not. In that sense my 'fall' was more glorious than my 'rise.' "

Heretics certainly have a better story to tell than the righteous and orthodox. The *Confessions* of St. Augustine would make less compelling reading had Augustine never sinned; and few of us would doubt that the young stand to profit more from the recantations of old Communists such as Arthur Koestler and Ignazio Silone than from the speeches of Ronald Reagan or Margaret Thatcher.

I am reminded of all this by Eduard Shevardnadze's book, *The Future Belongs to Freedom*.[3] Here is another man who spent many years in the Communist Party as a high functionary and is on record as having massively supported dogmatism and "socialism" in the style of Brezhnev. Yet there came a point in his life when the scales gradually fell from his eyes and, like Gorbachev, he began to feel "we just can't go on like this any longer"—a phrase he uses in his book on more than one occasion.

How would you describe the character of that seminal event in a believer's life when doubt is first encountered? Shevardnadze's moment of truth impresses me with special force because, within a few years of his discovery that the Soviet system was tyrannical, he was able to act on it and make history; for it is clear by now that the release in 1989–90 of Poland, Hungary, East Germany, Czechoslovakia, Romania, and Bulgaria from the "socialist camp" was actively promoted by the Gorbachev/Shevardnadze/Yakovlev leadership.

DJILAS   How, indeed, does the first element of doubt implode in the consciousness of a true believer? Speaking from my own experience, it first appears as a vague discontent with yourself as a man in the possession of power. You begin to see yourself as not very different from the type of objectionable person you once criticised as "bourgeois" and "feudal." You see yourself in the context of castles, villas, titles, decorations, prestige, and privileges of all kinds, which prompts you to ask: What am I doing in that environment? Wouldn't it be more honourable and truer to myself if I got out of this corrupting glamour and returned to my solitary work in literature and political thinking—if I took up any decent vocation?

But it is not easy to make that break. It is, you soon discover, almost impossible to turn your back on old comrades and abandon the job you have been put in. Then—you begin to waver. A fissure develops in your thinking and your determination: Isn't this hesitation, you ask, just temporary? Wouldn't it change with the progress of human consciousness under the new society?

Still, the gap between ideals and practice deepens. In my case (and I think other Communist believers underwent a similar experience) it deepened as I was exposed to unjustified attacks by the Soviet government and discovered weaknesses in the Soviet position. You develop an ambition to do better than the Soviets have done—to be truer to the faith and use more convincing arguments.

But while this conflict with the Soviet Union undermines the integrity of your faith, it is not strong enough to bring about a positive realignment—you have to convince yourself in practical life and by ideological consistency that the lies and slanders which have been mounted against you are, in fact, untrue. It is at this stage that your mind breaks through the self-imposed walls of ideology, that you first experience free spaces and find points of support in your new critical insights.

Then, as time passes, you go through a ruthless inner struggle which leads to painful reconsideration of everything you once believed to be true. You discover that Stalin was in deep error, that neither he nor Lenin curbed the fatal proclivities of the Soviet bureaucracy—that the Soviet system was not just bad but wholly unfitted to serve as a basis for the "new society." But even that is not enough: such critique loses its moral justification if it is not applied to your own weaknesses. There then follows a critique of your own life and work; but it is, as yet, a critique applied with some caution lest it undermine your own inner order and, with it, your ability to construct an authentically "new society."

But this intellectual and political struggle within yourself and with others cannot pass without profound psychological side-effects. It causes a deep psychic turbulence, you feel you are wholly at sea, you seek reassurance in daydreams, you search for ways of living in tune with your newly found truths.

And then comes another crisis: the denial, after the death of Stalin, of liberalisation, of free speech and the freedom of conscience by the new Soviet leadership. Your options are limited: Either you remain true to yourself, to your freshly developed critical insights, or you put on the mask of obedience, deceive the powerholders and wait for your opportunity.

There is something in man that resists the course of dishonour. What exactly it is, is difficult to say: perhaps the call of conscience, perhaps the spirit of disobedience, perhaps the need to repudiate erroneous beliefs and do penance for false actions. It is certainly a force stronger than will-power, stronger than mere hopes and desires, stronger than life itself. Is it a motivation that grips everyone? Perhaps so.

Depending on individual circumstances, it may take the form of small personal decisions, but it may also lead to decisions of a more universal character with wider impact, as it did in my case.

Whichever it is, the road from faith to heresy is a difficult one—it takes time, it is strewn with inner disturbances, with descents and ascents of the soul of excruciating cruelty. Like the heretics of earlier times, I find it easier to describe than to explain.

1991

Chapter 7

"The Best World We Have Yet Had"

A Conversation with Sir Karl Popper

On Optimism

URBAN Science-based social optimism is associated in the popular mind with the nineteenth century—with the expectations of the early French Socialists and with Marx and Engels. You reject in your celebrated books, *The Open Society and Its Enemies*[1] and *The Poverty of Historicism*,[2] the Marxist-Communist conceptual framework as "historicism," and show why it is dangerous for our freedom as well as philosophically untenable. Yet—as we know from several of your recent statements—you are almost as optimistic (and what is more, "scientifically" optimistic) about the state of our civilization as a practising Marxist would be. This seems to call for an explanation.

Marx was an optimist because he believed that his conception of history was scientific and could be employed to build a better world without using coercion. Man would recognize the grand design and march along with it. But *your* notion of piecemeal social engineering assumes no such thing. Piecemeal social engineering is simply another phrase in your vocabulary for muddling through. It is a curious phrase to use, but its meaning is clear: Man is disorderly, volatile and fallible. Where Marx thought that man would respond to the rational call of history and join the winning side, the most you expect of him is to cheat or evade his own imperfections.

Given his assumptions about history and the nature of man, I can see why Marx was an optimist, but given your assumptions, I cannot, with respect, see why you should be.

POPPER There are many possible senses of optimism. Optimists may be optimists with respect to the future; I am wholly neutral about the future. I do not make any predictions about the future because I believe the future is open and resists prognostication. In a different sense, optimism may refer to our judgement of the present. I am absolutely optimistic about the present, by which I mean the existing attainments of our culture and civilization. I know all the bad features of the present that may be brought up to qualify this judgement, but I also know the terrible things that happened in earlier times which endorse my optimistic reading of our present situation.

The worst offenders in our time are the intellectuals. They are, in their majority, ambitious fools who are not interested in the truth but are simply after maximum publicity. Time was when intellectuals had the guts of arguing with and opposing the majority. But now even that is gone. Their sole ambition is to move with the fashions hoping to be at least one step ahead of them so that they can capture the limelight. Schoenberg and the modern painters are good examples.

That you should be saying that I'm an optimist about the future shows that you have either misunderstood my work or that you are, deep down, yourself a hopeless historicist.

URBAN I sympathize with you when you protest that you are not an optimist in the future-oriented sense of the word. Yet your many statements on this topic have left a great many people (myself included) with the impression that your optimism is far-reaching and that it refers to the future as well as the present. It is indeed highly arguable whether one can be an optimist without in one way or another making or implying a statement about the future. If optimism is (as the *Concise Oxford Dictionary* tells us) "the theory that good must ultimately prevail over evil in the universe,"[3] then it is hard for me to understand how any optimist can restrict his hopeful disposition to the present, unless he assumes that evil has already been universally conquered and good is triumphant.

However this may be, in your celebrated three-part interview with Manfred Schell in *Die Welt*,[4] your optimism points cumulatively to the future even though you do not make predictions. You express great confidence in the liberating influence of technology (washing machines have done away with domestic slavery); you believe that our search for social justice is more intense and more successful than it has been in earlier ages; you assert "with real pride" that our attempt to make the world better has been "unbelievably successful," and you condemn those who take a more pessimistic view as propagandists who "tell us lies and slander our world in order to discourage us." May I put it to you that a reasonable man cannot read these judgements without thinking that your optimism points beyond the date of these statements in February 1990; and I also feel that the paper's editors, too, took your opinions with some scepticism, for they ran your second interview, tongue in cheek, under the quizzical headline, "Die Technik hat uns befreit. Was Soll die Hetze?" (Technology has made us free. Why all the agitation?)[5]

POPPER   I say explicitly in several of my writings that I am not a prophet; I can say nothing about the future; I am not a historicist. To quote from one of my lectures: "If I call myself an optimist I do not wish to suggest that I know anything about the future. I do not want to pose as a prophet, least of all as a historical prophet. On the contrary, I have for many years tried to defend the view that historical prophecy is a kind of quackery. I do not believe in historical laws and I disbelieve especially in anything like the law of progress."

I am an optimist in respect of our present time. We have achieved incredible things, but that doesn't mean that we'll go on achieving incredible things. Whether we do or do not depends on us—this is the essence of my teaching.

URBAN   If you say that we have made advances in many vital aspects of our lives over the last, shall we say, 100 years—and this is what you are saying—I find it slightly irrational to claim that as from this morning we can say nothing more about the likely future of these advances. Isn't your fear of making a prediction an overreaction to Marx? Wouldn't it be more reasonable to assume, with some modern non-Socialist planners (in France for example), that while forecasting may have to be handled with the utmost caution, reasonable extrapolations from existing trends are respectable and indispensable?

POPPER   No, it wouldn't. My whole teaching is that there is no such thing as a reasonable extrapolation. It is possible, of course, to discuss future possibilities, the likelihood of one contingency occurring rather than another, but there is no such thing as extrapolation. That, I repeat, is the fundamental teaching of history.

URBAN   I thought you have just said it was *your* teaching—

POPPER   Everybody with the exception of one great man always got the future wrong—and that exception was de Tocqueville. He foresaw how democracy in America was going to develop and many other things, but he was the exception.

You see, my antihistoricism makes it possible for me to be objective about the present. I give no hostages to the future and I do not consequently have to play up or play down the importance of any aspect of the present. But the great majority of intellectuals cannot be objective about the present because they have an investment in the future. They are constantly on the lookout for pointers to the future because they are committed to a *certain* future. And many of them are not satisfied with merely touching up the facts of the present to make them harmonious with their picture of the future, but they would also like to be one jump ahead of their rivals—to be the *avant garde* of the future. I remember Karl Mannheim, the ex-Hungarian philosopher, coming to the library of the London School of Economics every morning demanding from the librarian the latest books and essays on every conceivable topic. You see, he was anxious to be ahead of his time and to be one up on his colleagues. This is typical of the pride and vanity of intellectuals. My basic point is that we can perfectly well understand and judge what has happened to us over the last 20 or 50 or 100 years, but we are not entitled to use this understanding as a compass for the future.

URBAN   Isn't it a sign of an *odium philosophum* to assume that all intellectuals are in error except the speaker? And doesn't your whole teaching reduce the value of history, and arguably of all education, to the state of mental gymnastics or mere entertainment? For the first question any child worth his salt will ask after a history lesson is, "And what does all this tell us about the future?" The first question any concerned group of people is likely to ask after the rise of a Hitler or the death of a Stalin is, "Is this good or bad for our future?" Your teaching would, if I read you correctly, enjoin us to keep mum or offer only anecdotal conjectures.

POPPER   You seem to be such a stubborn historicist that you just cannot believe when somebody tells you, "No, I'm not a historicist. Historical predictions based on the alleged laws of history are nonsensical."

URBAN   With all due respect—I have, like you, spent the better part of my life fighting the idea that there are (in the mode of Karl Marx) inevitable outcomes in history, but I also believe that reasonable and cautious extrapolations are rational and necessary. We could not conduct our practical activities without them, nor could we teach anything worth teaching in our schools and universities.

But apart from that—I feel that you do yourself recognize the need to make certain broad predictions based on the evidence of the past. Let's not call them extrapolations if that offends you; let's call them expressing certain hopes derived from hopes realized in the past. You do so, for example, in your statement to *Die Welt:* "We have . . . an enormous amount of knowledge, and we can, under certain conditions, use this knowledge actually to influence things in a beneficial manner. For example, scientists and technologists have saved some of the great lakes from pollution such as Lake Michigan in America and Lake Zürich in Switzerland. It does not seem to me at all unthinkable that biology will find a solution to the hothouse effect, too, should this really become a threat to us."[6]

What I am saying is that your long statement in *Die Welt* leaves the reader with the impression that you take an optimistic view of both the present *and* the future. This may not have been your intention, but the large number of good things you identify in the present makes us think that those good things will go on happening in the future, too.

POPPER You must remember the context in which that interview was given. The Berlin Wall had been breached, the dictatorship in East Germany was collapsing. The Cold War was coming to an end and the world was suddenly facing the possibility of a friendly Soviet Union ready perhaps to be brought into the civilized world, as Churchill and Roosevelt had envisaged. I did not say that any of this would inevitably happen; indeed I listed all sorts of obstacles on the Soviet side that would have to be overcome, as for example the size and mission of the Soviet Navy, and Soviet arms sales worldwide. I was merely expressing a hope and a vague possibility. Nevertheless, speaking at the end of 1989, optimism was justified.

As to the passage you have just quoted, you conveniently omitted to stress the words "under certain conditions." To me these words are essential because they point unmistakably to the contingent nature of my hope. "Under certain conditions" we can, indeed, use our accumulated knowledge to good effect, but under other conditions we can't. My statements about the future are the expressions of hope; nowhere do I say that this or that *has* to happen. Let me, at the same time, re-emphasise my great trust in science and technology. Technology has indeed saved us. A few things about my childhood will illustrate my meaning.

Capitalism used to mean great wealth in the hands of the few, and great poverty for everyone else. It used to mean also rampant class contradictions between the rich and the poor, and I must say that Marx's description of this state of affairs in what he rather idiotically called the period of early-capitalism (all this labelling is silly and much to be rejected) was on the whole correct. But what has happened in our time makes nonsense of Marx's predictions. Capitalism had the good sense of reforming itself. It extended wealth and welfare to greater and greater segments of the population and exorcised the spectre of class warfare. In my childhood, I still experienced the unreformed, ugly face of capitalism, and that gives me a good yardstick for measuring the colossal advances we have made.

I get very angry when I hear feminists complain that women are an oppressed class in our society. They seem to have no idea of what women's lives and rights were like before the First World War or even between the two wars. One of the worst forms of slavery in the Austria I knew was domestic employment in the major cities. Every year in the autumn young peasant girls streamed into Vienna from the country-side seeking domestic service as chambermaids. But the employment they got was no employment in the modern sense. These girls were bound to the house in a form of serfdom. Their hours were unlimited with the exception of a fortnightly free day or free afternoon. They were subject to the discipline, not to say the whims, of their mistress, and not infrequently they were sexually used by the master of the house or his sons. I was about eight or nine years old when a girl in my family's service was apparently caught stealing something worth fifteen crowns. She was immediately dismissed and handed her servant's book without the usual positive recommendations to make her acceptable to another employer. It was not stated in her book why she had been given the sack (my mother was too compassionate to do that), but, as I say, neither did she get the habitual laudatory endorsement. This was in fact pronouncing a death sentence on the poor girl. Her choice was between starvation and prostitution, and not unnaturally many to whom this sort of thing happened ended up in prostitution. (I don't want to be too hard on my mother because in the contemporary context she was probably behaving rather charitably. One has to appreciate the mores of the time.)

URBAN The situation was much the same in neighbouring Hungary. It is perhaps worth recording that, in the 1920s, one of Hungary's

leading modern writers, Dezsö Kosztolányi, made what I consider to
be *the* classical statement on domestic slavery in his novel *Édes Anna
(Sweet Anna)*. Sweet Anna is horrendously abused; she is driven to
murder and ends up barely escaping the hangman's noose.

POPPER   This sort of thing can no longer happen. Technology with its
wonderful labour-saving devices has put an end to domestic slavery. I
consider the expiry of these shameful practices as cause for optimism,
and we should feel ourselves deeply in the debt of technology that has
made it possible.

URBAN   You have said predictions about the future are nonsensical
and indeed dangerous. Let me, using the example you have just given,
put it to you that tomorrow, next year, or fifty years from now probably
no one will be in a position to employ domestic servants in the manner
in which your mother did, any more than mine managers will be able
to send children down the shafts. In both cases, I am extrapolating
from existing facts. Would you not agree that "predictions" of this
kind are legitimate?

POPPER   All we can say is that a reversion of the sort you describe is
most unlikely to occur because a return to domestic and industrial
slavery would run into great popular opposition; but we cannot rule
out the possibility that, owing to some event or other, the unthinkable
might happen and even predictions of the kind you have just made
would turn out to be entirely false.

URBAN   This is surely so in theory, but doesn't your own optimism
and pragmatism induce you to think that if domestic service has been
gradually humanized and virtually eliminated over the last 100 years,
it will, in actual practice, prove almost impossible to restore or to
dehumanize where it manages to survive? And doesn't that statement
amount to an extrapolation or prediction? No one would expect it to
be a 100-percent fireproof prediction, but it is, I would have thought,
safe enough to make it possible for parliaments and governments to
think rationally about the future. It would fall somewhere between
"Utopian social engineering," which you repudiate, and "piecemeal
social engineering," which you support.

POPPER   It is immensely important to draw a demarcation line between
two problems—(a) judgements we make about our time based on our
reading of factors that worked towards it in the past, and (b) pointers
to the future. These are two entirely different things and we should not

try to combine them. Our curiosity about the future inclines us to identify this or that alleged pointer to the future as the one we ought to trust, but this is plainly foolish. There are, at any time, hundreds or thousands of different indicators, each pointing in a different direction, and we have no way of telling which of these, or what combination of these, might turn into reality. And because the future is entirely open—and this is the crux of my teaching—we have as individuals a moral responsibility to shape the future and not regard ourselves as mere flotsam and jetsam in some irresistible current of history. So, for methodological and moral reasons alone, it is of the highest importance that we should erect a distinct barrier between the past and the future and learn not to look at the past as a source of reference for the future.

The once-famous American historian, Henry Brooks Adams (grandson of President John Quincy Adams), said in his autobiography *(The Education of Henry Adams)* that the future can be predicted by a simple method: Select two points you could trust in the past, draw a straight line between them, and see which way it points. One could forgive a ten-year-old child if it came up with so unsophisticated an idea, but an accomplished diplomat and professor of history at Harvard University!

On Not Predicting the Future

URBAN Wouldn't you agree, though, that when a number of clearly observed trends are jointly considered, the result is a prediction, whether explicitly stated or only implied? Suppose we said: Serflike conditions in domestic service have gradually disappeared; child labour in the mines has been gradually eliminated; the disfranchisement of women has been gradually outlawed; progressive taxation is unlikely to be undone; the motorcar is unlikely to be banned; monarchy as a universal form of government is unlikely to reassert itself, and so on. Don't these observations about the past conjointly provide us with a curve which points to the future, not, to be sure, as a precise forecast which we could convert into precise political and economic action, but as an "envelope" indicator of considerable use to anyone concerned with the management of human affairs?

POPPER This kind of forecasting can be of interest—but I don't operate like that.

URBAN   But people concerned with our practical affairs do, and they have to.

POPPER   Yes, but I do not operate like that. When I think about the future I consider what ought to happen, what facts and opinions may be mustered against my judgements, what dangers and unintended consequences may wait upon my preferred future, and so on. That is how we should take our position *vis-à-vis* the future, and not look to fixed pointers as our guides. The future is open and we should avoid entertaining ideas that limit our choices and paralyse our will.

URBAN   But you would, I take it, agree with certain commonsensical predictions of the sort de Tocqueville, whom you have just praised, made about the U.S. and Russia becoming the world's two dominant powers. This was, to my mind, a typical "envelope" forecast. De Tocqueville saw that the U.S. and Russia were the only two continental powers with huge natural and manpower reserves, huge and underpopulated territories, internal lines of communication, and an unfulfilled desire for a rendezvous with history. He has been proven right. Would you repudiate de Tocqueville's prognosis, too, as an unwarranted extrapolation?

POPPER   All I can tell you is that my teaching points in a different direction.

URBAN   Allow me to pursue this a little further. I would have thought that we can, in 1991, make a reasonable envelope forecast about China without giving hostages to fortune or getting mixed up with historical determinism, Hegel or Marx. Seeing that China has always looked upon itself as the Middle Kingdom, that it nurses a longstanding grudge against the Western world, that it is the world's most populous country, that it is badly underdeveloped, that it is the home of an ancient civilization and an intelligent and industrious population, we can, I believe, say with reasonable certainty that after the demise of Communist rule and the arrival of Western technology, China will become a superpower and possibly a threat to its neighbours. A statement of this kind strikes me as little more than putting the facts of history, psychology and geography together and making an intelligent guess about their aggregate impact in the near or not so near future. Would you go along with this kind of "extrapolation"?

POPPER   No, I would not. A forecast is a forecast; it is always wrong. If *I* were pressed to make a "prediction" about China I would, on the contrary, cast about for ways in which a post-Communist modernizing China could be induced to cooperate with the Western world—for ways in which we might help China to turn itself into a free, prosperous, and peaceable society, and so on.

URBAN   I appreciate that this is what you would *like* to see happen—but what you are expressing is a mere desire which need not have any impact on what *will* happen.

POPPER   That is where you do not understand my teaching. One has to look to the future from the point of view of what one would like to achieve and think of ways of bringing it about.

URBAN   Which is what the Marxists say—

POPPER   The future is not an independent entity "out there" which will somehow happen whether we like it or not. It is part of a continuum.

URBAN   That is why I keep asking you at the risk of perhaps sounding unpleasant: If we can identify developments A, B, C, and D in the recent past and conclude that they all point in a certain direction, by what reasoning do we assert that this direction will stop being relevant to human affairs the moment we choose to talk about it? If the future is, as you say, tied up with the present, why this arbitrary caesura?

POPPER   You are now falling into the error of assuming that history is movement. Movement is a metaphor borrowed from physics and is inappropriate. History is no flow, it is no movement. Things happen in human affairs and we are among those who make them happen. That is all.

Among the many ways in which we influence history is the force of ideas. Ideas are an important factor, and probably the most important factor in shaping the successive activities of men. But they can be frustrated and destroyed. Many ideas that were current in Germany before the foundation of the Empire in Versailles in 1871 came up against a wall and led to nothing. There is no predetermined course in history. We have to think of it as the result of a great many forces, some conflicting with one another, others running parallel but independently, and so on. But history responds to no law, and the metaphor of movement, which is taken from physics, is absurd.

URBAN   But doesn't a philosophy so thoroughly based on the singular and particular give us a rather thin account of reality? If extrapolations are (as you claim) nonsensical, perhaps generalisations are nonsensical, too, in which case not only the study of history, but science too would be the great loser—

POPPER Generalisations are, of course, a necessary tool in science, but laws of history do not exist. And supposing they existed, we could not use them and rely on them. Let me put it like this apropos of a small book I recently published[7]: Lucretius with his thoroughgoing materialism tried to destroy the Romans' fear of the gods—*my* attempt has been to destroy the fear of determinism in the hearts of my contemporaries.

There is a view of the world which agrees with physics, chemistry, and especially biology, and which holds that our freedom of action coincides with the kind of freedom of action ordinary men and women have in their relations with one another in everyday life. For example, we know that we cannot do things which go beyond our financial capabilities, our physical strength, our linguistic ability, and so on. It is this limited view of our possibilities and of the future which I hold to be true and practical.

URBAN Wouldn't you agree, though, that while this view may be true at one level of thinking ("reasoning with the brain"), it fails to do justice to man's natural ambition to transcend his physical limitations? The finest things human beings have created in religion, music, the visual arts, and literature question and reject these limitations. In modern times, Unamuno's "tragic sense of life" and his "God-ache" are perhaps our most telling examples of this irrepressible *Sturm und Drang* in human affairs.

How would you answer those who find death and the thought of nonexistence an insult to their humanity and "rage," with Dylan Thomas, "against the dying of the light"?[8] What I am saying is that I doubt whether your happy disposition can be a reliable compass for the rest of us.

POPPER My answer is that we have already extended—enormously extended—our limits, and I would stress that it is a fine ambition for man to set himself the ever-increasing extension of our freedom of action as his target. We can now fly virtually anywhere we choose; we can communicate with one another in an instant from one end of the earth to the other, and with objects and human beings in space. We can use laser beams in the operating theatre and extend the span of life. More and more of our animal limitations have fallen away, and I am confident that one day all may go—not, mind you for the benefit of you or I, but of our successors. If anyone considers our limitations to be "tragic," he is free to do so if that amuses him, but Unamuno's "tragic sense of life" does not impress me. What is so tragic about our inability to live forever? Use the marvellous opportunities the world offers. My attitude to these things is diametrically opposed to his. I am grateful for the opportunities we have and I intend to use them.

URBAN   The man in the street may be forgiven for thinking that the wrangling of philosophers boils down to psychological types: If you are born with a happy disposition, you produce a philosophy in the manner of Sir Karl Popper. If you are born with "God-ache" in your heart, you write in the mode of Unamuno. Would you go along with that?

POPPER   No, I would not, but thereby hangs a tale which would divert us from the topics in hand.

URBAN   You stress that the future is open and the present shows great improvements on what has gone before—

POPPER   Yes, while the past has to be judged severely, we can only say that our Western society is, in every respect, incredibly superior to anything that happened in earlier ages. This should be clear to anybody with a smattering of history, although there are students of history—like J. Jonas, whom I hold to be an absolute fool—who claim the opposite.

Dante and the Old Testament

URBAN   Your use of the word "superior" puts me on my guard. Superior in what sense?

POPPER   Morally superior.

URBAN   May I put it to you that there are cogent reasons for thinking that a Christian in mediaeval Europe, with his sense of oneness with God, his membership of a homogeneous family-like community, his trust in salvation and resurrection, his place in a well-ordered hierarchy, was "morally superior" to ourselves, captives as we are of a shallow, materialistic, television culture? And when you add in the human and moral losses we suffered in two fratricidal world wars and in the camps of Stalin and Hitler, can we really claim that our age is morally superior?

POPPER You've got it all wrong. People in the Middle Ages lived under terrible conditions—

URBAN Terrible as we see them from our present point of observation—

POPPER No, we have evidence to show that our mediaeval forebears themselves realized that their lives were terrible. Take Dante's *Inferno* with its dreadful, sadistic imagery. It makes me breathless to think that those ghastly, refined tortures we read about in Dante's poem were supposed to be inflicted in support of a religion of love and forgiveness. Imagine the perverse public morality that induced Dante to think that the abysmal cruelties he describes were the will of God. Now, you do not have this in the Greeks, in Homer for example, although he depicts wars and fighting galore. The mentality of mindless killing and sadism stems from certain elements in the Old Testament and from distorted interpretations of the New Testament.

Take the Book of Esther where, inspired by a dream, Mordecai and his daughter, Esther, take terrible revenge on those suspected of having planned the destruction of the Jews of the Persian Empire. In addition to the plotter Haman and his ten sons, 800 were slaughtered in the capital city of Susa, and in the provinces the Jews "slew seventy-five thousand of those who hated them" (Esther 9:16). The Feast of Purim is celebrated to this day to commemorate these events.

Or take the punishment Moses metes out to Israel because of the golden calf incident (Exodus 32). He orders his law-and-order agents, the Levites, to " 'go to and fro from gate to gate throughout the camp, and slay every man his brother and every man his companion, and every man his neighbour' " (Exodus 32:27). Three thousand were killed that day, and in his admonition to the Jews Moses says, " 'Today you have ordained yourselves for the service of the Lord, each one at the cost of his son and of his brother, that he may bestow a blessing on you this day' " (Exodus 32:29).

You have to bear all these things in mind to appreciate the tolerant and humane society in which we live at the turn of the millennium.

But to come back to your question, I am not at all convinced that men and women in the Middle Ages lived deeper, more authentic, or happier lives than we do. The killing of Christians by Christians for alleged deviations from the faith are the darkest pages of the human story. Frightful crimes were committed in the name of fraternal love.

URBAN   Once we have accepted that man is frightful, his crimes should not surprise us—

POPPER   But man is *not* frightful—intellectuals are. The frightful crimes were committed because of the pretensions and vindictiveness of intellectuals. In the Middle Ages the priests were our intellectuals; today the intellectuals are our priestly class, but, whether the first or the second, intellectual pride and vanity (*Rechthaberei* is a good word for it) have been the causes of many of our most shameful deeds.

URBAN   I would put it slightly differently—intellectual pride combined with the love of power. I would have thought the corrupting influence of power is every bit as responsible for our collective crimes as the vindictiveness and *amour propre* of intellectuals.

POPPER   Well, the love of power is something I cannot comment on because I have absolutely no feel for it. My mind does not respond—positively or negatively—to the notion of power.

URBAN   But many intellectuals respond to it, and positively at that. Intellectual vindictiveness and the love of power are, to my mind, causally connected. If, as you say, the dominant motivation of intellectuals is to see their pet theories proven right by reality, then they must try to attain power, because only in the possession of power can they hope to bend reality to conform with their vision. Marxist intellectuals are, of course, our best example of this, but Henry Kissinger, with Metternich as his hero, is another. His balance-of-power politics was an attempt to uphold and to improve on the Metternichian model. Would you agree with that?

POPPER   The vindictiveness of Marxist intellectuals is certainly well-established. Kissinger is a different matter; whatever his model (if indeed he has one), he has done rather well both as national security adviser and secretary of state.

For a Piecemeal Change of the Soviet System

URBAN   The collapse of the Communist system in Central and Eastern Europe has been followed by a feverish search for a substitute. There is agreement on all sides that liberal democracy and a free market economy are the most likely answers, and, indeed, in Poland, Hungary, and Czechoslovakia liberal reforms are already being put into effect. But there is no agreement about one crucial detail—if detail it is—whether the change from the command economy should be by piece-meal reform or a sudden and sweeping transformation.

Those who have experienced the failure of piecemeal economic reform and piecemeal social engineering in Yugoslavia and Hungary over the last two decades argue that the new democracies in Central Europe must go for a speedy and thorough transformation, even if the arrival of a market economy should mean unemployment and social instability in the short term. Their view is shared by conservative economists and politicians in the West who feel that the lure of the Swedish and Austrian models must not mislead the new democracies into thinking that there is a halfway house to be occupied between socialism and a free-market economy. In other words, piecemeal social and economic reform is very much on the defensive—wholesale change is very much on the offensive.

I do realize that "piecemeal social engineering" for you was a predominantly sociological concept. It was meant to be a warning to democratic capitalist societies that their search for improved social institutions must be empirical and gradual. The nice question is whether you regard piecemeal reform and social engineering as equally commendable if pursued in the *opposite* direction? Should those countries which are now in the throes of change from Soviet-style socialism to a free-market economy and liberal democracy proceed by piecemeal social engineering, or would you advise them to embrace holistically, as it were, a laissez-faire capitalism on the argument that the general havoc wrought by the Soviet system is so profound that only the most radical solutions can help?

POPPER   I think you have misunderstood me again. It is not a question of substituting one social and economic system for another, but of learning to think in entirely different categories. We have to assimilate the idea that our actions have unintended consequences. It is, there-fore, useless for politicians and planners to design a fine theoretical programme and to complain when it misfires. They should start from the assumption that any ostensibly foolproof scheme *can* be fooled, and that it is their job to test it for potential weaknesses by trial and error. A slow, empirical type of approach is what is required.

URBAN   This, you tell us in your books, should be our approach when trying to rectify the social and economic inadequacies of a free-market system. But now our most pressing problem is the reverse: how to transform Utopian, holistic, formerly Communist systems into liberal free market ones. Is it still your view that slow and piecemeal change, with a kind of Swedish social democracy as its ultimate target, should be the reformers' aim in Central Europe and the USSR?

POPPER Yes, it is. But let me first say this: In the Soviet Union the holistic idea has suffered a clear and irreversible shipwreck. In making a fresh start, the state cannot do very much, but what it can do it must do. Foremost among the things it can do is the creation of a legal framework for the market economy—

URBAN Which Hungary, Poland, and Czechoslovakia, and what used to be the GDR, are busy doing—it remains to be seen with what success—

POPPER But, in the Soviet Union, legal reform is still in its infancy. This has to change. The reforms themselves cannot be decreed. The will to build a market economy, to induce respect for private property, including landownership, must come from the people, and the building of that will may be a very slow process. It makes me laugh when I read that a stock exchange has been opened in the USSR at a time when there are hardly any private companies, no stocks or banks capable of handling them. I find it equally appalling that the authorities should not permit a black market. Surely they must realize that the black market is black only because there are not enough goods to go around in the "white" market. Produce the goods, and your black market will turn grey and then white, but to ban it is like throwing your thermometer away for fear of discovering that you are running a high temperature.

URBAN Many of these ideas are already arrows in the quiver of Soviet reform intellectuals, especially those in the city councils of Moscow, Leningrad, and other major centres. Your critique would hardly strike them as surprising—

POPPER What people in the Soviet Union must absolutely abandon is any ambition to build a perfect society. This cannot be done either on the Left or the Right. That the Communist dream leads to both tyranny and poverty has been amply demonstrated. But it is also futile to imagine that capitalism is a wonderful thing. Capitalism is most definitely not a blueprint for the good life or the perfect society. Among capitalists there are just as many criminals as among the poor, and right now, in Britain, we have a fine collection of capitalist entrepreneurs serving prison sentences—not because they are capitalists, but because they broke the law. And when countries hitch their waggon to a capitalist economy, it would be naive to expect that a regime of spotlessly honest men and equitable dealings would follow.

The one thing people in the formerly Communist states must not do is dismantle their industrial system abruptly. Change takes time, often a great deal of time. Factories have employees who need employment; they produce something that *is* needed, even though this something may not meet international standards. When demand disappears and unemployment can be taken care of by alternative employment and an extended social safety net, then, and then only, should the old type of "socialist" enterprises be gradually phased out.

URBAN   In other words, you are for piecemeal social engineering rather than radical transformation even when it is a question of turning a totalitarian system into a free-market parliamentary society—

POPPER   No, not quite. The command structures must go, but the change must be gradual and natural. You must start with a new legal framework—this can be partly copied from Western models, but even that will take a tremendous amount of work and time because every article would have to be tested in practice and adapted to the climate of Russian opinion and traditions. Then you would have to allow your unnecessary and uncompetitive industries to splutter to a halt by a form of natural wastage while attracting, parallel with all this, foreign investment and know-how.

But you must be on your guard. When a Communist system is opened up, you are doing a revolutionary thing; you are opening your gates to everyone who has a fresh idea or wants to try new ways of advancing himself and his interests. This cannot be trouble-free. You must be prepared for corruption in places both high and low. There will be successful swindlers who will get a lot of money out of the poor in Russia and then disappear with their fortunes in Latin America—

URBAN   A form of free-market entrepreneurship in which Poland has already given a lead—

POPPER   And to keep these abuses within bounds, you will then have to tighten the law, build up your police forces again, bring in the anti-drug squads, etc., exactly as the West does; for let no one in the East of Europe run away with the idea that you can have capitalism without all these regrettable phenomena coming along with it. But while all this is happening, you will have to go on maintaining your old ramshackle factories and much of the system that goes with them, perhaps for half a century, until they grind to a final halt because no one is willing to buy their products. That is the way communism has to expire, not by suddenly dismantling what cannot be dismantled overnight.

URBAN   This really answers my question: Piecemeal social engineering, then, is a desirable thing, in *both* directions—an answer very much at odds with the thinking of radical reformers in the East and free-market politicians who support them in the West.

   But if caution is a virtue in reforming your command economy, might it not be a virtue in reforming your police forces, your thought-control machinery, your judiciary, your education system, too? Why the rush to de-Stalinize?

POPPER   The point is that the state can create a legal framework but it can do little else. It cannot make judges incorruptible or policemen dutiful; it cannot create inventive capitalists or a spirit of tolerance in multiparty politics. It cannot order wisdom and virtue.

URBAN   Does that mean, if in doubt, don't? In other words, are you saying that we'd better hang on to some of the certainties of the old system because the alternative might be anarchy? And wouldn't that argue for the retention of an authoritarian kind of socialism?

POPPER   You paraphrase my meaning too sharply. "Hang on" is the wrong phrase because, like it or not, the old things are *there* and cannot be changed by the stroke of a pen. I find it perfectly conceivable that it will take Russia fifty years or more before it gets over the first steps.

URBAN   Your words are greatly at variance with the sort of advice our newly liberated friends in Central Europe receive from us. Our principal message to them is to break with the Socialist economic system radically and swiftly because all the halfway house solutions that were tried have ended in tears, and we quote to them the Yugoslav system of self-management and the New Economic Mechanism practised under Kádár in Hungary as warning examples. And the East European and Soviet reformers themselves insist that the greatest danger lies in half measures, in trying to muddle through, in trying to combine the collectivist approach with private initiative. The Polish government has already rejected the mending-and-making-do kind of reforms, and the Czechs and Hungarians are in the process of doing likewise, with the Soviets, in theory at least, not far behind. None of this would seem to agree with what you have just said.

POPPER If you ask the wrong questions, you are bound to receive the wrong answers. Shall I change all my clothes in one go, or shall I take off my trousers only? This is nonsensical. You cannot change things by order. Can you produce people with a lot of money so that they can act as private entrepreneurs? Can you produce people who like to take risks? Can you produce judges who will not be bribed, or teachers willing and able to divorce their thinking from the Communist text-books and the old ideology? And what is this laughable scheme to reform the Russian economy "in 500 days"? Reform has to proceed empirically, with every change carefully tested against the prevailing reality.

URBAN But you would surely not advocate piecemeal change in the Communist education system, for example? I would have thought the education system is a target *par excellence* for rapid, merciless and "holistic" change. We have textbooks in Central Europe which point to Luther as a precursor of the Socialist system in what used to be the GDR, and others which impose on the reader Orwellian versions of the whole of human history. Should we make compromises with untruth?

POPPER Many of the history books in the Federal Republic of Germany are false, too—

URBAN But you would agree that the Soviet kind of totalitarianism of the spirit should be wiped out?

POPPER It should if one could do it, but educational reform is an especially difficult area; it is strewn with pitfalls because, before you can reform education, you have to re-educate the educators.

Seventy years of communism is a difficult heritage to get rid of, even if you are absolutely determined to get rid of it. People in the Soviet Union are disorientated. Having burnt their fingers with the Utopia of communism, they now imagine that capitalism is an incarnation of heaven on earth. They are, of course, tragically mistaken. I am convinced that our societies in the West are the nearest thing to heaven we have yet seen in history, but let me say in the same breath that our capitalists are still a very long way away from sitting near the gates of heaven. If and when the Russians get their capitalism, they will be in for a profound disappointment, for it will not be a rich capitalism. The capitalism of the supermarkets—and that is what they so fervently desire—will remain beyond their reach. Of course, the temptation to project their dreams onto capitalism is understandable: "Since communism doesn't produce a world of supermarkets, capitalism does. Why shouldn't *we* have it?" This is a frightful projection, and it will lead to sharp popular reactions when the dream is shattered.

URBAN   So our policy of trying to induce the Soviet Union to make a clean and swift break with "socialism" is itself a holistic, Utopian type of a plan which cannot succeed?

POPPER   Yes, it is. We should tell the Soviets the opposite. We should say to them, "You should go on with your system until another system has naturally replaced it." That is all that can be done, and it is irresponsible to suggest otherwise. *We* had to work hard for our supermarkets.

1991

Notes

Introduction

1. Geoffrey Barraclough, *An Introduction to Contemporary History* (New York, Basic Books, 1964), p. 231.

2. R.W. Seton-Watson, *History* 14 (1929): 4.

3. G.R. Urban, ed., *Stalinism* (London and New York: Temple Smith and St. Martin's Press, 1982), pp. 1–5.

4. Thomas Carlyle, *History of the French Revolution*, pt. 1. bk. 7. ch. 5.

5. Winston S. Churchill, "Speech on a United Europe, Zürich University, September 19, 1946," in Randolph S. Churchill, ed., *The Sinews of Peace: Postwar Speeches by Winston S. Churchill* (London: Cassell, 1948), p. 201.

6. Willy Brandt, *Berliner Lektionen* (Berlin: Siedler, 1988), pp. 72–88. For Brandt's explanation of *Lebenslüge*, see his open letter to Theo Waigel, "Nicht gegen die Einheit," *Frankfurter Rundschau*, 2 November 1990. Egon Bahr, Brandt's close associate and long-time adviser, spoke of the idea of unification as "political pollution of the environment" (*politische Umweltverschmutzung*); see Egon Bahr, *Reden über das eigene Land: Deutschland* (Munich: C. Bertelsmann, 1988), p. 108. For a masterly account of the West German Left's apologetics for the East German regime, see Melvin J. Lasky, *Voices in a Revolution* (Southwick, Sussex, England: Grange, 1991), pp. 8–9, pp. 18–21.

7. "Der Streit der Ideologien und die gemeinsame Sicherheit," *Frankfurter Allgemeine Zeitung*, 28 August 1987.

8. "Western partners now seem to be more concerned over problems of CIS [Commonwealth of Independent States] armed forces than some leaders of separate CIS countries and even certain military. Perhaps this extreme concern will help somehow to reassure leaders now seeking to split the army as soon as possible in a downright barbarous way, and to create their own armed forces." Marshal Yevgeniy Shaposhnikov, commander in chief of the armed forces of the CIS, quoted in *ITAR-TASS*, 6 February 1992.

9. Karl Popper, *The Poverty of Historicism* (London: Routledge, 1957). See especially sects. 19–24.

10. "Introduction," *Fourth Annual Report 1978, the Board for Interna-*

tional Broadcasting (Washington: Government Printing Office, 1978), p. 4. See also *Fifth Annual Report 1979*, pp. 31–32.

11. *Fourth Annual Report 1978, the Board for International Broadcasting* (Washington: Government Printing Office, 1978), p. 50. The same stipulation appeared in several other *Annual Reports* in the 1970s and early 1980s.

12. Jerry F. Hough and Merle Fainsod, *How the Soviet Union Is Governed* (Cambridge & London: Harvard University Press, 1979), p. 548.

13. Ibid., p. 277.

14. Ibid., p. 554.

15. Alexander Zinoviev, "Why the Soviet System Is Here to Stay," in G.R. Urban, ed., *Can the Soviet System Survive Reform?* (London and New York: Pinter, 1989), pp. 45–107. Andrei Amalrik made a more inspired forecast. Writing in 1969, he asked *Will the USSR Survive until 1984?* He got it wrong by a mere seven years. Andrei Amalrik, *Will the USSR Survive until 1984?* (London: Allen Lane; New York: Harper & Row, 1970).

16. Stephen F. Cohen, *Bukharin and the Bolshevik Revolution* (Oxford, England: Oxford University Press, 1980), pp. XV–XXIV.

17. *Frankfurter Allgemeine Zeitung*, 29 September 1984. Earlier Greene had written, "If I had to choose between life in the Soviet Union and life in the United States of America, I would certainly choose the Soviet Union." *The Guardian* (London), 7 August 1969. See also Graham Greene, [Letter to the editor], *Daily Telegraph* (London), 25 February 1987.

18. "Even if they [members of the non-Communist Left, ed.] sharply condemned Stalin and all his works and crimes, their hope was in that direction. Socialism which has gone wrong but is still socialism—a corrupt perverted workers' state, but a workers' state; Lenin saved the Revolution; Bukharin was an honest Communist—Stalin and Beria were monsters, and yet the left looks hopefully to socialist countries—even Israel." Sir Isaiah Berlin, "Prophet of Liberalism Laments Ailing Left," *The Guardian* (London), 7 March 1992 (an extract from Ramin Jahanbegloo, ed., *Conversations with Isaiah Berlin* [London: Peter Halban, 1992]).

19. Tim Sebastian, "Dialogue with the Kremlin," *The Sunday Times* (London), 2 February 1992.

20. See, for example, Louis J. Halle: "As with the conflict between Christendom and Islam centuries earlier, the slow churning forces of secular change were transforming the conditions on which the Cold War had been based. The question arose, then, whether the old conceptions of the Cold War were still relevant to the changed times. . . . The Cold War constituted . . . a spasm in the conflict brought on by a collapse of the Western power structure. . . . By the end of 1962 the spasm appeared to be over." *The Cold War as History* (London: Chatto, 1967), p. 410. Halle's well-intentioned folly, though substantial, eventually was dwarfed by Francis Fukuyama's somewhat analogous claim in 1989 that, with the expiry of Sovietism, history had "come to an end" ("The End of History," *The National Interest*, Summer 1989, pp. 3–18).

For an inspired discussion of Fukuyama's claim, see Anthony Hartley, "On Not Ending History," *Encounter*, September/October 1989, pp. 71–73.

21. Ceausescu's royal honours included the Great Collar of the Leopold Order of Belgium, the Order of the Elephant of Denmark, and the Seraphim Royal Order of Sweden.

22. I was myself at first highly sceptical of the usefulness of signing human rights accords with the Soviet Union and our ability to see them enforced. I changed my mind after the 1980–83 Madrid conference, mainly in the light of Max Kampelman's farsighted leadership of the U.S. delegation, which set the tone for the whole round of conferences. The events of 1989–91 have fulfilled the most sanguine hopes of the architects of Helsinki. See "Can We Negotiate with the Russians?" [Max Kampelman in conversation with George Urban], in G.R. Urban, ed., *Can the Soviet System Survive Reform?* (London and New York: Pinter, 1989), pp. 1–44.

23. A similar view is expressed by Richard Pipes: "Why is it desirable for Russia to keep on disintegrating until nothing remains of its institutional structures? Because this is the only way of ridding the country of its patrimonial mentality and the Communist cadres which embody it. This kind of radical surgery is a prerequisite for any genuine progress." "Russia's Chance," *Commentary*, March 1992, p. 30.

24. Speaking in the United States in May 1992, former president Mikhail Gorbachev uttered similar sentiments: "In pushing forward to a new civilisation, we should under no circumstances again make the intellectual, and consequently political, error of interpreting victory in the cold war narrowly, as a victory for oneself, one's own way of life, one's own values and merits. . . . This was altogether a victory for common sense, reason, a victory for democracy, a victory for human values." Speech at Westminster College, Fulton, Mo., 6 May 1992.

25. Michael Bourdeaux, *Religion and the Collapse of Soviet Communism*, The Hugh Seton-Watson Memorial Lecture, Centre for Policy Studies, London, 29 April 1992.

26. Quoted by Heinz-Joachim Fischer in *Frankfurter Allgemeine Zeitung*, 4 March 1992.

27. For Eduard Shevardnadze's answer to this question, see Eduard Shevardnadze, "Rückfälle in das Lagerdenken," in *Die Zukunft gehört der Freiheit* (Reinbek bei Hamburg: Rowohlt, 1991), pp. 203–231. For a perspective on the Gorbachev leadership's benevolent attitude toward the gathering forces of reform in Hungary and Poland in the period 1985–89, see "A rendszervaltas elokeszitese" [Preparing the change of the system], a conversation with Imre Pozsgay in *Hitel* (Budapest), 13 May 1992, pp. 6–11.

28. V.I. Lenin, *Selected Works* (New York: International Publishers, n.d.), 10:127.

29. In the reading of Anatoliy Sobchak, mayor of St. Petersburg, Gorbachev "had two moments when he could have changed history. The first was

at the 28th CPSU Congress, when he could not make up his mind to split the Party. At that time a real multi-party system could have arisen, and the formation of the new system of power could have proceeded by a more civilized path. The second moment was at the beginning of 1991 when the conservative forces went on the offensive. If he had then resolved to throw in his lot with the democrats, his own fate could have been different too." *Komsomolskaya Pravda* (Moscow), 3 March 1992.

30. Joachim Fest put this with elegance: "Once again [as after the collapse of the Nazi period—ed.], wherever we look we run into denials and losses of memory. We yet have to see a single member of the Politburo who would make an attempt to justify his past activities in the name of the historical mission of which so much was spoken until yesterday. . . . Wherever we look, we run into renunciations and the belittlement of the roles played. Instead of seeing men who acted out of a sense of conviction, we encounter men . . . caught in the act of cattle-rustling." "Schwacher Abgang," *Frankfurter Allgemeine Zeitung*, 6 March 1992.

31. Jean François Revel, *How Democracies Perish*, trans. William Byron (Garden City, N.Y.: Doubleday, 1984). Original work published 1983.

Chapter 1

1. New York: Harper & Row, 1987.

2. New York: John Day, 1943.

3. "For some reason, philosophers have kept around themselves, even in our day, something of the atmosphere of the magician." *The Open Society and Its Enemies,* 5th revised edition (London: Routledge, 1984), p. 30.

4. See "Philosophy and Human Conduct," in *The Quest for 'Being'* (New York: St. Martin's Press, 1961), and *Pragmatism and the Tragic Sense of Life* (New York: Basic Books, 1974) *(passim)*.

5. New York: John Day, 1933.

6. Popper, vol. 2, p. 339, footnote 9.

7. Reprinted in Maude Aylmer and Ronald Sampson, trans., *Tolstoy's Writings on Civil Disobedience and Non-Violence* (New York: Signet, 1967), pp. 181–190.

8. Carbondale and Edwardsville: Southern Illinois University Press, 1980.

9. Quoted in Sidney Hook, *Out of Step: An Unquiet Life in the 20th Century* (New York: Harper & Row, 1987), p. 318.

10. Van Nostrand: Princeton, N.J., 1955.

11. Ibid., p. 124.

12. Ibid.

13. "Out of the crooked timber of humanity no straight thing can ever be made." Immanuel Kant, *Ideen zu einer allgemeinen Geschichte in weltbürgerlicher Absicht.*

14. Max Eastman, *Enjoyment of Laughter* (Darby, PA: Darby Books, 1981). (Original work published 1937)

15. London: Secker and Warburg, 1957; especially in "Conclusion."

16. Alexander Solzhenitsyn, *Lenin in Zurich* (London: The Bodley Head, 1975), p. 221, quoted as document 31 from Werner Hahlvreg, *Lenins Rückkeht nach Russland 1917,* Leiden, 1957.

17. Walter Warlimont, *Im Hauptquartier Der Deutschen Wehrmacht: 1939–1945* (Frankfurt: Bernhard und Graefe, 1962).

18. "In my opinion, the thought of what the Americans can and will do disturbs them all, and the Germans [at the Hitler-Mussolini conference at Klessheim Castle] shut their eyes in order not to see. But this does not keep the more intelligent and the more honest from thinking about what America can do, and they feel shivers running down their spines . . ." Galeazzo Ciano, *Ciano's Diary,* ed. Malcolm Muggeridge (London: Heinemann, 1947), entry for 29 April 1942, p. 462.

19. Joseph Goebbels, *The Goebbels Diaries,* Louis P. Lochner, ed. (London: Hamish Hamilton, 1948), p. 277.

20. Adolf Hitler, *Hitler's Table-Talk: 1941–1944,* intro. by Hugh Trevor-Roper (Oxford: Oxford University Press, 1988), p. 587 (paperbound edition).

21. "One may accept or reject the ideology of Hitlerism . . . but everybody should understand that an ideology cannot be destroyed by force, that it cannot be eliminated by war. It is, therefore, not only senseless but criminal to wage such a war as a war for the 'destruction of Hitlerism' camouflaged as a fight for democracy." From V. Molotov's speech on the partition of Poland at the 5th extraordinary session of the Supreme Soviet, 31 October 1939.

22. "What experience and history teach is this—that peoples and governments never have learned anything from history, or acted on principles deduced from it." From G.W.F. Hegel, *The Philosophy of History,* J. Sibree, trans., vol. 10, Introduction, p. 6 (1899).

23. George Urban, "A Conversation with Lukács," *Encounter,* October 1971, p. 35.

24. Fyodor Burlatsky, "What Sort of Socialism Do the People Need?," *Literaturnaya Gazeta* (Moscow), 20 April 1988.

25. Leonard Schapiro, "Some Reflections on Lenin, Stalin and Russia," in *Stalinism,* ed. G.R. Urban (London: Temple Smith, 1982), p. 417.

26. Nina Andreyeva, [Commentary], *Sovetskaya Rossiya,* 13 March 1988.

27. Brown v. Board of Education, 347 U.S. 483 (1954).

28. "Who never ate his bread in sorrow,/. . . He knows ye not, ye heavenly powers." From *Wilhelm Meisters Lehrjahre,* 2:13.

29. In William James, *Memories and Studies* (New York: Greenwood, 1968). (Original work published 1911)

30. Ibid., pp. 287–288.

31. Zürich, 1917.

32. Sidney Hook, *Pragmatism and the Tragic Sense of Life* (New York: Basic Books, 1974), pp. 13–14.

33. London: Hamish Hamilton, 1935.
34. London: Hutchinson, 1988.
35. Frankfurt: Frankfurter Hefte, 1951.
36. Stuttgart: Seewald, 1978.
37. Zürich: Opprecht, 1950.
38. New York: Dover Publications, 1954. (Original English translation published 1921)
39. *Out of Step,* p. 228.
40. Ibid., p. 170.
41. Ibid., p. 174.

Chapter 2

1. Mikhail Petrovich Pogodin, "Letter on Russian History," in *The Mind of Modern Russia,* ed. Hans Kohn (New Brunswick, N.J.: Rutgers University Press, 1955), pp. 66–68. (Originally published in 1837)
2. Marquis de Custine, *Journey for Our Time: The Journals of the Marquis de Custine,* ed. Phyllis Penn Kohler (New York: Pellegrini, 1951), pp. 72–73.
3. Ibid., pp. 12–13.

Chapter 3

1. Elie Kedourie, *Nationalism* (London: Hutchinson, 1980), pp. 20–31. (Originally published in 1960)
2. Hugh Seton-Watson and George R. Urban, "The Fall of Multinational Empires in our Time" in *Communist Reformation,* ed. G.R. Urban (1979), 276–7.
3. Hugh Trevor-Roper and George Urban, "Aftermaths of Empire," *Encounter,* December 1989. See chapter 2 of this volume.
4. L.B. Namier, "1848: Seed-Plot of History," *Avenues of History* (1952), 53.
5. Friedrich Engels, *Neue Rheinische Zeitung,* Cologne (13 January, 15 February 1849).
6. "Saying the Unsayable about the Germans" [Interview with Nicholas Ridley], *Spectator* (London), 14 July 1990, p. 8.
7. John Maynard Keynes, *The Economic Consequences of the Peace,* (1919), 31, 33.

Chapter 4

1. Ernst Trost, *Das blieb vom Doppeladler. Auf den Spuren der versunkenen Donaumonarchie.* (rev.) (Munich: Wilhelm Goldmann, 1981). (Originally published in 1966)

2. Assen Ignatov, *Studien zur Mentalität der herrschenden Schicht in der Psychologie des Kommunismus* (Munich: Wewel, 1985).

3. Hugh Seton-Watson, "Aftermaths of Empire," *Journal of Contemporary History* 15(1) (1980): 197–208.

Chapter 5

1. Richard Pipes, *Russia under the Old Regime* (New York: Scribner's, 1974).

2. Boris Shragin and Albert Todd, eds., *A Collection of Essays on the Russian Intelligentsia,* Marian Schwarte, trans. (New York: Howard, 1977). (Originally published in 1909)

3. Ibid., p. 38.

4. Ibid., p. 148.

5. Ch. 2, the present volume.

6. In 1988, Adam Ulam published a fictitious reconstruction of Sergei Kirov's murder under the title *The Kirov Affair* (San Diego: Harcourt, Brace, Jovanovich).

Chapter 6

1. G.R. Urban, "A Conversation with Milovan Djilas," *Encounter,* December 1979; reprinted as "Christ and the Commissar" in G.R. Urban, ed., *Stalinism* (London and New York: Maurice Temple-Smith, 1982).

2. G.R. Urban, "Djilas on Gorbachev," *Encounter,* September/October and December 1988; reprinted as "New Utopias for Old" in G.R. Urban, ed., *Can the Soviet System Survive Reform?* (London: Pinter, 1989).

3. London: Sinclair-Stevenson, 1991.

Chapter 7

1. Fifth revised edition, London: Routledge, 1984. (Originally published in 1945)

2. London: Routledge, 1957.

3. R.E. Allen, ed., *The Concise Oxford Dictionary of Current English* (Oxford: Clarendon, 1990).

4. Manfred Schell, [Interview with Sir Karl Popper], *Die Welt* (Hamburg), 19, 21, 23 February 1990.

5. Ibid., 21 February 1990.

6. Ibid.

7. *A World of Propensities* (Bristol, England: Thoemmes, 1990).

8. *Do Not Go Gentle into That Good Night* (1952), lines 3, 9, 15, 19.

Authors

Milovan Djilas was, until his expulsion from the League of Communists in 1954, a vice-president of Yugoslavia, president of the Federal Parliament, a member of the Politburo, and one of Tito's closest associates. He is the author of *The New Class; Land without Justice; Conversations with Stalin; Njegos; The Unperfect Society: Beyond the New Class; Memoir of a Revolutionary; Wartime;* and *Tito: The Story from Inside.*

Otto von Habsburg (Archduke Otto of Habsburg) is member of the European Parliament for Bavaria and a citizen of Germany, Austria, and Hungary. He is the international president of the Paneuropean Union and Speaker for the Christian Democrats in the Political Committee of the European Parliament. He is a fellow of Jerusalem University and has honorary doctorates from Nancy, Ferrara, and other universities. He has published i.a. *Zurück zur Mitte; Macht jenseits des Marktes—Europa 1992; Die Reichsidee—Geschichte und Zukunft einer übernationalen Ordnung;* and *Europa, Garant der Freiheit.*

Sidney Hook was the author or editor of more than thirty books, including *Towards the Understanding of Karl Marx; The Hero in History; Political Power and Personal Freedom; Pragmatism and the Tragic Sense of Life;* and *Out of Step.* He taught philosophy at New York University and was, after his retirement in 1972, a senior research fellow at the Hoover Institution on War, Revolution, and Peace, Stanford University. He was a founding member of the International Congress for Cultural Freedom.

Elie Kedourie taught politics at the London School of Economics and held the chair of politics, University of London. He was a fellow of the British Academy and had been a visiting professor at Princeton, Harvard, Monash, Columbia, and Tel Aviv universities. His publications include *Nationalism; Nationalism in Africa and Asia; The Chatham House Version and Other Middle Eastern Studies; Islam in the Modern World and Other Studies;* and *The Crossman Confessions and Other Essays in Politics, History and Religion.*

Sir Karl Popper is emeritus professor of philosophy at the London School of Economics. He is a member of the British Academy, guest professor of the theory of science at the University of Vienna, and a senior research fellow at the Hoover Institution on War, Revolution, and Peace. His publications include *The Open Society and Its Enemies; The Poverty of Historicism; The Logic of Scientific Discovery; Conjectures and Refutations,* and *A World of Propensities.*

Hugh Trevor-Roper—who sits in the British House of Lords as Lord Dacre of Glanton—was Regius professor of modern history, Oxford, and master of Peterhouse, Cambridge. His publications include *The Last Days of Hitler; Hitler's Table Talk* (ed.); *The Rise of Christian Europe; Hitler's War Diaries* (ed.); *The Age of Expansion; The European Witch-Craze of the 16th and 17th Centuries; The Goebbels Diaries* (ed.), and *Catholics, Anglicans and Puritans.*

Adam B. Ulam is Gurney professor of history and political science at Harvard University and director of its Russian Research Center. He is a former Rockefeller fellow and Guggenheim fellow. Among his books are *Lenin and the Bolsheviks; Titoism and the Cominform; The Unfinished Revolution; Ideologies and Illusions; Stalin: The Man and his Era; In the Name of the People,* and *The Kirov Affair.*

G.R. Urban is Bradley international fellow of the Heritage Foundation, former director of Radio Free Europe, and a former visiting fellow at the University of Southern California and at Indiana and Harvard universities. He is the author or editor of *The Nineteen Days; Kinesis and Stasis; Eurocommunism; Can We Survive our Future?; Détente; Communist Reformation; Hazards of Learning; Stalinism;* and *Can the Soviet System Survive Reform?*

Index

Second World War
  alliance against nazism, 131
  Bulgaria, 93
  Japan, 26–7
  Versailles Treaty and, 7
  Yugoslavia, 94, 187–8
self-determination. *See* sovereignty
Serbia, Serbs, 94, 121, 140, 179, 180,
    182–91 *passim,* 194
Seton-Watson, Hugh, xviii, 109–10,
    171
Seton-Watson, R. W., xii, 137
Shachtman, Max, 64
Shakespeare, Frank, xxvii
Shaposhnikov, Marshal Yevgeniy,
    221
Shevardnadze, Eduard, xxix–xxx,
    115, 198, 223
sin. *See* evil
Siqueiros, David, 42
Slovenia, Slovenes, 120, 140, 186,
    189
Smith, General Walter Bedell, 84
Sobchak, Anatoliy, 223–4
social consciousness, history of, 138
"social fascism," 3–4
socialism, socialists (*see also* com-
    munism), xiii, 20
  ethical motivation, 11
  and First World War, 34–5
  religious-totalitarian incrustations,
    164
  Soviet type discredited, 170–1,
    179–80, 191
Solzhenitsyn, Alexander, xx, 57–8,
    162
Sonnenfeldt, Helmut, xxvii
sovereignty, independence, 87, 89,
    92–3, 101–5
Soviet Union (*see also* Russia), xii–
    xviii, 66–7, 95, 101, 113, 115,
    179–80
  between the wars, 13–14, 28
  camps, 57–8

collapse of, xii, xxiv, xxviii–xxxv,
    106, 120–1, 147–52; not inevita-
    ble, xxviii; piecemeal change
    now needed, xvii, 214–20; rea-
    sons for, xxviii, xxix, xxxiv;
    West and, xv, xxix–xxxi, xxxiii–
    xxxv, 167–8
  collectivization, 158
  communism (*q.v.*) in, 147, 155–9
  economic reform, 95
  human rights in, 3
  "pluralistic," xxi
  "Russian" and "Soviet" distin-
    guished, 155–65
  stability provided by?, xvi, 86, 90,
    92–3, 97, 133–6, 167–8
  totalitarian, xxi, 2, 45
  West and, xv, xviii–xxviii, xxix,
    xxxiii–xxxv, 92, 128, 167–72
  See also Afghanistan; Bolshevism;
    Cold War; Gorbachev; Lenin;
    Red Army; Stalin; Trotsky; War-
    saw Pact; *and under* Christian-
    ity; communism; Habsburg Em-
    pire; ideology; Jews; Marxism;
    nationalism; Nazis; Ottoman
    Empire; socialism
Spain
  Civil War, 33
  empire, 80
  recent history, 152, 153–4
Sparta, 83
Spinoza, Baruch, 17
Stalin, Stalinism, xxviii, 3–4, 28, 38–
    40, 53, 96, 161, 173–4
Steed, Wickham, 137
Stone, Norman, 91
Strasser, Gregor and Otto, 27
Strauss, Franz Josef, 146
Struve, Peter, 162–3
subsidiarity, 144–5

Taine, Hippolyte, 19
technology, value of, 205–7